Walking the Himalayas

Also by Levison Wood

Walking the Nile

Walking the Himalayas

Levison Wood

HODDER &
STOUGHTON

First published in Great Britain in 2016 by Hodder & Stoughton
An Hachette UK company

1

A CIP catalogue record for this title is available from the British Library

Hardback ISBN 978 1 473 62624 9
Trade paperback ISBN 978 1 473 62625 6
Ebook ISBN 978 1 473 62627 0

Typeset in Bembo by Hewer Text UK Ltd, Edinburgh
Printed and bound by CPI Group (UK) Ltd, Croydon, CR0 4YY

Hodder & Stoughton policy is to use papers that are natural, renewable
and recyclable products and made from wood grown in sustainable forests.
The logging and manufacturing processes are expected to conform
to the environmental regulations of the country of origin.

Hodder & Stoughton Ltd
Carmelite House
50 Victoria Embankment
London EC4Y 0DZ

www.hodder.co.uk

For my parents

Ishkashim

AFGHANISTAN

Wakhan Corridor

Gilgit

KASHMIR

Islamabad

Srinagar

PAKISTAN

Dharamsala

Indus River

Lahore

Amritsar

Shimla

Rishikesh

Haridwar

Delhi

Ganges

I N

Border

Disputed border

Town/city

Capital city

Route

0   250

Miles

Contents

I

Pokhara, 2001

Without warning, a man burst into the internet café, pulling down the shutters behind him and plunging us into near darkness. He was desperately out of breath and shouting something in Nepali.

As my eyes became accustomed to the dingy light, I made out the anxious face of the skinny white teenager who'd been sitting next to me. Clearly just out of school and on his first solo trip abroad, his loneliness all too apparent, he was now trembling. The screens of the twelve ancient computers, the only gateway to the outside world, flashed and the roar of computer fans filled the room. Dust sparkled in the sliver of light that crept in through a high window. Outside it was eerily quiet.

The man forced a smile and walked a little closer to the weather-worn woman who ran the café. She and her baby were both shrouded in the faded, thinning silk of her sari. All eyes were on him, as he stood there sweating in his white string vest and an old pair of grey suit trousers.

'Army, police, they coming now. Shooting, killing. You need to leave, now, go.'

I looked across at the boy next to me. He hesitated nervously, wanting to move but paralysed by fear. I got up, but the man gestured in the direction of the door.

'Wait. Stop, too late. Not now.'

As he spoke, there was the unmistakable rattle of gunfire somewhere in the street outside. It sounded close, but it was impossible to tell, as the din of a hundred shouts grew nearer. I had no idea if it was the police or the army, or just another angry mob.

'Riots,' whispered the man. 'Stay here for now, too dangerous outside.'

I tiptoed towards the front window and peered through a crack in the shutter. The noise outside was deafening. I couldn't see much in the blinding sunlight, except people shuffling past. Some were running and some waving big red flags.

'Who are they?' I asked the man, who was busy attempting to reassure the nervous mother. The child remained fast asleep.

'Protestors. They no like government. Maoists.'

I'd heard about the Maoists when I arrived in Nepal just a week earlier. There was already a curfew in the streets after nine o'clock in the evening, but most people in Kathmandu seemed to pay lip service to it, particularly in the backpacker enclave of Thamel. I certainly had, walking alone through labyrinthine alleyways back from a boozy tavern in all my teenage irresponsibility. The newspapers were full of warnings about these communist insurgents, but until now they'd been confined to the countryside and mountains. In more recent months, the Maoists had spread to the towns and cities, causing mayhem. The government had cracked down and violence was on the rise, but I was not prepared for this – a full-blown riot outside my shabby hotel. This was turning out to be a rather unusual gap year.

A civil war had been raging in the hills of Nepal for six long years and hundreds of people had been killed. In the months before my visit, dozens of policemen, soldiers and government officials had been hacked to death by angry mobs and many more had been victims of improvised bombs hidden in cars and haybales. Over three hundred Maoist insurgents had also been gunned down. Some had been executed without trial by the security forces in revenge for the chaos. Since 1996, the Maoists, or members of the United People's Front of Nepal, had taken up arms in protest at having been excluded from the political process. They launched a 'people's war', fighting against the government and monarchy, employing communist guerrilla tactics of torture, assassination, bombing and extortion in an attempt to gain power. By 2001, the insurgents numbered in their thousands and were active in fifty of the seventy-five states of Nepal. At the time though, I was blissfully unaware of the political situation; I was just there to enjoy the Himalayas.

After half an hour, the noise outside died down and the whirring of the fan became apparent again. The man in the string vest ventured to the door and pulled up the shutter, revealing the blinding rays of the midday sun, which poured into the filthy room. With my eyes adjusting, I peered around the door to see the street virtually empty. Across the road, a water buffalo munched away at a soggy cardboard box. All that remained of the riot were a few broken bottles and the tatty remnants of a red banner.

A motorbike spluttered past; the rider cannot have been older than twelve. An even younger boy clung haphazardly to his brother's back and I watched as the pair darted in between the parked cars, swerved around the occasional cyclist and narrowly avoided a bullock cart. Overhead, the wonky electricity poles threatened to crash down at any second, and the spidery tangle of wires dangled menacingly above the heads of passing pedestrians. On the other side of the road, a shopkeeper pulled up his shutters, let loose an enormous throatful of phlegm into the street and dragged a trestle table covered with fruit back onto the pavement, patting it delicately with a feather duster. Pineapples, oranges, mangoes and a giant Indian jackfruit wobbled precariously as he replaced his sign offering 'fruity lassi', the yoghurt drink found across the subcontinent and favoured by backpackers and hippies on the trail. It reminded me I hadn't eaten anything yet and I was hungry.

I thanked the woman who hadn't moved from her broken plastic seat during the whole episode, the baby still fast asleep. I handed her twenty rupees, despite the internet not working; yet again I'd failed to send the email promised to my parents. I said goodbye to the skinny teenager, who had a kind and innocent face. I'd felt sorry for him when I saw his fear, and in it had recognised my own. But he was at the start of his journey and I was near the end of mine, so in a way I also envied him. He was leaving Pokhara tomorrow anyway, back to Kathmandu, before continuing his world tour. Encounters were often like that. You'd meet a likeminded soul and even share an hour of intense, life-changing experiences, you'd joke and laugh and bond, and then ... move on, perhaps never to see them again. Then again perhaps you would; in another world, in another time, perhaps in another internet café.

As I walked towards the lake, I watched normality resume. Open-engined tractors driven by smiling farmers started to rattle by and women picked rice from the paddy fields as if nothing had happened. I contemplated how to spend the afternoon. My hostel was dreary and there were no foreigners to talk to, so for two days I'd avoided it, preferring instead the lakeside district, which was full of small shacks serving dal bhat and samosas to backpackers, hippies and trekkers. I was only nineteen and still shy. Even though I'd already been on the road for five months and seen three continents, it still required all my courage to sit next to a stranger and strike up a conversation.

I ambled north along the main street with the lake to my left,
a cool breeze wafting from the emerald waters, a welcome break
from the mugginess of the monsoon. Perhaps a storm was
coming. Clouds had settled around the tops of the foothills so
that the jungle seemed to fade upwards into heaven and the
mountains beyond became invisible. The sky was nothing more
than a dirty white pillow. The height of the rains was the worst
time of year to be in Nepal. More often than not, you'd be
confined to your hotel terrace as sheets of water pummelled the
gardens beyond, with an aggression that needed to be seen to be
believed. There was little to do but watch and wait. You'd play
cards or chess or just drink as the downpour began and cabin
fever set in. Outside, the feeble drains overflowed and motorbikes skidded through the streets. Dogs lurked pathetically, shivering in flooded doorways and chickens pecked their way to
shelter. Women in saris desperately scuttled from shop to shop,
drenched through, the silk clinging to their bodies. But today it
was still dry – the Maoists had the good sense to only protest in
good weather; their demonstration done and dusted in good
time – but I knew that as the afternoon wore on, the inevitable
would happen. I needed to find shelter.

The lakeside was great for people-watching. I found a small
shop, ordered a banana lassi, and settled in. I gazed vacantly out at
passers-by; eternally lost dreadlocked backpackers going in circles
round the world to find themselves; determined trekkers dressed
in waterproof trousers casting ambitious and longing glances at
far-off peaks; opportunistic and happy-go-lucky Nepali shopkeepers with persuasive grins on their faces; playful children, leap-
ing in and out of the lake, with winning smiles on their faces. I
continued my stroll, wondering whether to return to the hotel or
carry on walking, perhaps even take a rowing boat onto the lake.
I hadn't ticked that box yet. But then on further consideration I

thought better of it. The lightning yesterday had been spectacular but I didn't fancy being on the receiving end of it. In my five-month trip I'd managed to survive getting mugged in Zimbabwe, stranded in a broken-down jeep and surrounded by lions in the Kruger, almost being arrested in Australia and being hounded down the beach by a mob of very angry lady boys in Thailand. The last thing I wanted in my last couple of weeks away was to be frazzled by a rogue lightning fork in the middle of Lake Phewa. I was supposed to be starting university in September and I'd worried my parents quite enough.

Instead, I went down to the water's edge, just beyond the outskirts of town, where a few small and rickety shacks flanked the lakeside. Here the fishermen and farmers rested in quiet solitude among the half-built concrete walls that kept the buffaloes in their grazing pastures.

'Hello. Where are you going?' said a voice behind me.

I turned around and saw a fresh-faced Nepali man about my age in grey trousers and a baggy blue T-shirt. He could hardly have been out of his teens. His hair was curly and a little greasy, but he had a friendly smile and an honest look about him.

I've been conned, ripped off, taken for a ride more times than I can remember while travelling, and it's usually the same story. A man walks up and offers his services as a guide, or a translator, or perhaps just wants to show you a temple, or for you to teach him some English. Before you know it you've handed over a month's budget and all you have to show for it is a few beads and a guilt trip that you didn't donate your life savings. After a while it becomes a bit tiresome and, wrongly or rightly, you learn to adopt selective hearing. You're forced into cynicism. But even so, I was nineteen, naive and wanted to believe the best in people, so inevitably I'd stop and chat. I didn't have much money to give anyway and time was on my side, so I figured that I hardly had much to lose. The experiences, stories and new friends were usually well worth the few rupees, baht or pounds it sometimes cost.

'Hello,' he said again, smiling and walking up alongside me. 'Do you want to see the mountains?'

'They're covered in cloud. Isn't it going to rain?' I said.

'Not today.'

I eyed him dubiously. The clouds were low and menacing and getting darker by the minute. I was convinced it would rain.

'Not today,' he repeated. 'Come to Sarangkot.' He pointed towards the enormous hill to our right overlooking the lake. The hill, like the others, was shrouded at its peak by the mists that made it impossible to estimate its true height.

I looked at my watch. It was mid-afternoon already and I wasn't sure it was even possible to get to the top of the hill before the rain began.

'Very easy, two hours.' He smiled. It was a natural, innocent smile, and I was determined to trust him.

'Okay,' I said. It was either that or slip back into my routine of waiting for the heavens to open from my cheap hotel. And after the drama of the riot I didn't want to risk being stuck inside again. So we walked. And walked, and walked. At the beginning it was in silence as I struggled to keep pace and catch my breath. The trail wound through the rhododendron bushes and monsoon forest, often disappearing into the tangled vines that battled to suffocate man's pitiful interference. I enjoyed the feeling of putting one foot in front of the other, of leaving the concrete and dust behind. I'd spent far too long recently confined to the backpacker ghettoes, listening to the same reggae music in tourist bars and lounging on cushions, as I flicked absent-mindedly through a Lonely Planet guidebook. It's all too easy to forget the real world beyond the enclaves, and I relished the thought of disappearing into the misty forest above the town for a while.

We passed a few small houses; little more than one-room shacks with thatched roofs and mud-brick walls. These were usually surrounded by small gardens where the villagers grew potatoes, bananas or mangoes. In the surrounding trees, the black faces of langur monkeys could be seen furtively glancing from the safety of their green camouflage. An array of tropical birds thrashed about the canopy, warning of the oncoming human beings, with squawks and squeaks and sudden flourishes of brightly coloured wings. It became a steep climb and the young man could see I was ready for a breather.

'Not far now,' he reassured me with an almost paternal tone. But in between the thick trunks and shrubbery, all I could see was mist. Below, the path disappeared into a grey soup of fog and I wondered what I had let myself in for.

'What's your name?' I asked the boy.

'Binod Pariyar,' he said. 'I am twenty years old, how old are you?'

'I'm nineteen,' I said, resting on a fallen log, unaccustomed to working my legs on steep hills.

Binod chuckled. 'Nineteen? You're younger than me. I thought you were twenty-five. And you're not even fit.' He reached out his hand with a concerned look on his face and pulled me up. 'Do you have hills in England?'

We reached the top of the hill at half past four and I was exhausted. But as we emerged from the forest, the hillside opened up. On the far side of the slope from which I'd climbed, unfurling beneath the canopy, the mist had cleared to reveal a scene more stunning than I could have imagined, and one I would never have encountered were it not for agreeing to the serendipitous hike.

The stubborn monsoon fog had finally lifted. A valley, some three or four miles across, now stretched out before us, dissected by a river and lined on both sides by the sleepy town of Pokhara itself. Rice paddies gave the valley floor a bright and verdant shimmer and spiralling plumes of smoke curled out from wood-fires in the villages below. Above us, a lone hawk soared through the damp, still air. As the foothills rose on the far side, a dark green expanse of patchwork carpeted the view. Beyond this rose something wild and untamed. Something so sublime in its proportions, and gargantuan in its raw, unwieldy beauty as to give the impression that it was floating in mid-air, somehow unattached from the green and brown hills and valleys below.

There, above us all, was the mighty Himalaya and at the fore, the snow-laden peak of Machhapuchchhre – the fishtail mountain. Perfect in its assymetry, it rose like a gleaming shark's tooth into the endless blue above. I stared hard in silence and saw what Binod had promised me – the twin peaks, just like a fish's tail, as everyone said. In the background, on either side, were its guardians the Annapurnas, less striking but equally noble. It all looked so close from here, yet at the same time utterly removed; impossible to touch. Holy, infinite, heaven incarnate. I turned around after what seemed like an awe-filled eternity to look back down the other side of the ridge, back towards the lake which glistened in the afternoon light. Binod was right. There would be no rains today.

'Come, brother, there is somewhere that I would like to show you.' The path fell steeply away from the top of the ridge and I trod slowly in fear of slipping on the rocky trail. In the sharp afternoon light the path suddenly felt real and the clarity brought with it scale and the realisation of altitude – and with it, peril. Binod led and shouted encouragement. 'We are nearly at my village.'

9

Ahead, a few hundred metres down the slope, a collection of huts jutted out of the hillside. There was a cow tied loosely to a tree that seemed to grow straight out of the brick wall. The scene was medieval to me. The cow was trying desperately to reach the leaves of a nearby plant with its steaming tongue. As I got closer and caught up with my new guide, I noticed with disbelief that the tall plant, like all the plants in his garden, was cannabis. Distinctive finger-like leaves pointed out in all directions from the thin stalks which danced with the breeze.

'Welcome to my garden. It's all for my own use,' he said with a wink.

'Is it legal?' I asked in my naivety.

Binod smiled and shrugged, plucking a handful of spindly leaves from the top of a bush and crushing them in the palm of his hand with a thumb. 'It's wild. It grows everywhere and anyway the police don't come up here. They're too lazy. And if they did I'd just roll them a joint and they'd forget all about it.' He rubbed the crushed damp leaves between his fingers until it was a mushy ball and held it out for me to smell. The odour was sickly and distinctive.

At that moment a flash of red moved within the hut. I glanced over Binod's shoulder into the dark room.

'That's my wife, Chandra,' said Binod. 'Bring the boy,' he shouted in the direction of the gloomy doorway. A tiny figure appeared in the form of a flowing red sari topped by a woman clutching an infant. She could hardly have been older than sixteen. The shy girl bowed her head and with her hands clasped together around the baby whispered the Nepali greeting. 'Namaste.'

I saw her hands were covered in gold rings; heirlooms and presents – the entire family wealth wrapped around a few fingers.

Binod took the boy from his mother and held him up in both hands and kissed him on the red nose.

'This is my son, Bishal. He will grow up to speak better English than me, and I want him to know how to use a computer. I hear of something in town called internet. I want him to use it and get very rich.'

Binod was the man of the house. His father had died at a young age and Binod had married at the age of sixteen to a bride two years his junior. Like most of his generation it was an arranged marriage, but he assured me it bore no relation to his happiness. 'She is my wife, we do everything together. Of course we are in love.' He said it in such a matter of fact way that I decided not to ask any more daft questions. They all lived in the same room – man and wife, grandmother and baby – a smoke-filled chamber no more than ten feet wide, where a pile of flea-ridden blankets formed a communal bed.

Chandra disappeared for a moment to fetch tea but as she placed it down beside us she put a reverent hand on Binod's shoulder and whispered something in his ear. She looked sullen. Binod, until then all smiles and cheer, looked serious and shook his head in disbelief. I could tell something was wrong.

'What is it?'

He looked agitated and said something back to Chandra, and then looked around towards another house some few hundred metres away, before remembering me.

'Oh, nothing, well, I don't know, I need to find out more. I don't know,' he repeated. 'Oh God, it's terrible,' he said, still shaking his head. 'If it's true, it's bad, it's worse than I thought. What kind of a world will Bishal grow up in?'

In the couple of carefree hours it had taken us to climb to Sarangkot, Nepal had been rattled by tragic news which had spread like wildfire among the villagers of the hills and valleys.

'The King is dead,' said Binod, with a solemnity I didn't expect. 'Murdered with his whole family. The country will fall apart.' He handed the child back to his mother. 'Let's go and find out what's going on.'

We drank our tea and with that, we were off. Binod was silent now, only occasionally muttering to himself. He was a young-ster, forced all too early to become a man, and just recently a father. His world had been shattered by news so grim that he foresaw his own country falling apart. Despite having no formal education and little care for a political system that looked after the status quo, he was perceptive enough to realise that this news signalled chaos, destruction and, ultimately, danger for his family. Taking a longer but easier path to the east, we descended the mountain and reached lakeside by dusk, where the town was awash with gossip. Men sat haunched around the tea shops, speaking hurriedly and with a gloom I hadn't seen among a people normally so happy and stoic. They were busily sharing what little they had heard, before the inevitable dispersal at eight p.m., when the nightly curfew was enforced by the army. And no doubt tonight it would be strict.

'Nobody knows who did it yet. There's a lot of rumours going round. They think it was one of the Princes,' said Binod, as we eavesdropped on a conversation between a taxi driver and a mango seller.

I picked up an English-language newspaper, discarded by a tourist. The news was that regicide had been committed by the King's son Dipendra. Annoyed that his family had not approved of his choice of bride, he had gone on a killing spree in the palace, slaughtering his parents, cousins and uncles, before turn-ing the machine gun on himself. But nobody seemed to know the truth of the matter – there were so many unanswered ques-tions. Perhaps it was a conspiracy by the communists after all?

Nobody had any idea what the repercussions would be. One thing was clear though.

'The cities will become bloodbaths,' said Binod grimly. 'You need to get out of here now. The police will be on the rampage, wanting to use this as an excuse to round up any terrorists. And the Maoists will see this as their best chance of claiming power. There will be fighting and much killing.'

As I looked up from my paper, the boy I had seen at the internet café earlier in the day walked past with his rucksack on his back.

'Mate, have you heard the news?' I shouted after him.

'Yes, of course I have. Everyone has.' He looked even younger than I remembered, just a boy, like me, barely out of school and now lost in a war zone – caught up in a massacre. 'The embassy is telling everyone to leave the country. There's a flight this evening; I was meant to be going tomorrow but I've just changed my ticket. I've had enough, I'm going home. But be quick, I don't think there's many left.' With that he scurried on, his pasty white legs looking faintly ridiculous in their crisp, new shorts. I assumed he was headed in the direction of the bus station so that he could get to the airport.

My heart sank. I didn't have my passport. In the chaos and confusion of the last few days, I had left it with a travel agent, who had promised to get me an Indian visa. I was supposed to be travelling overland from Nepal but I hadn't got my paperwork sorted out yet.

Binod followed me back to my hostel where I asked the receptionist's permission to use the telephone. I called the number on a tatty business card that I'd been given by the travel agent, only to be greeted by a recorded message. 'Due to the incident today, the office will be closed for the next week, or until normality returns. Please contact me in due course.'

I looked at Binod nervously. For the first time in my life I was literally stranded in a foreign country with nowhere to go. Short of banging on the walls of the British embassy, I didn't know what to do.

'Don't worry, my friend,' he said. 'We will head for the hills. It isn't safe here any more but in a few days we will sort all this out. Go and pack your bags and we will return to Sarangkot.'

'But Binod. I don't have any money, I can't pay you as a guide.' I was serious. I was nearing the end of my journey and almost completely out of money.

'I don't want your money, brother. It would be my honour to host you until you can escape.'

And so I hastily packed my bags and followed my new friend out of town as the sun set behind Poon Hill, casting its last rays of golden light over Lake Phewa. The country fell into darkness except for the flickering glow of small fires that were burning like stars in the villages above.

2

Fourteen Years Later

'Are you looking for anything in particular, sir?' asked the wiry car salesman in a sharp suit and a fat knotted tie. I thought it best not to give too much away at this point and carried on squinting at the tyres as if I knew what I was looking for.

'Not too many miles on the clock,' I muttered, with studied disdain. The last time I bought a vehicle it had four legs and a hump, in more ways than one, and I was determined to get a good deal this time.

'She's a good runner. Only a ton behind her,' said Archie. I knew he was an Archie even before I had noticed the glinting name badge. Perhaps it was the slick haircut, or the gold cufflinks which twinkled as he held his hands behind his back, lolling between the customers in the showroom.

As I pretended to read the small print on the price tag, Archie rested a hand on the bonnet of the Land Rover. It was ten years old, black and very shiny. I liked it a lot but took great care not to show even a glimmer of emotion.

'That's a third of the way to the moon,' I told him. 'It's literally driven around the world four times. And the leather looks a bit worn.' I peered in through the window hoping to catch a glimpse of the salesman's reaction in the reflection.

Archie didn't flinch. Archie knew the routine.

'It's well loved, no rips or tears; Land Rovers last for ever. How about a test drive? If you take her today I'll throw in the wide-rim alloys.' His blue eyes stared knowingly. The bastard had me. He was as good as any Bedouin camel dealer, even if he had failed to offer me a glass of tea with six sugars.

I'd promised myself a car for five years but hadn't been able to justify it. My nomadic lifestyle coupled with an unhealthy amount of time spent overseas meant that I hadn't really needed one until now. I mean, I still didn't need one but I figured that where I lived in Fulham, while being a delightfully quiet part of London, was still London and that if I had a car, at least I'd be able to escape the city at the weekends, catch sight of some greenery and go and see my friends who had left the big smoke.

So I bought the car. Archie shook my hand and I signed the vehicle registration document. It was a happy moment and I drove home through town, craftily avoiding the congestion zone, only to be nobbled with a parking ticket when I stopped to do my good deed for the day and drop off some clothes at a charity shop.

I had in fact grown very fond of my little garden flat in spite of everything. There was no internet because the walls were too thick. The oven hadn't worked in weeks and the shower rail threatened to impale anyone who dared risk the alternating trickle of ice-cold or boiling-hot water. There simply was no middle ground. To make matters worse a family of mice had decided to take up residence somewhere in the masonry of number 110 Edenvale Street. I was less bothered about them than Emily, my housemate, who went so far as to procure a cat called Gracie specifically for the task of eradicating the unfortunate squatters. Gracie performed her duties admirably and was rightly proud of her achievements, so much so that on more than one occasion she decided to show us how clever she was by depositing a semi-incapacitated rodent in each of our duvets. But soon enough the mice opted to relocate and peace resumed. I had also considered getting a dog, which I thought would make an excellent addition to my new suburban domesticity. I soon realised though that dog ownership would involve fairly substantial daily walks, which really undermined the point of getting a car. Deep down I'd already made my decision: enough was enough; I was fed up with being a pedestrian.

Still, despite the travails of everyday London life, it was nice to finally be settled. After almost five years of being basically homeless, all I wanted to do was put my feet up and enjoy a nice pint by the fire. There's a place in Fulham called the Sands End. It's a good pub and they let you take your dog in. But, of course not having a dog of my own I had to content myself with eavesdropping from one of the comfier chairs with my laptop as a diversion. Gaggles of leggy blonde estate agents would paw away at minuscule, bug-eyed chihuahuas while their boyfriends discussed the relative merits of buy-to-let mortgages.

'Everyone in Fulham works in property, darling,' I heard one of them say, as her chihuahua leapt from her clutches towards a scotch egg the size of its own head. It seemed to be true. The entire economy seemed to be based around rich people selling houses to each other.

But that's Fulham for you. You only have to walk along the New Kings Road to notice that every shop is selling hand-painted doorknobs or lampshades with a three-figure price tag. I suppose the good thing about Fulham though is that at least it isn't Chelsea where the lampshades have a four-figure price tag.

Sunday afternoons in the Sands End were invariably busy. Red-faced youths with floppy hair shouted lispy profanities to each other through extraordinarily big teeth, much to the chagrin of the ladies.

'My word, Jonny, it is *rough* in here these days,' said a woman attached to a black Labrador. She was talking to her boyfriend sitting nearby but the words were for the benefit of everyone within earshot.

It was around three o'clock and drizzly outside, just as the last of the gourmet sausage rolls were being delicately arranged on a mahogany chopping board at the end of the bar by a bored-looking waitress.

'Four pounds fifty?' squealed the Labrador woman. Jonny sighed. He was resigned to perch on a bar stool with a pink dog lead as the rugby team tried to muscle in for a one-armed grope of his girlfriend's prize pooch.

'How very reasonable,' said the chihuahua lady as she pushed in front of the first, looking down her nose.

Despite Fulham's pink shirts, red chinos and fox-fur hand warmers, I had grown to like this little bend in the river. It's where the bishops of London used to live in the Middle Ages, and on sunny days I'd go for a stroll along the river.

If you keep walking on the north bank of the Thames, past the Putney Bridge Premier Inn there's a medieval church with a stone tower. In the graveyard outside I took morbid pleasure in trying to find the oldest headstones. Some displayed skull-and-crossbones, carved into the stone, not unlike the ones you'd see on the flags of pirate ships. I'd try to imagine the ragged congregation six hundred years ago crossing the river by rowing boat, and at low tide having to wade up the sand-bank covered in mud.

Now of course a neat stone embankment sealed off the road and the church and the rest of man's construction from the river. That didn't stop valiant middle-aged men in wellies and deer stalkers, shirking their husbandly duties, and venturing out on an intrepid quest. They would hunt for whatever hallowed object it was that Princess Ethelburga dropped on the beach while on her way to beg forgiveness for her extramarital affair with brother Cederic. Armed with leather satchels, trowels and highly expensive metal detectors, legions of amateur archaeologists would patrol the mudflats every Sunday morning, weaving between the houseboats left high and dry by the low tide, in search of ancient gold coins, iron swords and silver bracelets. More often than not, of course, they'd return only with a bag of ring pulls and an aggravated hernia but I sometimes envied their sense of purpose.

The river, whether high or low, continued in its glorious, brown inexorability, steadily dragging the remains of the day east. Athletic men in Lycra sped past in tiny boats, preparing their spindly frames for the forthcoming University boat race. Whatever the weather, there would be joggers pounding the pavements as if to warm up for the apocalyptic morning commute, when they would all pour into the black hole that is Putney Bridge tube.

If you carry on along the river a bit further and know where to turn off the riverside path you will find the old manor house hidden by tall trees, a secret rural idyll that few Londoners have even heard of, let alone visited. At the weekend Fulham Palace is the sole domain of pretty young mothers who travel in pairs each with a small infant attached to their chest by means of a vastly overpriced harness. There's a tea shop in the grounds where a sea of yoga pants and cashmere shawls blends seamlessly into the mountains of double buggies, each with its own built-in frappuccino cup holder – essential for those longer expeditions beyond Parsons Green.

But it seemed that even the mothers didn't know what lay beyond the high brick walls of the Bishops Park vegetable garden. Through the little archway it's impossible to imagine that humdrum suburbia is only metres away and for a moment you can be transported into another world. Like a scene from

Alice in Wonderland you are momentarily pulled into fantasia and surrounded by tall roses and grapevines and lavender shrubs where it's possible to finally breathe. Then, as if by magic, bright-green parakeets populate the park, descendants of a hardy subtropical pioneer who escaped his cage and spawned an immigrant community of squawking expats who have wisely selected the SW postcodes as their patch. It is rumoured that in the 1960s Jimi Hendrix let a pair of these gaudy birds loose and that they bred rampantly, presumably feeding their brood on the left-over brioche and smoked salmon that litters the lawns of the Hurlingham Club. Who needs to travel anyway when you have such wonders in your back garden?

It had taken a while but I'd fallen back in love with London after a time when I worried that I was destined never to settle. The previous year I'd spent walking the length of the Nile, a journey that had taken nine months and almost all of my will-power and mental energy. I'd said to myself I'd had quite enough adventuring for one lifetime, and more close calls than I wished to remember.

'Haven't you used up your nine lives already?' said my dad on the phone. He didn't like London. 'Too many people,' he said. 'And your mother and I could do with some grandchildren soon. If you leave it much longer, we'll be too old to remember their names.'

I had it all planned out. Twelve months in London: it was to be a hectic social calendar: the German Christmas Market, the Real Ale festival, New Year's eve in St James's, Putney Bridge for the boat race, Army vs Navy rugby match, tennis at Wimbledon, and maybe even try to understand cricket. If not this year then next. I'd get my adrenalin fix from nice short trips away with the army reserves, and take up a silly hobby, like paragliding or yoga; anything but walking. I'd find a dog, get married, buy a little flat with a garden and earn my money spinning yarns in the City and writing a travel column about nice places with beaches and wine and comfy beds.

Things had been going rather well in fact. I'd started to write more articles, had a few pieces commissioned by the newspapers and public-speaking requests were coming in thick and fast. My book was selling well and I had a bit of money saved up. For the first time in years I'd spent more than six months living in the same house, and even gone so far as to hang things on the wall. There they were, a big tattered antique map of Africa that showed names such as Zaire and Rhodesia in large black text. My bookcase, which had suffered a decade-long sabbatical, gathering dust in my parents' garage, had made a glorious return; reinstated in pride of place in my tiny bedroom, adorned with hundreds of books I had almost forgotten I owned. One grey Sunday afternoon I took great pleasure in arranging them in thematic order. There were lots of history books, plenty about travel, a whole host of guidebooks dating back to my first travels in 2001, atlases, maps, biographies and a respectable amount of fiction too. Sometimes it was hard to categorise. Everyone who's read anything by Bruce Chatwin would struggle to know whether its rightful place lies within the realm of fact or fantasy. There were the old classics by Marco Polo and Ibn Battuta, and a whole host of more modern, and lesser-known travellers: Norman Lewis, Eric Newby and Redmond O'Hanlon, whose ramshackle Oxfordshire cottage I one day hoped to replicate.

On the wall above the bookshelf I hung the sword I'd bought from a nomad in Sudan who claimed it had lopped off many British heads at the battle of Omdurman, and beneath it the Mundari spear I'd traded for a cheap mobile phone in the Sudd swamp. The built-in shelves by the window housed the rest of my tat: a pair of naval binoculars that once belonged to a British sailor in the First World War; an old prismatic compass in a desiccated leather pouch; some crocodile teeth; a Soviet belt buckle; some ancient Greek coins and an Uzbek skull cap; a Congolese witchdoctor's mask; prehistoric flint tools from the Sahara and my medal from Afghanistan, and another one I'd been given for working with the Americans in Burundi. Glinting from behind the smeared glass sat a *kukri*, the long curved war knife used by Gurkha soldiers; this one, according to the old SAS trooper who gave it to me, had seen action in Korea in 1951.

It was a humble little shrine, and of course completely out of place in the grey surroundings of South West London, but it was my path to redemption. A reminder of all my youthful wanderings and attempts to live a life of my own choosing, even if it did seem a hundred years too late. It was my own way of celebrating the past by surrounding myself with it. I found that by placing within arm's reach an item with a story of its own, I immediately felt comforted by that sense of perspective; of relative humility; and an acute reminder that life is short. How many people before me had taken inspiration from the roughly cut pages of the second edition of T. E. Lawrence's *Seven Pillars of Wisdom* that sat like an idol on my bedside table? Or shared in the forgotten prayers chanted as the high-pitched song emanated from the Tibetan brass bowl that I'd uncovered beneath piles of antique masks in a market in Kathmandu? How many warriors had depended upon the Ethiopian shield that leant against the bottom of my bookcase? And how many feet had trodden on the silken Uzbek rug that covered the wine stains on my floor? I was no collector of things of value, in the monetary sense, only things that I felt had a soul; they were what I wanted in my home. And now I had enough. I'd walked the Nile and climbed mountains and crossed swamps and explored jungles, and I'd got the scars and photos to prove it. I had a house full of treasures and a head full of memories. It was time to hang up my walking boots. For the foreseeable future, at least.

From now on I'd decided to become an armchair traveller. I had an Amazon wishlist as long as my arm which I wanted to get through and I was tired of being on the move. For now my adventuring days were over, and I had nothing left to prove. The Nile had defeated me and turned me into a fatalist, and I was all the happier for it. I had enough experiences to last a lifetime – a hundred lifetimes – and I'd seen everything I wanted to of the world. I wasn't cynical – merely realistic and content; what's more, I was alive to count my blessings. Besides, I had a car now and I was damned if I paid tax on the thing and didn't mean to use it. No, my mind was made up. The only expedition I would be going on any time soon would be to spot deer in Richmond Park. Winter had fallen on London and I looked forward to the season of mulled wine, mince pies and getting fat.

3

We Are the Pilgrims, Master

The doorbell sounded and as usual I was greeted with the unbridled enthusiasm of a man on a mission. My friend Ash Bhardwaj had just taken a tube from East London where he spent his time hanging out in trendy bars and watching immersive theatre, in between running a production company and writing articles about pop-up coffee shops. He was wearing his distinctive black skinny jeans, a garish shirt with the top button done up and pointy brogues. His hair was very fashionable and he was sporting a solid black beard that gave him the appearance of a rather dashing hipster. I'd happened to mention on the phone a few days before that I was thinking about getting a dog. He insisted on seeing me right away.

'You can't do it, Lev, you simply can't,' said Ash. 'Suburbia just isn't for you. You need to do another walk. At least one more. '

'Absolutely not,' I reassured the man with whom I had travelled on and off for five years. He knew me like a brother and was one of the most positive, thoughtful and considerate gentlemen I'd had the pleasure of getting to know. He was also far too enthusiastic about me going away again and I wondered what he was up to.

'You need another challenge. You've been in one place for six whole months now, don't you have itchy feet? You'll be bored out of your mind if you keep on hanging around here.'

'I'm quite content, thank you very much,' I said. 'I'm beginning to enjoy London. It'll be spring soon and then we'll all cheer up. The last thing I need is another walk; my feet have almost recovered and my toenails are only black at the tips now. I'm going house hunting this week, a lovely little two-bed has just come on the market. It needs a bit of work, I mean, a whole new replaster and plumbing, and probably a kitchen, but it can all be done in a month or two. It even has outside space.'

'Outside space? Wood, have you heard yourself? You mean a bloody garden? You sound like you've been living in Fulham too long. I'm worried about you. You wouldn't know what to do with a spanner if it hit you in the face. You're not a plumber. And if you want outside space then I hear the North Pole has some. Forget about the house, go on another journey into the wilds, and then you can settle down in another year or two. We're still young.'

'I've made up my mind, Ash. If you want an adventure, then go on one. I'm done. Let's go to New York and get drunk, that'll be an adventure.'

Ash shook his head. 'Forget it, let's just get drunk here.' But I suspected he hadn't forgotten anything.

'Fulham?' I said, more to wind him up than anything.

'There's no way I'm drinking there – it's a fiver a pint and full of arseholes who work in property. Let's go to Hackney.' For the sake of our friendship we had to negotiate the same deal every time. We'd either take it in turns and visit each other on our own turf, or meet in the middle.

'I'm not going to East London,' I said. 'It's still full of arseholes and they don't even do pints there. I'm not drinking craft ale from a bottle.'

'Well then, we'll have to do central.' We both hated central, as it was always too busy and also full of arseholes. And it was still a fiver a pint.

'Central it is.'

For March the weather was unusually mild and it was decided that we would take a walk from Charing Cross station, running the gauntlet down Villiers Street, avoiding the charity pitches and overenthusiastic buskers, to Gordon's Wine Bar.

Gordon's is a London institution. Nestled between Victoria Embankment and the Strand, it's a stone's throw from Trafalgar Square and right opposite the offices of PricewaterhouseCoopers, which explains the abundance of accountants on dates with their secretaries. Mind you, who could blame them? With its underground bar in the ancient wine cellar and rough brick walls illuminated only by candlelight, it has a certain old-world charm. The wobbly wooden stools, melted wax and vaults covered in yellow newspapers from days gone by, whip you straight back to Victorian London. The chairs are so close together you can't help but feel an intimacy towards whoever you're with – possibly because you're reluctant to touch the dripping mould that grows from the walls. Getting a table in the dungeon is virtually impossible unless you're first in, and since there's no beer, you're guaranteed to have polished off a couple of bottles of burgundy before the sun has even set; the ideal venue for a date.

Ash and I thought we'd leave the lovers inside to it and instead claimed a corner of a table in the garden, where we plonked ourselves with a cheese board and vintage port.

'You'll get gout if you stay any longer.' He chuckled as he gulped down a full glass of tawny. 'When was the last time you went for a run?'

For some reason I looked at my watch. 'December,' I said ruefully, realising that in the havoc of London life, amid the whirlwind of parties and talks and charity functions, I hadn't so much as broken a sweat in over two months.

'You should be ashamed of yourself,' said Ash, tutting.

He had me there. I needed a way out. An excuse. Something to pacify him. 'All right, all right. I won't get a dog. I'll take up waterskiing instead. Happy now?'

'No, not until you agree to another journey. Remember the Nile? Wasn't it incredible? The simplicity, the lack of choice, of having to make do, that's what happiness is all about. Look around us. People spend their lives worrying about little insignificant decisions. Pointless choices that really don't matter, that's what makes people unhappy. You need to get away again and have a bit more of the simple life. And I want to come along for a bit.'

I'd had enough of his persistence but I knew he wouldn't give up.

'Fine,' I conceded. 'Let's go for an adventure. I'm not walking though. Let's drive somewhere,' I said, more to keep him quiet than anything.

'That's more like it. I've been thinking . . . how about the Silk Road?' said Ash excitedly. There it was. I knew he was up to something.

I thought about it for a minute. Ash knew all too well that I'd wanted to revisit Central Asia since I hitched to India in '04.

'Think about it. The Silk Road would be fantastic, I've always wanted to see Persia.' He beamed.

'Iran,' I corrected him.

'Where's your sense of romance? It'll always be Persia. The minarets, the deserts, the great palaces at Bukhara and Samarkand, the bazaars in Herat and the high mountain passes in Hunza. Get your phone out, let's plan a route.'

'Tomorrow perhaps. More port?'

'There's no time like the present. Go on. We can draft a proposal. How about something like "the Silk Road By Any

Means"? You can drive, or go on horseback, motorbike or whatever you want. I'll meet you for bits along the way. You could start in Turkey and go all the way to China. You could do it in six weeks, eight max, and then you can retire and live in suburbia.'

I had to admit he'd piqued my interest. I felt a familiar shiver of simultaneous excitement and dread rattle down my spine. I knew, right then, that the cogs of destiny were about to make another turn and there was nothing that I could do but play my part.

I took out my phone and looked at Google maps. The route looked simple enough. I could retrace part of the route I took when I was twenty-two, from Istanbul through the Caucasus and Iran and head north through the 'Stans and cross the Taklamakan desert to get to Western China, and if I drove fast enough I could even make it all the way to Beijing. Easy. I drafted a note to my agent Jo and got back to the more important business of sinking the port and listening to the clamour of London.

It was dusk now, but the crowds showed no sign of abating. If anything, the bar was getting busier and with it a shifting feeling of proximity ensued. People were crowding closer, strangers talking to each other as disparate groups of drinkers converged because table space commanded a premium. Pile upon pile of crumbs of cheese and flakes of Parma ham were stacked on plates that awaited collection by frantic waiters who seemed resigned to the continual destruction of wine glasses at the hands of increasingly intoxicated patrons.

Perhaps it was fate, or just serendipity, but as I went inside to order another bottle, I happened to look upon a faded plaque that clung – against all odds – to a wall adjacent to the bar. It boasted the fact that once upon a time, when this grimy cellar was used for its original purpose of storing wine, Gordon's used to be the London residence of that most acclaimed of Victorian writers, Rudyard Kipling. The moustachioed author and imperial correspondent happened to have lived upstairs from 1889, when he was twenty-four, until 1891 while writing his desperately sad and semi-autobiographical novel *The Light That Failed,* the tale of a stricken young writer and adventurer, who suffered blindness and the subsequent loss of his fickle lover.

It was Kipling's short stories that had first inspired my teenage fascination with Britain's colonial past, especially her involve-ment in the Indian subcontinent and the high mountain passes that led to the interior of Asia. *The Man Who Would be King* and the classic novel *Kim* sent my young mind spinning, making me half wish I had been born a hundred years earlier. I devoured all I could read about long-forgotten skirmishes on the roof of the world. I encountered the likes of Younghusband, Curzon and a whole host of other bold, hirsute romantics who went off in search of glory and adventure under the banner of a tattered regimental colour, or the patronage of an aristocratic President of the Royal Geographical Society. The period known as the Great Game soon became an all-encompassing passion. Over the years I'd tried to put aside these fanciful studies in favour of more useful and contemporary issues. At university I read modern history and got my teeth firmly sunk into political theory and the basics of philosophy. But I found myself return-ing to those obscure texts dealing with the intrigues of an impe-rial past that has so often been disregarded and misunderstood. It seemed to me that in those histories perhaps a lesson or two might be learnt about our world today after all. For what happened in the aftermath of that fateful day in September 2001 and the events unfolding in Afghanistan in the early years of the new millennium, were a direct consequence, and in many ways, continuation, of a battle between civilised and uncivilised, West and East, invader and invaded, secular and fanatic that has repeated itself time and again, in the deserts and mountains of High Asia.

I remembered the chilling words of warning Kipling issued to the British soldier fighting on the frontier a hundred and thirty years earlier. They were just as relevant today to the tommies I'd fought with in the same dusty defiles that harboured Ghazis and Pathans in 1880.

> *When you're wounded and left on Afghanistan's plains,*
> *And the women come out to cut up what remains,*
> *Jest roll to your rifle and blow out your brains*
> *An' go to your Gawd like a soldier.*

But where there is darkness, I'd also found light. Years of travelling out of uniform in war zones had taught me a few lessons. So long as you're not armed and come in peace, you're willing to adopt local customs with sensitivity to culture and tradition and try not to judge too much – however tempting – you'll generally be fine. People in the most dangerous parts of the world had gone out of their way to make me feel at home, sometimes regardless of whether I'd wanted to or not. With a smattering of language, a spot of homework, a bit of fancy dress (and knowing when it's wise to grow a beard or not), I'd somehow managed to blend in, survive, and what's more, make some good friends along the way. From the minefields and mountains of Kurdistan, to the swamps of Sudan and the forests of Rwanda, from the frontlines of Burma to the deserts of Syria I'd met a fascinating bunch of likeminded souls. I'd found that by putting myself through the same hardships as those that live in a place I'd been invited to see its secrets, and it's the secrets, I think, that make travelling worthwhile.

As I tried to shove through the throngs of tourists and accountants, great wafts of Stilton fumes floating over the haze of humanity, I reached an impasse in the form of an enormous Frenchman who was blocking half the bar and something occurred to me. I quite liked walking. Despite my outward complaints, I supposed that I must enjoy it at least a little since I spent quite a lot of time doing it, and it was through walking that I'd had the opportunity to meet so many people that had given me faith in the world. It was a minor epiphany but an important one and I rushed outside with an acceptable vintage to tell Ash the news.

'I'll do another walk. But this is the last one,' I said, gravely.

'Wonderful, but you do realise the Silk route at its shortest is at least five thousand miles. You don't want to be walking all that, do you?' he said.

I racked my brain as I imagined the winding path, and he was right. There was a lot of yellow on the map – vast empty stretches of desert and barren plateaus. The Silk route stretched from the edges of Europe all the way to China, and passed through a heck of a lot of 'Stans. Sure, it would be possible to walk it all but it would take a couple of years, and I wasn't getting any younger. No, it was too far. I needed a route that was more contained but just as interesting.

If I were to walk at all, it would need to be an expedition as iconic and sublime as the Nile, if not more so. I carried on look-ing at the map glowing from the screen of my phone with a sense of squinting bewilderment. As I looked harder, a faint outline seemed to stand out, an outline that seemed to smile from the screen of the phone in an upward arc of white, purple and green, a creased and crumpled bevel of such magnitude and dominance, as bewitching as it was threatening. It was of course, the Himalayas.

It was an area I knew well and it seemed absurd that it hadn't occurred to me before now. I wondered for an instant if anyone had succeeded in walking the entire length of the mighty range, from one end to the other.

Perhaps it was the port addling my brain, or just the sense of excitement that accompanies the dawn of a new idea. This adventure had suddenly manifested itself as a tangible, realistic goal and I felt alive again, ready for a new challenge. It was as if Ash had known all along that this is what I had wanted and been lacking in my recent suburban interlude.

'If I have to walk then it has to be the Himalayas,' I said, and without a word Ash simply smiled and raised a glass.

The Himalayas have attracted a steady stream of mountaineers, adventurers, conquerors and empire builders for thousands of years. Something about these majestic peaks has been irresistible to armies, traders and vagabonds whose attempts to conquer and subdue them have become synonymous with a kind of sadistic futility. Humans have lived and travelled in the Himalayan foothills since time immemorial, fatalistically pitting themselves against some of the harshest conditions in the world and often failing. But in spite of the knowledge that men have always looked up to mountains and not the other way round, they come back time and again to see for themselves the power and majesty that these sublime thrones seem to radiate.

It was the same forces that drove me to want to see the Himalayas for myself at the age of nineteen, and once hooked, I knew that I would have to return.

After Binod bade me goodbye at Pokhara bus station that fateful summer, I made a promise to return one day to Nepal and repay his kindness and hospitality. He had rescued me from the deadly after-effects of the royal massacre and the rioting in Pokhara and looked after me in the foothills until a normality of sorts had returned and I was able to reclaim my passport and escape to India. He'd done all this in exchange for no money, because I had none left, and by way of gratitude I wanted to show him that I was a man of my word. I told him that in a few years I would come back on an expedition where he would be my chief guide and I could pay him properly. He told me that his future was in the hands of God and that if I chose to come back and pay him, great, if not, no matter. It made me all the more determined to keep my promise.

It was to be another eight years before I saw Binod again. In 2009 I had reached the rank of Captain in the British Parachute Regiment after four years of service around the world, including a short stint in Afghanistan. I had been posted to the darkest depths of Yorkshire, to the Infantry Training Centre in Catterick where it was my duty to instruct new recruits in, among other less important tasks, the art of shaving and how to avoid venereal diseases. After the excitement and adventure of combat duty in the deserts and mountains of Southern Afghanistan, it was a huge disappointment to find myself giving PowerPoint lectures on personal hygiene to seventeen-year-olds, even though I'd been assured it was a great addition to a junior officer's CV. The previous three years had been a rollercoaster ride of action-packed exercises in the forests of East Africa and jungles of Belize as I learnt the ropes at commanding soldiers. I'd thoroughly enjoyed escaping the confines of Sandhurst and getting my teeth sunk into proper soldiering, and with the campaign in Afghanistan in full swing by that time I knew that sooner or later I would see action, and I wasn't disappointed. Four months of patrolling the battlefields of Kandahar province may have been a drop in the ocean in the grand scheme of things, and my wartime exploits pale into insignificance compared to many of my colleagues' who deployed on two or three full tours, but it gave me a taste for action and I relished the experience of living life on the edge. The danger, the unknown and total immersion of being alert 24/7, constantly on the lookout for the enemy and roadside bombs might sound like hell, but ask any infantry soldier and they'll tell you it was the best time of their life.

But now it had all changed. I was suddenly promoted from the blissful joys of field soldiering to the litigious mire of welfare and teaching, which I soon realised were not for me at all. As a result I found myself looking for any opportunity to escape, and failing that, amuse myself with a new challenge that would see me through to the completion of my contract.

I wasn't the only despondent soldier in Catterick. While it is a convenient posting if you happen to hail from the north-east, or if you're married and need a break from the rigours of tours of duty, for a keen young soldier eager to gain experience in the field, it was like a prison sentence. Most of the other Platoon Commanders felt the same, as did many of the junior corporals and sergeants instructing the soldiers.

The one benefit of working at the Infantry Training Centre (ITC) was that you were working on a fixed rotation according to teaching terms. In that respect it was similar to being a teacher and for the first time in my army career, I was in the very strange position of knowing exactly what my diary was going to be like for six months at a time. There was planned leave and therefore the opportunity to book holidays in advance, a precious luxury I'd almost forgotten existed.

One such bout of downtime came in October 2009 at a time when, due to some administrative balls-up, there hadn't been enough soldiers to fill a platoon and as a result I and a number of NCOs found ourselves with the forthcoming prospect of almost an entire month with nothing to do. Ordinarily, the army would conjure up some inconceivably pointless task with which to fill the time. Luckily my Commanding Officer, who appeared to be just as upset as the rest of us, was unusually forward thinking enough to be receptive to the ideas of junior Captains such as myself.

I knew that in order to avoid being sent on a course designed to inflict upon the student a greater knowledge of Maslow's *hierarchy of needs* I had to think fast and come up with a plan. It suddenly occurred to me that this was an ideal opportunity to do my bit for the morale of my team and have a little adventure in the process. In Catterick, the Infantry was sharply bisected into two camps, as the main garrison was divided by a road and high fences. On the north side of the roundabout was the Line Infantry headquarters where soldiers destined for the regional regiments were quartered. This included the likes of the Rifles, the Yorkshires, the Scots and the Welsh, or, as we Paras liked to call them, *hats*, in honour of the multitude of silly headgear worn by the provincial regiments. To the south of the roundabout only three types of soldier were based. The Foot Guards, the Gurkhas and the hopefuls of the Parachute Regiment. While the Guards and the Gurkhas, according to strict Para sensibilities, were also technically *hats*, at least both of them had some sort of a selection process, even if for one of them it was merely the ability to stand up straight for long periods of time and walk in a straight line. To the Commanding Officer of the Second Battalion ITC these were his chosen few.

'Sir, I'd like to take eight soldiers and climb Mera Peak.' I stood to attention before the wild-eyed Colonel. This, as I saw it, was the perfect opportunity to return to Nepal and fulfil the promise I'd made all those years ago to Binod.

I knew that not only did the Colonel have Gurkhas under his command but also that he'd travelled to Nepal himself and was very fond of the country. Even armed with this insight, I couldn't have been more surprised at his enthusiasm.

'Good. There's money in the pot so the blokes shouldn't have to fork out themselves. Just don't kill anyone.'

Coming from a grizzled Para that was as positive as it gets.

For the first time in months I was excited to be in the army. They were going to let me lead an expedition and repay my debts to Binod at the same time. I asked for volunteers and they were forthcoming, as soon as I mentioned that it was free and they could escape Catterick for a few weeks. Two of the sergeants had climbed before but the others were all novices and I looked forward to showing them the mountains for the first time. Training consisted of an hour on the gym climbing wall and a weekend in the Lake District where a professional mountaineer instructed us in the art of not impaling oneself with a crampon or ice axe.

The expedition was a success – well, almost. Only two of the team summited the mountain, which stands at 6,500 metres making it one of the tallest trekking peaks in the world. Those who made the top were Geordie Taylor and Phil Kew, the two Senior NCOs who actually had mountaineering experience. The rest of us got to within a couple of hundred metres of the summit, before being forced to turn back to base camp due to extreme weather and the onset of frostbite. After that I swore I'd never set foot on a mountain again. While there was some disap-pointment for some of the team having not reached the top after a two-week trek I had no sense of let-down. For me, it had been all about having Binod along for the journey and to have fulfilled my promise. He was of course over the moon to be invited to be the chief guide and translator. The money he earned in that fortnight would keep him going for several months to come and, as a bonus, in my team he earned himself several new potential clients. It also reaffirmed a long friendship between him and me which I was sure would continue for the rest of our lives.

In the years that followed, Binod and I kept in touch and I helped him where I could, sending him small gifts of money and essentials for his family and children. During my first visit to Nepal in 2001, Binod had just one son, a few months old, but now he had a daughter too, and another baby boy. A dispute over land rights to his shack in Sarangkot and the fact that he belonged to a low caste, meant that he was always short of money. I became aware that the cost of a few nights out in Gordon's for me, amounted to a lifeline for him and the future of his family. Naturally, I took him under my wing, as he had done for me all those years ago.

I left the regular army to try my hand at new things and for a few years found myself pottering. I tried everything from wedding photography to charity work, until I finally settled on the rather insecure life of a full-time travel writer. And then I decided to walk the length of the Nile, after which I swore I'd never walk anywhere again.

Time, it seems, is a great healer. Or at least it helps fade the bad memories. After I'd sobered up from Gordon's and the idea of walking the length of the Himalayas solidified, I found myself once again trawling through the archives of the Royal Geographical Society for maps and routes and browsing the diaries of explorers past and present. I studied the mountains intensely, looking for a way through and soon realised that while I could potentially complete this expedition in a much shorter timeframe than the Nile, walking the Himalayas was going to be the biggest physical and bureaucratic challenge of my life.

For a start there is a dispute over what constitutes the beginning and end of the Himalayas. Strictly speaking the westernmost anchor of the range is the mountain Nanga Parbat in Pakistan, where the northernmost bend in the Indus river heralds the gateway to the snowcapped peaks. But one only has to look at a map or a satellite image to see that the white swirls and geographical contortions begin much further west, where the Karakorum, Pamir and Hindu Kush all collide, in a massive uplift that forms the borders of Afghanistan, China and Tajikistan. Likewise to the east, the spinal column of Asia appears from above to change during its progress from a narrow ridge into a sprawling fan of gigantic proportions as it departs Bhutan and spills across eastern Tibet, India and Burma. It seemed an almost impossible proposition. How could one hope to cover it all and do it justice?

The scale of the undertaking suddenly hit me and I realised that whatever I was hoping to achieve would need to be focused and limited in its goals. I decided that the aims of this expedition wouldn't be to climb mountains, or to try to break any records, or even to attempt to cover as much ground as possible, but instead use this opportunity to explore, on foot, the valleys and foothills that were inhabited by the various communities and tribes that called the Himalayas their home. For me it was about the people I encountered that attracted me to travel, and travelling on foot is the only way to explore the backcountry and villages that are hidden from the main trails and roads. It is also the way people have travelled in these regions for millennia and there seems to be a common bond between pedestrians everywhere. The physical hardships, the risks, the utter vulnerability mean that on the whole you will be looked upon as a fellow human being, rather than a foreigner, or worse, a tourist. So with that in mind I planned to travel more or less the extent of the mountains from the western-most fringes in Afghanistan, a country I knew well, all the way through its main arteries via the countries that were currently so presumptuous to claim ownership – Pakistan, India, Nepal – and finish up in either Tibet or Bhutan, depending on which of the two infamous regions happened to be feeling sporting enough to let me in.

It sounded simple in theory – all the best ideas do – but even with as vague an aim as that, the journey was likely to be riddled with enormous and varied challenges. On top of my first visit in 2001 and my first forays into mountaineering with Mera Peak in 2009, I'd also travelled briefly into the Indian Himalaya in 2004 as part of an overland journey from Europe and had completed a five-month hitchhike ending in the foothills of Himachal Pradesh. Here I almost froze to death after a nightmarish few hours in a cave, convinced that if the cold didn't finish me off, the wolves and bears would. The route that I proposed would pass through the same region, and I was acutely aware that what lay ahead wouldn't always be pleasant.

Insurgency in Afghanistan, landslides in Kashmir, Maoists in Nepal, grizzly predators throughout and that's without the heavy rains of the monsoon; rabid dogs; rabid monkeys; rabid bureaucrats and a whole host of equally terrible ways to meet your end: leeches, scorpions, hypothermia, snakes, spiders, leprosy, leishmaniasis, malaria, typhoid, altitude sickness, avalanches, dysentery, bad roads, worse brakes and terrible drivers.

The travel advisory on the Foreign & Commonwealth Office's website wasn't exactly reassuring either: 'The FCO advises against all travel to Afghanistan'; 'The FCO advises against all travel on the Karakorum Highway between Islamabad and Gilgit'; 'There is a high threat of terrorism, kidnap and sectarian violence throughout Pakistan'; 'The FCO advises against all travel to Jammu and Kashmir' ... These were all places I wanted to go to. As for Tibet, the British government assured me that the border could be closed without notice and that under no circumstances would the Chinese allow me to go off wandering without an official minder. In Bhutan I was faced with an almost empty page. Nobody knew anything about Bhutan.

To make matters worse, on 25 April 2015 the unthinkable happened. A 7.8 magnitude earthquake struck the very heart of Nepal, killing and injuring thirty thousand people and rendering hundreds of thousands homeless and destitute. In a country that was already terribly impoverished, the disaster was apocalyptic.

As a result, the general consensus among everyone I spoke to was that the walk was unachievable and that I would almost certainly be killed. And it did occur to me that on this occasion the naysayers might just be right.

I thought back to the Nile – the endless days on the road, being swarmed by mosquitoes, eaten alive by tsetse, sleeping among the roadside filth and being chased by dogs, rats and crocodiles. I remembered how I said I'd never do it again; once was most definitely enough. It all came flooding back: the loneliness, the pain of walking every day, of blisters upon blisters, the isolation and the bitter frustrations of dealing with officious little policemen and the fear that one night you'd wake up to the grinning face of a machete-toting madman above your bed. Suddenly the idea of staying in Fulham seemed much more sensible.

4

Kabul

The last time I flew into Afghanistan things had been very different. We had flown in under cover of night so as to avoid being shot up by the anti-aircraft guns hidden among the craggy rocks of the hills around Kandahar and had to wear body armour for the landing. I remember it like it was yesterday. The tense silence, the blackness outside, the red flashes of light from the RAF Tristar transporter's wings, the acrid smell of sweat from a hundred Paratroopers, many of them flying into battle for the first time.

This time it was marginally more peaceful. The sun had risen over the appropriately named *Dasht-I-Margo* – the Desert of Death – as we began our descent, and a pale light shone across the faint undulations of the barren wastes of central Afghanistan. As we got lower, I craned my neck to make out the foothills of the Hindu Kush through the window. I thought for a moment that the entire landscape was covered in snow, such was the brilliance of the white, rippling sheen beneath us as we descended on Turkish Airlines Flight 455 into Afghanistan's blighted capital.

The plane was full of men: Afghans in shiny suits and pointy black shoes with slick black hair and the almond eyes of the Tajik. These were the wealthy classes – businessmen, diplomats and economic migrants returning to their homeland. Only a couple of the older men wore beards, the rest were clean-shaven and suddenly I felt self-conscious at having grown mine in an attempt to fit in. In my khaki expedition shirt and grey Craghoppers trousers, I may have felt ready for action, but I was also far and away the scruffiest person on the plane.

It wasn't until we were below three thousand feet that I realised the milky panorama wasn't snow at all – it couldn't be, this was the height of summer – but the distinctive fine hanging dust that envelops everything in this country. From the twig-like poplar trees and the patchwork of mud-brick villages to the rows upon rows of MI8 Russian helicopters that were parked in front of the military side to the runway, nothing was immune to this filthy blanket.

It was the first week of June and very hot. As the doors of the aeroplane opened, a fierce, dry wind blasted through the cabin. It felt like a hairdryer to the face. I prepared to roll up my sleeves and was astounded to see the Afghans actually put their coats and jackets on.

Everyone seemed impatient to get off and the men spilled out of the front doors and down onto the tarmac in mere minutes. Slightly hesitant, I let them bustle past me. As I stepped off the last rickety stair, onto the ground that shimmered with the incredible heat, the memories came flooding back. This was no ordinary airport, it was the gateway to Afghanistan, a world I thought I'd left behind.

Kabul airport was busy. Former Soviet soldiers sauntered across the runway in luminous vests, spectres of a communist past that never seemed to disappear. American Special Forces operators and government agents loitered by the entranceway to the main hangar. They were hardly covert, wearing tight T-shirts that hugged hulking muscular frames, developed over a decade of doing pull-ups on home-made gyms set up in secret mountain bases. They all wore dark wrap-around sunglasses and khaki cargo pants and brown military-style rucksacks, with a karabiner attached to a webbing clip. Regimental and Unit tattoos were half revealed under short sleeves. They could hardly have looked more military if they'd been in uniform. Despite the NATO troop withdrawal six months before, it was obvious that foreign forces were still coming and going quite freely.

And, of course, there were Afghan soldiers everywhere too. Uniforms of every colour and style of camouflage were draped on fierce-looking men in varying states of hairiness. Some were armed with American-made carbine assault weapons and wore brand new body armour over menacing black overalls, their faces covered in balaclavas – these were the secret police and the special militias. The personal bodyguards of warlords under the thinly veiled pretence of national authority. Others, moustachioed and provincial, wore drab, grey service dress, an outfit designed twenty years ago when the Soviets had invaded, with Kalashnikovs dangling loosely from leather slings. These were the regular police – underpaid and undertrained. And there was every variety of mismatching states of dress and professionalism in between. Plain-clothes spies wearing Ray-Bans and black shiny shoes, pistols secured in sling holsters, or, for the most nonchalant of officers, stuffed down the front of ill-fitting jeans. Everywhere there was a sense of machismo and showmanship; it was as if Kabul had held a competition to see who could dress in the most alarming fashion in order to terrify the latest visitor.

I carried my pack and pushed a trolley through the hallway where swarms of officials rifled through bags, ordered the filling out of forms and generally carried out a myriad of contradictory bureaucratic duties.

'You must be Lev.'

I heard a voice shout out above the tumult of Persian. I looked up and swerved the trolley laden with my bags, narrowly missing a throng of chattering women in black chadors.

A man stood in front of me looking just as conspicuous as the rest of the shady Westerners. He too wore the uniform of the mercenary: faded jeans, a tight polo shirt and trekking shoes; an engineer's penknife in a black pouch, and of course, the wrap-around shades. But he was most definitely British rather than American. He had none of the swagger of a US operative, and his hair, although cropped on the back and sides, wasn't quite a 'high and tight'. But it was the accent that distinguished him. Even in his opening remarks I discerned the faintest twang of a Birmingham drawl.

'Martin,' said the tall 'security contractor' in front of me with a firm smile. He raised his shades to reveal a pair of grey eyes beneath a wide, thickset forehead. He shook my hand with the grip of a former military man.

'Let me help you with that.' He commandeered my trolley and did a three-point turn between the sea of Afghan luggage that covered the floor of the arrivals hall. Unusually, I was relieved to be in the presence of a minder. Martin had been recommended as 'the go-to man in Kabul' by an old army mate, and these days you couldn't be too careful. Violence had been on the rise; kidnaps and murders were rife and suicide bombings a daily occurrence. Already this year 5,000 civilians had been killed or wounded, a higher number than at any time during the actual conflict over the past fourteen years. It was wise for someone to have your back and I'd been told Martin would look after me for the twenty-four hours I had in Kabul before setting off into the mountains.

'Oh, I almost forgot, this is your man,' said Martin, as he barged a customs official out of the way.

Meekly trailing behind Martin was a small, thin man with an ageless face. He was old, I thought, or at least much older than me, but I couldn't be certain. Weathered, with deep-set creases around his eyes that betrayed a lifetime of laughter and smiles, I liked him at once.

'Malang?' I asked. As with Martin, I'd only ever had phone communication with this diminutive Afghan and had no idea what to expect. I'd spoken to him once after a friend had said that he'd make an excellent guide. I knew that he was a Wakhi tribesman, a shepherd from the mountains of the north and had been selected as a porter for a mountaineering expedition a few years before. He had impressed the Italian climbers so much by his indifference to hardship, that they had insisted he join them on the next trip to the summit of Mount Noshaq. The successful expedition, summiting Afghanistan's highest peak, made him the first Afghan in history to accomplish the feat.

Since then he'd become a famous man in his country, appearing on the news and even being flown by his European mentors to the French Alps to receive formal training. For a man who, until the age of twenty-nine had never left the sight of his own flock of sheep, this could all have been a touch overwhelming, but my first impressions of Malang suggested that he took everything in his stride.

'*Salaam Alaikum*,' he said formally, with an iron handshake. It turned out he wasn't meek at all, just respectful. He was wearing a salwar kameez, the long robe-like shirt with a woollen waistcoat over the top, and a black and white checked scarf wrapped loosely around his neck. His hair was fiercely black and receding slightly, but under the beads of sweat that were forming on his domed forehead, glowed the most piercing set of silver eyes I'd ever seen. At first glance I sensed intelligence and humour, and an indefinable madness. I knew right then that he would make the perfect walking companion.

'The car's this way,' said Martin, as he led us through a maze of bomb-proof concrete chicanes, security barriers and check-points. The heat was phenomenal and within seconds I was drenched in sweat, my khaki shirt clinging to my body like a wet rag. Now I remembered why the Afghans wore their jackets and coats. Dressing down was futile. You may as well cover up and at least look respectable.

Malang helped steer the laden trolley between bollards and down ill-placed kerbs as we entered a car park that was packed with every kind of vehicle.

We passed row upon row of swanky white Toyota Land Cruisers. Some were unmarked and others were plastered with the logos of their respective aid agencies: United Nations, Save the Children, Halo Trust. Some had national flags emblazoned on the bonnet or rear doors. Norwegian, Danish, Romanian, Canadian, British. Sand-coloured American Humvees domi-nated the space with their colossal chassis and aggressive forms. We came to a halt near the exit of the car park, where a tall white pole displayed a flaccid Afghan flag. There was no wind today, just a still and powerful heat. Everything seemed scorched in the unrelenting sun, which, even though it was barely break-fast time, was high and punishing.

I looked at the car and wondered if Martin was joking. There in front of us was a battered estate, covered in scratch marks, with the paint peeling off around the trim. He smiled knowingly.

'It's safe, mate, don't worry. We're not like Yanks, driving around in those monsters.' He gestured to the Humvees nearby.

'It's all about being covert. Under the radar.' He winked, slamming the boot down to cram in my bags.

'After you,' said Malang, opening the creaky door for me.

'What a gent,' smiled Martin.

I was stuck in the middle, as a large duffel bag took up the right seat and Malang followed me in, securing the best seat and the most legroom. He threw me a cheeky grin.

'See, if you cut about in some fancy-pants, shiny new motor, the Taliban know you're a foreigner and you make yourself more of a target,' Martin informed me from the front passenger seat. 'Let's go.' He nudged the driver. The silent Afghan simply nodded and turned the key in the ignition, roaring the battered car into life.

'But with this beauty, everyone thinks we're just a plain old taxi and will leave us alone.'

The logic made sense to me; I've always found blending in is the safest option. Even if it did seem counter-intuitive. There was no bulletproof windscreen or bombproof body armour on this machine, but then again, if you're invisible, why would you need it?

The car pulled out of the airport compound and we were immediately sucked into the chaos of the city. Unpainted concrete villas lined roads that were packed with cars identical to the one we were in. Boys rode horses down the pavements and old men beat skinny donkeys with leather whips as they staggered under heavy loads of timber and bricks. Armed policemen in peaked caps directed the traffic on roundabouts and there were people everywhere. The concrete villas had upturned roofs and looked faintly oriental in their architectural style – a stark contrast to the endless, drab apartment blocks that also dominated the city, a legacy of the Russian years and the only evidence of urbanisation in this vast country.

Kabul is surrounded by the majestic Hindu Kush mountains. Beyond the sprawling, beige suburbs and through the haze of dust and smog, I could just about discern their outline. The mud-brick villages beyond the city seemed to go on for ever, shacks stacked upon each other, clamouring for space on the rocky hillsides. Everything was dust-coloured except the doors and windows. Startling hues of lime green and turquoise shone from the otherwise adobe terraces.

On top of an escarpment overlooking Kabul sit the bullet-scarred remains of the Darul Aman Palace where the kings used to live, its vast neoclassical shell now crumbling into dust. The 1920s mansion, once a symbol of wealth and reform, in a country that was well on its way to becoming one of the most prosperous and liberal in the Muslim world, was now charred and empty. Pye-dogs were now the royal rulers and squatters the only visitors, stealing the copper and iron fixtures, to sell in the markets in town. From the hill looking down across the plain, I could see three large military surveillance balloons floating high above the city, like the levitating sentries that guarded London during the Blitz. It seemed that warfare hadn't changed all that much. It was a stark reminder that Kabul was still a city under siege.

We were soon in the thick of it. The congested road weaved through the central bazaar where traffic ground to a halt. I looked out of the window, which was smeared with grime, and found myself feeling remarkably vulnerable. I put on my sunglasses and wrapped my cotton scarf around my ears, not for warmth but as an automatic defence against looking remotely foreign. All the men wore scarves here, loosely draped over a shoulder, or around the neck; they were multi-purpose accessories – sweat rags, turbans, dust shields and sometimes a colourful fashion statement.

Even the extremists weren't immune. The Taliban wore black turbans and scarves. Al-Qaeda preferred pure white. But most men chose pastel shades – beige and yellow and sky blue. Some had stripes, others chose the popular black and white Iraqi, or red and white Palestinian-style *Kiffiyeh*.

As far as hats went, there seemed to be just three options: loose turbans for the pious and provincial, white skull caps for the young and urbane, and for the men of action, it was the flat, woollen pancake-shaped hats called *Pakol*. Made famous by the Mujahideen, the *Pakol* came in a mind-boggling range of styles and colours, each with its own special significance and symbolism. Some were known as *Chitrali* caps, rolled with ribbed patterns in the rim, named after the famous valley in Pakistan. The Afghan variants were mock-ups of the Pakistani versions, and were still mostly made in small shops in Peshawar across the border. Imported across the Khyber Pass, they were a reminder of the fluidity of the Afghan-Pakistan borders and the close-knit community of the Pashtun tribes that dominate the cultural landscape. It has been suggested that they were introduced to the Hindu Kush by Alexander the Great, whose Greek army wore a remarkably similar style of hat two thousand years or so ago.

'I wore one to the top of Noshaq,' said Malang. He was referring to the mountain that had brought him fame. 'I never normally wear one though. Only people with guns usually wear them. The Mujahideen and Taliban. But they're kind of comfortable, and people like to see an Afghan wearing one. It's what they expect.'

The markets were heaving. Butchers' shops displayed entire carcasses of cows, their severed heads displayed morbidly on wooden benches outside, overrun with swarms of flies. The acrid stench of death filled the streets and rats ran about unmolested among the open sewers. A withered hand emerged from beneath endless folds of material, some poor widow begging on the street. Men on scooters honked their horns and women in sky-blue burkhas scuttled about in total anonymity. The clamour of stall vendors filled the air, but nothing could outcry the legions of goats being coaxed about by ragged shepherds, out of place amid the urban sprawl. The dry bed of the Kabul river formed the city centre, and in it were hundreds of the beasts, devouring piles of litter and human excrement. Narrow-eyed Hazaras, descendants of Genghis Khan, had set up shop on the pavement, selling fake DVDs of Bollywood films and rip-off Levi's jeans.

The car shunted on and I was glad that the air-conditioning worked. I think Martin noticed the trepidation in my silence.

'Busy is good,' he said. 'Normally word gets out if there's going to be an attack and people stay at home. You wouldn't believe the power of the jungle drums. Back in the old days, the terrorists would use code words on walkie-talkies, so their mates wouldn't get blown up. A bit like Guy Fawkes. Now it's all done on WhatsApp and Twitter.'

I looked at the back of his upright form and wondered about the man. I knew nothing of him and he hadn't volunteered to share his military background. I wondered if he was ex-Special Forces, but I had a hunch he was more likely an Intelligence specialist or a military policeman with expertise in close protection.

'Still. Best to be careful,' Martin continued. 'We always mix up the routes that we take, and avoid the embassy road, where we can. That's where all the big attacks happen. Oh, and the hotels. It's best to avoid anywhere that Terry Taliban reckons he can bag an infidel. I did a spreadsheet the other week to try and figure out, statistically, when most attacks happen. I mean, what time of day.'

'And?' I asked.

'Eighty per cent of suicide bombings happen at morning rush hour, between nine and ten o'clock. The bastards have a fancy last meal, usually bag off with some Chinese pro and get themselves a good night's sleep before getting strapped up at first light. They say their prayers, and then boom! It's off to Allah and their seventy-two virgins, right outside the American embassy. It's downright rude, really. The road gets blocked up for at least a couple of hours while the poor street cleaners are left picking up fingers and toes all day long. And you know what?'

He stared at me. The smile hadn't left his face.

'Nine times out of ten, the only person the stupid bugger kills is himself. Oh, and half a dozen Afghan taxi drivers, and they're probably his bloody cousins, anyway.'

I looked at my watch. It was exactly nine thirty in the morning.

We emerged, relieved and unscathed, from the bazaar and into the wide avenues of Wazir Akhbar Khan, a supposedly safe district in the north of Kabul. At the bottom of a big, brown hill that used to be referred to as the tank graveyard, I remembered how, when I first came here in 2004, the cratered streets were flanked with crumbling houses, shelled to destruction first by the Taliban and then by the Mujahideen. Littered with the remnants of war, the streets had been full of burnt-out armoured cars and the twisted husks of tanks and artillery pieces.

But now, like the roof girders of the royal palace sold for scrap, they had all been cleared away. The streets had been swept clean and shiny three-storey mansions had sprung up to house a new invader – the hordes of foreign aid workers, UN bureaucrats and 'consultants'. We were heading to a nondescript house, hidden from view and obscured from the main road by an even larger, more vulgar residence.

'The whole block is owned by Dostum,' said Malang, peering out of the window as we pulled into the tall gates of a walled compound. An Afghan guard brandishing an Uzi submachine gun saluted as we rolled in.

'Correct,' said Martin. 'And the rest. All the buildings you can see on this hillside are part of his empire. He's even got his own army.'

I'd read about General Abdul Rashid Dostum before. One of the numerous warlords who had influenced Afghan politics since the 1970s, it's fair to say his record of power play and duplicitous intrigue is unmatched. Even amid the complex situation of Afghanistan, where double-dealing politicians were ten-a-penny, Dostum was about as machiavellian as they come.

An ethnic Uzbek, born of peasant lineage, Dostum became a communist and joined the Russian-sponsored Afghan army in 1978, fighting against the Mujahideen in a number of battles. After the Mujahideen victory and the humiliated Soviet departure, his days may have seemed numbered, but Dostum contrived a miraculous U-turn. He joined forces with the famous Mujahideen commander Ahmad Shah Massoud to capture Kabul and establish the Northern Alliance. For a while, he had fifty thousand men under his command and an entire region of Afghanistan made up his own private playground. The man even printed his own currency and founded an airline as a little sideline business.

Soon the Taliban came along and he took up arms against them too. It was a good move, especially when the US-led invasion occurred in 2001 and he was given bucketloads of cash to fund his army. Despite assassination attempts, exile in Turkey and a wary elected government, Dostum has managed to maintain his secretive power base and wealth, and, more impressively, his life.

Nobody knew where he was now, but you only had to look at the soldiers patrolling the streets to see where their allegiances lay. Rough-looking militiamen guarded street corners, dressed in Afghan army uniforms, with their scarves wrapped around their faces, so that you could only see their eyes. On their body armour, above the ammunition belt, they all displayed the same thing: a photograph of the man himself. Like Buddhist monks who roam the Himalayas with an image of the Dalai Lama, these warriors wore a photograph of their military commander like a religious icon by their hearts. Symbols of his invincibility perhaps, like the man himself, who had somehow managed to navigate the impossible politics of one of the most dangerous countries in the world – and survive.

'He's a safe bet,' said Martin. 'He pays off everyone out of his own pocket and he's left alone. Nobody would dare blow themselves up around this neighbourhood. Dostum would sort them out. He doesn't mess around. They should let him be President, it's what they need. A strong man. He'd wrap the Taliban up in six months flat. Anyway, like I say, it's safe here, you needn't worry.'

As we got out of the car and stretched our legs in the safety of the garden, I noticed something. As Martin bent down to open the boot of the car, the handle of a pistol jutted out of the back of his jeans. He quickly tucked his shirt over the top and glanced around to see if anyone had noticed. I thought it best to avert my gaze and just follow him up the steps and into the house.

A pretty Afghan maid greeted us. She was unveiled and her colourful, loose headscarf kept slipping down onto her shoulders as she *Salaamed* Malang and me. She offered us sweet black *chai* on a flimsy aluminium plate.

'Drink up and I'll give you the brief,' said Martin, eager to show off the compound he'd just 'acquired'.

'So, welcome to Flashman 2. Flashman 1 was the last one, but it was too small and too close to the main road. This is much better.'

I appreciated his choice of naming the pad after George MacDonald Fraser's infamous fictional character, a Victorian anti-hero who finds himself in all sorts of trouble in Kabul in the 1840s. It was a light-hearted reminder that foreign invaders had been attempting to tinker with Afghan affairs since time immemorial.

The main reception room was bare except for some big faux leather sofas. Like all the other furniture in Afghanistan, these were probably smuggled goods that had made their way west, following the course of the Himalayas, from the smoky factories of urban China, over the Tibetan plateau and down the Karakorum Highway through Pakistan. It was the Silk Road of old, now supplying Asia and the rest of the world with a steady stream of cheaply made junk.

We walked past the kitchen where the maid had returned to cook lunch. The delicious smells of freshly baked Afghan bread and the sizzle of chicken from the tandoor oven wafted into the hallway. I peered around the door, impatiently salivating at the prospect of the chopped salad she was expertly handling.

'On the off chance anything does happen,' said Martin, as we walked up the marble staircase, 'we will go into SOPs.'

'What is SOPs?' asked Malang, whose grasp of English didn't extend to army lingo.

'Standard Operating Procedures,' said Martin as we reached the open landing.

'This is your bedroom. And yours.' He nodded at Malang. The rooms were large and plain, and I noticed all the windows had metal grilles on the outside of the glass.

'They're RPG-proof and you'll see all the doors are double bolted. We have a direct line to the quick reaction force and I have Dostum's local commander's number stored on my phone. If we get in the shit, they'll be here inside ten minutes.'

He handed me a phone, a vintage Nokia from the early 2000s.

'Still the best on the market. There's nothing that can go wrong and the battery lasts for days. It's got an Afghan SIM and all the emergency numbers are stored on it. If we get separated call me. And if we really get in the shit and Terry comes knocking, get yourself in here.'

He led us past the bedrooms to a vast, metal door that resembled a giant bank safe. That's exactly what it was. A bullet-proof, bomb-proof safe room. An impregnable vault that could be locked from the inside if necessary, with no windows and no doors.

Martin turned on the lights, proudly revealing his *pièce de résistance*. Laid out in perfect uniformity was a plethora of survival tools that could readily stand up to any zombie apocalypse. Along the far wall, there they were: flashlights, candles, waterproof matches, cyalumes. Next up were the emergency food rations – enough for a few days at least – and endless crates of drinking water. A handful of black Kevlar helmets, capable of withstanding a bullet at point-blank range and several sets of body armour were stacked in the corner.

'Stick that kit on when you hear them climbing over the walls.'

The hairs on the back of my neck stood up at the prospect of locking myself in a dark room while a mob of fanatical extremists poured over the garden wall.

'What's in the ration packs?' said Malang as he glared at the bright-orange foil bags, more concerned by the menu than the idea of being hacked to pieces by a murderous gang of psychopathic insurgents.

'And if it comes down to it ...' said Martin, now beaming. 'Help yourself.'

At this he whipped open a canvas duffel bag to reveal half a dozen military-style, pump action shotguns and piles of loose ammunition.

'Does this say chicken or lamb?' murmured Malang.

5

A Short Flight in the Hindu Kush

I'd slept fitfully that night. Every car horn heralded danger, every dog bark a warning of lurking terrorists and every bang of a hammer was a bomb going off in the dark recesses of my imagination.

There was a knock on my door at seven thirty sharp. 'Breakfast's ready.' It was Martin. 'Quiet night last night. Only a few gunshots, did you hear them?'

I couldn't tell if I had or not. I was just glad that we hadn't been overrun in the night. I went up to the roof to get a view of the city. It was brilliant sunshine and the air was unusually clear, momentarily free of dust and sand. Away to the north, I could see the mountains looming, brown jagged peaks that pierced the blue sky. This was where it began. Somewhere up there, in a north-easterly direction, were the first glaciers and snow clad summits that heralded the Wakhan corridor, a narrow valley that juts out from the main body of the country like a mysterious tumour and acts as a buffer between Tajikistan, China and Pakistan. It was the wildest, most remote and inaccessible part of Afghanistan. It was also where my walk would begin; the very start of the Greater Himalaya range, where the Hindu Kush clashes in a violent upsurge with the Pamirs, and beyond them the Karakorum. A twisted knot of rock and ice, forced upwards by a tectonic clash, fifteen thousand feet high.

But first I had to get there. Malang had warned me when we spoke the first time that an overland route was out of the question for foreigners. He knew the dangers all too well, having driven the road from Ishkashim down to Kabul only a few days before.

'It's full of Taliban. The whole of Nuristan and the Panjshir is off limits. I had to dress up in my salwar kameez and hide in the back of a van the whole way. Two days!'

This morning though, he was dressed in trekking gear, with top-of-the-range Altberg boots and a Craghoppers fleece. He held a bright blue rucksack up to show me. He looked every inch the mountaineer.

'See this. They'd cut my head off just for having it. They'd call me an infidel. Just talking to foreigners is a crime up there.'

I shivered at the thought.

He burst out laughing. 'But I do like these trousers, so I don't mind. The Taliban can go screw themselves.'

With the overland option out of the question, we returned to the airport to start our journey.

'Don't forget to tip the pilot,' shouted Martin. 'They like whisky better than vodka. It gets them drunk faster.' He smiled mischievously and waved goodbye from beyond the concrete chicane.

A Turkish soldier thumbed my passport carelessly. The Turkish army had been given the mandate by ISAF of protecting the airport. It was a dull job in the scheme of things and the bored-looking man at the checkpoint waved me through without even making it to the visa page. We were inside the Military Zone now, and tall, concrete walls covered in razor-wire flanked the dusty road. The words 'No Parking' were painted everywhere. With the exception of a pregnant dog limping down the gauntlet, there was no one to be seen until we reached another gate, where a freshly painted barrier heralded the start of the runway.

I was on the back seat of a minibus with Malang, who was gazing thoughtfully out of the window. The sullen driver to whom Martin had relinquished his minding duties had barely uttered a word to us.

Once we were beyond the Turkish lines, he spoke up. 'These bastards are so annoying. I see them every day. I'm white, I don't wear a turban and still they demand to see my papers,' he complained, with an unmistakable South African accent. I noticed the name badge pinned haphazardly to his high-vis jacket. Mike. That's all it said; no surname, no job title.

'Hang on a minute. Aren't you the guy who walked the Nile?' Mike turned around and looked over his sunglasses, directly at me. Before I could speak, or express my surprise, he thrust an enormous, hairy hand towards mine and pumped energetically.

'Yes, yes, it's you, you won't remember me, but we met in Bedouin last year. We got pissed with Belcher.' It clicked immediately. He was referring to the hotel where I had stayed in Juba, South Sudan. He was right. I didn't remember him, but it didn't surprise me. Juba, like Kabul, had a habit of attracting misfits and mercenaries.

He eyed me up and down. 'Shit, you were a lot thinner then, weren't you? Making up for lost time in London I guess.'

The minibus rumbled across the runway towards a vast, white helicopter with *Mi-8, MTV-1* written down the side. Positioned at the bottom of the steps were three men in immaculate khaki uniforms with gold epaulettes and insignia. We met Oleg, our Moldovan pilot, who resembled a Bond villain and never deigned to remove his Aviator shades. I managed to provoke one smile, when I asked if any of them had been to the Wakhan corridor before.

'Never!' he exclaimed. 'Normally we only fly gangsters around Kabul, and sometimes take UN on sightseeing trips to Bamian. Same thing really. But we never go that far north. I hope she'll make it.' He grinned and patted the nose of the thirty-five-year-old Russian aircraft.

Malang looked queasy but did his best to hide it.

'I've never been on a helicopter,' he said.

'You're in for one hell of a ride,' said Oleg. 'We have to fly over some big hills.'

The 'big hills' to which Oleg so casually referred were the infamous Hindu Kush mountains – or the Hindu *Killers* – so named because of the vast numbers of Indian slaves who died while being transported through them en route to the Khanates of Central Asia, during the Middle Ages.

Oleg sparked up a cigarette on the runway, as his co-pilot, a hulking man who looked like a wrestler, tinkered absentmind-edly with a spanner on the fuselage. The final uniformed Moldovan threw our rucksacks into the helicopter with utter disdain and then simply nodded at us to follow.

'Get in,' said Oleg. 'We're good to go.'

No safety brief, no dos and don'ts, no seatbelts. Just 'get in'.

So we did. Malang climbed up the few steps into the main body of the Mi-8. As far as helicopters go, it was pretty spacious inside; apart from our bags, it was virtually empty. The seats were basic, fold-down types, and the cushions and carpet that had been thrown in gave the whole thing an air of alarming apathy.

On closer inspection, these had probably been added as draught excluders; the holes in the wooden floor and gaps in the metal work revealed the wheel arches below. The windows had latches on them so that you could open them, and Oleg said he'd leave the slide door open 'for a better view'. A 'gunction box', was the only thing discernible in (attempted) English. I presumed it was a spelling mistake, but couldn't be sure. It was painted grey, like everything else inside the machine, and they were the only words I could read. Everything else was in Russian.

Oleg donned a set of headphones, connected by wires for intercommunication with his two co-pilots. The wrestler was perched on a control box between the two front seats, his shoulders pressed up against his countrymen. He removed his shirt and handed it to Malang.

'Put it on the hook,' he ordered, and Malang did as he was told. The wrestler, now comfortable in just his string vest, chest hair sprouting through every gap, flashed us a gold-toothed grimace and pressed a button.

The deafening roar of engines disturbed the relative peace as the rotor blades swung into action. They began to spin, slowly at first, then faster and faster, until they were going so quickly they appeared to be going the opposite way. We began to move. The helicopter shuffled forward, tentatively bouncing about on the runway, teasing us with its ineptitude. It jolted back down to earth. I glanced at Malang to see his reaction. I'd been in plenty of helicopters before, but I could only imagine what my new shepherd friend was going through.

He forced a smile but immediately looked back out of the window across the runway, past the rows of military aircraft and the hangars towards the brown hills beyond. Finally we began to move in earnest; this time it was forward, driving on the wheels, but worryingly, very much attached to the earth. For a moment it seemed as though we might take off like a plane. Speed and momentum gathered and we tore along the runway. Thankfully, it wasn't long before we lurched into the air. Up we went, right above the airport and the road we'd been stuck in traffic on only yesterday.

I gripped tightly onto my seat as we wobbled through the thermals above the city and distracted myself with the views out of the open door. Soon the irregular shapes of shanties and walled compounds gave way to fields, irrigation ditches and jaunty, angular dirt roads that dissected the agricultural lands. Tall, earthen chimneys poked up from farms. These were the rustic factories that produced homemade mud bricks. Trees were few and far between; only spindly poplars lined the streams. Levees and mounds signified centuries of human habitation along the banks of the Kabul river that meandered out of the mountains.

Our flight path was due north, and we screamed out of the city airspace, past Bagram airport, and with it, the last flat plains I would see for the next couple of months at least. The brown hills rose sharply and we darted up and over them with the freedom and unsteadiness of a sparrow finding its wings for the first time.

We flew just low enough to make out the crumbling huts and watchtowers nestled amid defiles and craggy ledges, and the occasional figure of a lonely shepherd with his flock. Soon enough, the relentless brown hills transformed into real mountains, topped with glistening white snow. We almost skimmed ghostly peaks, which seemed to close in on all sides. The helicopter sped through gorges, up and up, over a snow-capped pass, and into the notorious Panjshir Valley.

Below, a scene of violent beauty unfolded. Sheer cliffs fell into deep crevasses and brown sandstone dipped into patches of iridescent green terraces. Rivulets and streams crashed down in untamed passion from the glaciers above. On the valley floor, sporadic settlements interrupted the natural wilderness. Pencil-thin sheep tracks connected habitations of high-walled fortresses and ancient castles. It was a scene of fearsome isolation.

As Malang had warned, the Panjshir was full of Taliban. It translates as the valley of the five lions, and harks back to the days when the roar of Asian lions could still be heard among the rocky outcrops. In more recent times, it was the domain of equally ferocious predators. This was the hidden homeland of the Tajik warriors who formed that backbone of the Mujahideen and fought the Russian invaders of 1979. The valley became synonymous with bloody ambushes and Soviet defeats at the hands of the guerrillas, led by the revered Afghan hero, Ahmad Shah Massoud – the lion of the Panjshir.

I looked down and wondered just how many terrified Russians had met their end among the boulders and ridges during the war. And also, of more concern, how many Mi-8 helicopters had been shot down by their stinger missiles over the years. It was a chilling prospect.

Nowadays, the Mujahideen had become indistinguishable from the Taliban. As I learnt during my own days fighting them in the south, they were no longer a cohesive force, but rather gangs of fighters; usually mercenaries or just criminals, willing and able to fight for whoever paid them the most. The old adage was true; the Afghans simply loved fighting each other. But when foreign powers dare to invade, they have a habit of putting their differences aside and ganging up to oust the invader. Most of them weren't, and still aren't, particularly inspired by religious fanaticism, but rather an innate sense of war, one that is in the blood after centuries of violence.

After all, the Soviets were by no means the first foreigners to try to tame the Afghans.

Afghanistan has been a battlefield for millennia. Its geographical position – at the crossroads of Asia – has made invasion an all too frequent feature of Afghanistan's history.

It was no coincidence that Rudyard Kipling decided to set his novel *The Man Who Would be King,* in the country that unfolded beneath me. The Panjshir, and the high passes to north and east, used to be known as Kafiristan – the land of the unbelievers. It was so named by the Muslim rulers because they had failed for hundreds of years to conquer the hostile tribes of the region; parts of the area didn't succumb to Islam until as late as 1895. Even now, shamanist undertones bubble away. In the nineteenth century their physical isolation, combined with a formidable reputation for violence and barbarity, gave the inhabitants an almost mythical status among the Afghans, who were already notorious in Asia for their warrior skills and savagery.

In the story, Kipling sends a pair of maverick British ex-soldiers into Kafiristan as they attempt to flee charges of minor fraud and extortion during the heyday of the Raj. The pair of rascals have a plan – to use their soldierly cunning and English charm to make their way over the high mountain passes into a land that no white man had ever passed. On the way they convince the warring tribes to unite and in doing so they establish a new kingdom and get rather rich in the process.

In a predictable show of hubris, the overzealous duo fail to read their history books; legends of invaders have abounded here since time immemorial. Their almost perfect plan comes crashing down when one of them takes it a step too far and attempts to pass himself off as a reincarnated Sikander, the Asian name for Alexander the Great.

Without wishing to spoil the ending to Kipling's novella, it serves as a tale of warning for anyone who thinks it's a good idea to invade Afghanistan, and one that successive armies really ought to have taken heed of. The British in particular.

Legends of Alexander have flourished in these mountains for over two thousand years. Allegedly, this was where the great conqueror first felt fear, doubting his ability to subdue the natives. Perhaps then, choosing his bride – the princess Roxanne,

unrivalled in beauty and fairness – from these valleys, was a tacti-
cal decision. He became so enamoured with the untameable
landscape that he left garrisons of his men stationed in clifftop
castles, even after he carried on east in his efforts to invade India.
He never returned to collect these men, and so they stayed,
marrying the local girls; a new hybrid civilisation, the Gandhara,
was formed.

Half Asian, half Greek, it lasted a thousand years. Archaeologists
have dug up coins from these same mountains that bear reliefs
of Macedonian warriors' heads on one side, and humped buffaloes on the other. In Taxila, on the far side of the Hindu Kush,
now in Pakistan, you can still see ancient statues of Buddha, but
they are unlike images to which we are accustomed. The living
god is draped in a Greek toga, with Greek eyes and wears a
thick, curly Greek beard. It's no coincidence either that *Pakols*,
the flat woollen hats worn by all the mountain men in Afghanistan
and Pakistan, are almost identical to the ancient Macedonian
Kausia. The Gandhara legacy is still alive today; you only have to
browse through pictures of the people that live in Nuristan and
the Kailash valley to see the piercing blue eyes and Mediterranean
faces of a tribe that lost its way.

Maybe it was Alexander's descendants then that made up the
dots beneath us, standing motionless in the fields, gawping up at
the big white metal bird that tore through their skies.

We were heading beyond the Panjshir, beyond even Nuristan,
to Badakhshan – the country's most isolated province. Nestled
between the natural boundary of the Hindu Kush to the south
and the Amu Darya river to the north, Badakhshan is a forgotten corner of the Himalayas. The Amu Darya is the local
Persian name for what the Ancient Greeks called the Oxus, the
famed river of classical civilisation; synonymous with being the
edge of the known world. Beyond its banks lay nothingness – a

dark, savage wilderness, so extreme in its environment that nobody who entered would ever return. It was a place from which no real news was ever received. Vague and strange myths sometimes returned, of dog-headed men, strange horned beasts, hairy giants, cave-dwelling tribes, human blood drinkers, devil-worshippers and other practices too brutal to contemplate.

'It hasn't changed much,' shouted Oleg, over the noise of the engine.

'I thought you said you've never been?' I shouted back.

'My uncle fought these monsters back in '85. He never made it back; they couldn't find his body. It's down there somewhere. Word has it, they stitched his balls into his mouth and made him bleed to death.'

He grinned. I had no idea if he was saying it for effect or whether it was true.

The strangest bit of Badakhshan though was our destination, the thin protrusion of the Wakhan corridor. The long valley follows the Oxus all the way to its source near the Chinese border. To the north is Tajikistan, once the Soviet frontier – where Oleg's ill-fated uncle would have come from in his tank and the direction in which the last of the Russians fled, when they finally gave up the ghost in 1989. This is the route that Marco Polo took on his epic journey to the court of Kublai Khan in 1229, naming a breed of sheep after himself that survives to this day. To the south were the equally notorious valleys of the northern regions of Pakistan, where it was thought Osama bin Laden fled to in the wake of 9/11.

The reason that this remote strip of land belongs to Afghanistan is that it provided a convenient buffer zone during perhaps the most intriguing of all the political conflicts of recent times: the Great Game. A term coined by the British, this was the period in the nineteenth century that should really be known as the original cold war. As the Tsarist Russian Empire grew and took over more and more territory in Central Asia, so did the British in India. Both sides deemed it prudent to have a no-man's-land, and the mountainous wilds of the western Himalayas provided an obvious natural barrier. But it wasn't impregnable, and in a half-century-long bid to gain the upper hand, both sides sent in their hardiest soldiers and spies to reconnoitre the high passes on the 'roof of the world'.

It was the height of imperial designs and a golden age of exploration in Asia. Young European eccentrics dressed themselves in rags and furs and passed themselves off as Pashtun horse traders or Hindu preachers, all the while sketching secret maps on yak hide canvases for the glory of their respective emperors. I'd read extensively about these brave and intriguing young romantics in my youth and I could barely contain my excitement now at the prospect of following in their footsteps, on my own Himalayan adventure.

We flew further north-east, over the settlements of Rukah and Pukh – now nothing but a collection of mud huts, but once important waypoints in an ancient trade route that had all but disappeared. The mountains appeared as brilliant white diamonds on either side, blinding and sublime. I looked out of the window. We'd already been flying for about two hours before I laid eyes on something I'd waited for a decade to see. Rising from the Hindu Kush was a triangle with a sheer face; a mountain called Mir Samir. At just over nineteen thousand feet it isn't a particularly high Himalayan peak, and is really a dwarf compared to Mount Noshaq, which Malang had conquered in 2003. But it fascinated me because it was the peak made famous in the book that had inspired me most to make my own forays into the mountains.

A Short Walk in the Hindu Kush is one of the most celebrated pieces of travel writing from the mid-twentieth century. Written by Eric Newby in 1958, it describes the hilarious account of his failed expedition to summit the unconquered peak with his companion, the British diplomat Hugh Carless. The pair of amateur hill walkers encountered all sorts on their journey, from gun-toting bandits to murderous policemen, and even bumped into that most eccentric of explorers – Wilfred Thesiger, who famously called them a 'couple of pansies'.

Newby sadly died in 2006, but I met Hugh Carless on a few occasions before he also passed away five years later.

It was the spring of 2008 and I was about to deploy to Afghanistan with the army when my friend Will Charlton invited me to lunch with his eighty-one-year-old grandfather at the Royal Mid-Surrey Golf Club. This was something not to miss. Hailing from a family of very respectable, very learned and utterly bonkers individuals, Mr Michael Charlton had had a long and very successful career as a news broadcaster, cricket commentator and war correspondent, covering live in his heyday Kennedy's assassination, Vietnam and the Moon landings.

'I've got a very special guest coming today, my boy,' he said with a refined, Australian lilt, slapping me on the back. 'You'll have a lot in common. Tell him where you're off to.'

I was surprised to find the subject of Newby's classic tale of adventure sitting at the table, already nursing a whisky and soda. In his early nineties, very frail and unsteady on his feet, he rose to greet us. There was no smile on his lips, but his handshake was firm and his eyes as young and sparkling as I imagined they were the day he set off into the Panjshir in 1956.

'Sit down, Ambassador,' said Michael. Will gave me a nudge, clearly enjoying the formal display of affection.

'So you're off to Afghanistan?' said Hugh, raising an eyebrow.

Before I could reply, Michael interjected, 'He most certainly is, Ambassador. Down south, where Lord Roberts went. Kandahar. Terrible business it is, Ghazis everywhere. Hasn't changed a jot.'

'I went there you know,' said 'the Ambassador'.

I did know. I must have read *A Short Walk* half a dozen times and felt like I knew Carless all too well, such was the vividness of Newby's writing. It was hard to reconcile the fearless, youthful character of the story with the old man sipping his whisky in front of me.

'I spent a bit of time in Kabul,' he said.

By 'a bit of time' I assumed he was referring to his two years as third secretary at the embassy, not to mention several expeditions into Nuristan and the Panjshir, including the famous 1956 journey.

Michael joined in. 'He was in Tehran too; there isn't a bit of that godforsaken place that the Ambassador doesn't know. Speaks the lingo too, don't you, Carless?'

'Oh, I've forgotten it all now,' said Carless.

'Don't be so modest, 'course you haven't. Aren't you jealous of this young chap though?' He slapped me again. 'Heading off to the war to have a snipe at the Ghazis. I can almost smell it. The crack of musketry, the wails of anguish. Oh God, I do miss it all now.' Michael, a man of stocky stature – and presumably in his youth, strength – had closed his eyes, daydreaming of the romance of battle. I was a mere twenty-three-year old lieutenant; I was excited, but equally, terrified of the prospect of war.

'Leave him alone,' said Hugh. 'He'll have his fun, that's for certain, but we mustn't be nostalgic. It's all changed now. Robots and drones and smart bombs.' He uttered the words 'smart bombs' with disdainful, clipped precision.

Over lunch we spoke at length of how Afghanistan had changed over the years and yet at the same time just how remarkably constant some things had remained. He told me about his war years in the Middle East and Italy, and his days in the Foreign service, and finally about his companionship with Newby and the famous meeting with Thesiger.

'He was an odd sort of fellow,' said Hugh. 'Very aggressive man. Used to box at Cambridge and never lost, or so I'm told. I don't believe he was a homosexual, but he did have a habit for bringing young African boys to the Travellers' Club. Dressed them up in good tweed too. Damned expensive business whatever it was.'

Before we parted, Carless gave me some of his maps from Afghanistan and some sage advice about how to silence a donkey if the enemy are nearby (a quick snip to the vocal cords apparently isn't necessarily fatal). He promised to write. True to his word, he did. While stationed in Kandahar, I received long and often hilarious letters, mainly referring back to the exploits of Victorian spies and lamenting the loss of full regimental dress as a valid battlefield uniform.

Hugh Carless was representative of his time and age and belonged to a long tradition of mountaineers and explorers.

Before the twentieth century, there had been a vague interest in mountaineering by Victorian aesthetes, but it was generally confined to the Alps, and high-altitude walking was regarded as a healthy hobby rather than a serious pursuit. The Victorians saw the mountains of Asia as a point of strategic consideration and little more. There were valleys to be mapped, snowy passes to be navigated and Russians to be stopped. But why anyone would bother to scale a summit for any reason other than to gauge whether it might make a decent gun emplacement, was beyond Victorian sensibilities. The Himalayas were regarded as a mere buffer zone between empires; a no-man's-land of mystery and intrigue. The harsh, unforgiving environment was viewed by most as unconquerable and best left to the unfathomable tribals that lived there. And anyway, the Holy Grail for romantic exploration in the mid- to late nineteenth century was of course the hunt for the source of the river Nile in Africa.

The turn of the century though heralded a newfound interest in mountains. There seemed to be a shift brought on by nationalism across Europe. Suddenly all eyes were on Asia and everyone wanted to reach the top of the world. It was the beginning of the era of mountaineering.

Other than a brief hiatus during the war years, the first half of the twentieth century was a period of intense exploration in the Himalayas that saw a number of great expeditions undertaken.

Mount Everest, of course, took centre stage. The tragic 1924 expedition which saw the disappearance of Mallory and Irvine captured the public imagination. Then there was the 1950 ascent of Annapurna (the first successful 8,000-metre peak) by Maurice Herzog and the subsequent first ascent of Everest by Edmund Hillary and Sherpa Tenzing Norgay in 1953 which brought the most acclaim. There were many more world records broken in this period too and they symbolised the last great mountaineering expeditions. As the century wore on, individuals and teams of British, European and North American climbers finally conquered virtually all the major summits.

After the great expeditions of the mid-twentieth century though, everything changed. China invaded Tibet, opening up one of the last great secrets in nature (only to close it down and keep it for themselves); the hippy trail of the 1960s and 70s saw thousands of Europeans pour into the mountains in search of enlightenment and cheap weed. Later, with the advent of mass tourism, facilitated by cheap commercial flights and the downfall of the neighbouring Soviet Union, the 1990s heralded an era of unsurpassed development in travel to the Himalayas. Nepal, once a secretive enclave that refused entry to foreigners, became the great backpacker hub of the continent. Northern India too, with its holy rivers that flowed out of the mountains, drew the crowds. Which gap-year student hasn't hung around the Dalai Lama's monastery in Dharamsala hoping for a glimpse of His Holiness? Even Pakistan, with the building of the Karakorum Highway, now sees a steady stream of hardy trekkers heading into the hills.

Climbing has undergone a kind of post-modern transformation – more contrived, more manipulated. Speed challenges, supported and unsupported, with or without oxygen, flying off the top of ... the list goes on. Of course, it doesn't make the endeavour any less impressive, and even now, tens if not hundreds of people make it to the summit of Everest each year, not to mention a thousand other mountains – despite the very clear and present dangers.

I'd decided to bookend my journey with perhaps the two most unknown and sealed countries in the Himalayas – Bhutan, and here – the north-east of Afghanistan. I wasn't here specifically to climb mountains (although I imagined it may be unavoidable at times), but to dig around beyond the clichés and figure out just what the appeal was to visitors and more importantly what the mountains meant to those who lived here.

Malang had been fumbling in his pocket as I pondered all of this and I watched him put his phone to his ear. He began shouting into the microphone in the Wakhi language. Before I could ask him who on earth he could be chatting to, and how on earth he had managed to get a signal in a chopper flying at fifteen thousand feet, he jumped up and whooped with joy and ran across the cabin towards the open door. I grabbed him by his jacket.

'Careful, you lunatic, you'll fall out.'

'Look!' he said, smiling like a mad man. 'Ishkashim. It's my home. I'm home!' he shouted. With that he shoved his head right out of the door, clinging precariously to a rope attached with a clip to the roof of the helicopter, and waved down furiously.

'That was my mum on the phone, she can see us.'

I looked down to see the patchwork brown and green of a small town straddling the Oxus river and surrounded to the north by the Pamir mountains. We were right on the border of Tajikistan, and with it the entrance to the Wakhan corridor.

6

Bam-I-Dunyan

An hour later we had flown almost to the very end of the valley. With the Oxus as their guide, Oleg and the Moldovans had navigated the helicopter to within just a few miles of the Chinese frontier. The Pamir mountains loomed large and forbidding on either side. We'd left the last permanent civilisation behind – not even jeep or motorbike tracks could be seen down on the wide steppe-like landscape below. We had entered another world. Devoid of trees, houses and roads, it appeared as a wilderness like no other. Virtually untouched by man, yet unloved by nature, the barren emptiness was spine-chilling. It really was the roof of the world.

Malang shouted as we banked around, 'The Afghans say that the Pamir is so high, even the birds must cross on foot.'

As the chopper slowly but surely hovered above the stony meadow the rotor blades blasted the earth and sent sand, dust and terrified yaks in all directions. We bounced and bumped and finally came to a standstill, but because of the extreme altitude – we had landed at almost four thousand metres – Oleg said he needed to keep the engines running while we threw out the bags into the dirt and dashed away to a safe distance. Oleg stayed in the pilot's seat while the wrestler got out to take a piss. While he was there he took out his phone and started taking selfies of himself with the helicopter in the background. I'd almost forgotten that these airmen had never travelled this far before and it was as foreign to them as it was to me. He took one last look in my direction and shook his head.

Holding onto my hat I turned around to wave back at the helicopter and Oleg gave me a thumbs up from the cockpit. As quickly as it had landed, the machine sped up into the air, sending Malang's scarf flying off into the dirt. Within just a few seconds the helicopter was just a tiny dot high above us and the noise died away gradually to a faint hum that disappeared into the clouds. Our transport was gone and from now on, we would be on foot.

I was eager to meet some of the Kyrgyz nomads that live in these mountains and asked Malang if he thought we might.

'Did you see their tents from the helicopter? Not far, let's walk to the other side of the valley. We better be quick though, as this time is the *Kutch*.'

A *Kutch*, Malang explained, was the biannual nomadic migration where the families pack up their earthly belongings, yurts and all, and move, according to the season, in search of better pastures for their animals. June heralded the summer *Kutch*, when the tribe shifted from the lower camps in the valleys, to higher up into the hills where the grass was greener now that the snow had melted.

We hunched under the weight of our bags and set off in the direction of the settlement Malang had seen. It took almost an hour to reach the lowest point in the valley where my map indicated a stream and a series of tiny ponds. What I actually discovered were not insubstantial lakes, presumably because the snow melt had filled them to bursting point. Remarkably they were full of little fish. I wondered how on earth they got here. Some of the pools were completely isolated from the others, not fed by rivers, and yet life abounded. These must have been the descendants of creatures that have lived in these puddles of water before even the mountains were lifted out of the sea.

Malang had a better suggestion. 'God put them here to feed the Kyrgyz, but they are too stubborn to fish. All they care about is horses and goats.'

A lake stretched out in front of us, barring our route to the settlement on the far slopes.

'It's not deep, come on,' said Malang pointing into the cold, clear water.

Up here, the unbearable heat of Kabul had given way to a pleasant balminess. The sky was clear but occasional gusty winds blew up the valley, warning that the weather was liable to change at a moment's notice. But for now at least I was happy to follow my new guide. I took off my boots and rolled up my trousers and in we went, shuffling under the heavy loads of our packs. The water was just above freezing and Malang squealed with delight.

'Much nicer up here, no? Mountain water, cool and fresh.'

He stooped down to scoop up a handful of the chilled pond-water and threw it into his mouth. We plodded on, the water reaching our waists now, and I was beginning to regret my decision. Walking around the lake would have only added on an extra hour or so, and we could have forgone the unpleasant sensation that comes from submerging your crown jewels in an ice bath.

Yet at the same time it was a lesson learnt. We had far too much stuff. Our rucksacks were bursting with ration packs and technical gear: cameras, satellite phones, water bladders and spare clothes. We needed to reach the camp soon, if only to get help carrying the bags.

On the far side of the water, the land began to slope upwards. It wasn't steep, but bumpy, with large undulations and dips and hillocks strewn among the gravelly plains. It meant that even though the landscape inside the valley looked fairly flat from above, at ground level it would be easy to lose the trail. Behind one such mound we came across an astonishing sight.

'Wakhis,' said Malang, pointing down.

I strained my eyes into the speckled morass of green, grey and brown, which reminded me of the British army camouflage pattern, only on a much vaster scale.

Then there was movement and I spotted three figures, walking about half a mile away. They were moving slowly and then I realised why. They were surrounded not by boulders, as I'd presumed, but by around five hundred sheep and goats, grazing from the short grass that flourished between the stones.

'I thought this was Kyrgyz territory,' I said. 'And anyway, how can you tell from here?'

'It is. But they are Wakhi. They're walking, and the Kyrgyz never walk anywhere.'

We sat down on a boulder and waited as the mass of animals slowly drifted towards us, and with them the three men.

Malang shouted towards them and they sauntered over. They were teenagers, filthy dirty and dressed in nothing but rags. They bore sticks – prize possessions in a land without trees.

'They work for the Kyrgyz. They look after all these sheep and goats.' Malang grabbed a goat by its neck and picked it up, hugging the bewildered beast as it bleated protestations.

'Where are you going?' I asked the boy.

Malang translated. They were the vanguard of the *Kutch*, the Kyrgyz apparently strung out across the valley somewhere behind. We would see them soon.

So we stood still, letting the herd pour around us. Hundreds and hundreds of fat-tailed sheep and skinny little goats with coarse black and white hair. After ten minutes more figures appeared from behind the hills. A man was riding a minuscule pony with his infant son in front and his wife trailing behind on a donkey. The scene was almost biblical. The woman wore a long red velvet dress and a tall white hat. All of them had dusty,

weathered faces and cracked lips, and unlike their Wakhi servants, had narrow eyes – a reminder that these people are the
Central Asian descendants of the Mongol horde. Some of the
last true nomads in the world, they were now cut off from their
former grazing lands by politics, border disputes and all the
other restrictions of the twentieth century.

The family ignored us completely. In fact they barely regis-
tered our presence. Malang strode up to the man and asked him
something which I couldn't understand. The Kyrgyz muttered
something in return, and my guide returned to me.

'So miserable, these people. Never say hello. They won't talk
to us until we are introduced to the chief. He's coming now,
look.'

Behind the convoy of sheep and donkeys, there were a couple
more families, all riding, some were even on yaks. They all
ignored us. At last, we spotted a solitary figure at the back, lurch-
ing about on a wretched donkey half his size. He looked ancient
and withered, with a hunchback that was barely concealed by a
filthy blazer. As he approached I tried to discern a face but small
dark glasses covered his eyes, and with them any form of expres-
sion. In one hand he held a long wooden stick and from the
other trailed a rope attached to three of the shaggiest beasts I
had ever seen. These were bactrian camels, and unlike the short-
haired dromedary found across North Africa and Arabia, these
fantastical looking creatures had two humps and were designed
for the mountains. They were laden with enormous stacks of
painted wood that I assumed must be framework for the yurts,
as well as felts, carpets and sheepskins.

'I met him before,' said Malang of the chief. 'They call him Ir
Ali Bhai. It means very rich man. He doesn't like me.'

'*Salaam Alaikum*,' we all chimed as the chief approached. He
grunted and raised his stick above his head and gave Malang an

almighty whack across the buttocks. Malang simply smiled and grabbed the chief's hand and held it tightly.

'Who are you?' The chief spat the words through horrible stumpy yellow teeth. 'Are you Taliban or Daesh? Who's this one with the beard and strange clothes?' He flicked a crooked finger in my direction.

Malang kept smiling.

'It's me, Malang Darya, from Ishkashim. We're not Taliban, we're tourists. This one is a foreigner from Inglistan.'

Malang went to embrace the chief but received another whack for his efforts.

'Ouch . . . Come on, Ir Ali Bhai, you blind old goat. Give us a cup of tea and stop messing around.'

The chief grunted again and handed the reins of the camels to me and trotted off in the direction of the herd. I was slightly bewildered as to what had just happened but Malang just laughed.

'Let's go, English. He invites us to his new house.'

We trailed the convoy for an hour over the rough plains and the camels followed me in silent obedience. They were far better behaved and had much better breath than my Saharan companions.

By the time we crossed the valley to a flat hillock at the base of the mountains, some young men were already at work setting up a yurt. We helped unload the camels – the red poles were indeed the frames for a further two of these habitations. A total of five yurts housed four families. The women of the clan were allowed their own cooking tent. All of the women wore red dresses, each covered in elaborate decorations of cowrie shells and trinkets and other eclectic jewellery choices such as small shards of mirrored glass, beads, toenail clippers, bells and silver amulets. Unlike anywhere else in the country the women here go about unveiled, only wearing enormous top hats covered with a white or red scarf. White for married, red for a virgin. Some of them were very striking, although I found it virtually impossible to identify how old they were; most of them did not know themselves. With little more than a thousand Kyrgyz remaining in the Wakhan, there are few options for marriage and most will marry their first cousins so as to stay within the family group. Sealed off from the rest of the world they lead a secretive, unsupported existence where the year of one's birth is of little consequence.

It wasn't long before the yurts were up and ready. Ir Ali Bhai beckoned us into his house. Rugs had been laid out and an old stove lit with a pipe that extracted the smoke through a hole in the roof. An ancient hunting rifle dangled from a sling and a baby slept peacefully beneath it in a handmade basket. A wireless radio was the only reminder that we hadn't suddenly transported into the thirteenth century. The old man wobbled across the floor aided by his stick and bade us to sit cross-legged with our backs to the wall of the yurt. I was amazed at how colourful it was. Dazzling gold and red blankets lined the sheep-felt and camel-skin walls. The chief sat down and stared at us through his dark glasses.

Malang followed and sat next to him. The chief grimaced and went for his stick, threatening to clobber Malang around the head, but my guide pre-empted the horseplay and confiscated it, pushing it just out of the old man's reach. The chief was not amused.

'These are proud people,' said Malang, 'but they are forgotten. They get no help. No government here. They are sad.'

The Wakhan is in fact the most impoverished region in Afghanistan. Farming is virtually impossible because of the harsh climate and there are no roads. All of the borders are closed and so trade is limited to that which occasional merchants can smuggle over the high passes from Pakistan or China – which isn't much. As a result, there's no need for currency and people simply barter a yak for some sheep, or a guard dog for a rifle. There's just a few basic school houses, although none for the Kyrgyz, and there are no clinics or medical facilities. The Wakhan has the highest rate of infant mortality in the world – every second child dies at birth; the average life expectancy is under forty.

A woman walked in. She could have been sixteen or thirty, it was impossible to tell. Her face was round, childlike but her body full and buxom. She bent down and distributed cups of milky chai in chipped porcelain. She didn't say a word or look us in the eye. She walked out and left us alone.

'The wife,' said the chief, and for the first time I detected a smirk.

I tried to conceal my horror. The old man claimed to be sixty-two, and had become chief by way of outliving every one of his peers. He therefore had his pick of the women, and had somehow outlived four previous wives.

'They all keep dying, so I have to find new ones. It's no good, they are so expensive to buy.'

I took a sip of tea as I listened to the wrinkled rascal and almost spluttered it out onto the floor. It was salty and rancid. Malang burst out laughing.

'It's the way we like it. Lots of salt. It makes you powerful with the girls.'

'It's disgusting. Ask him if we can borrow some yaks,' I said to Malang, remembering the purpose of our visit was to secure some pack animals for the onward journey.

'No,' said the cantankerous old man.

'What does he mean, no?' I asked. 'There's loads outside. Not to mention three camels and half a dozen horses.'

'He just says no. We can have donkeys.'

'I don't want donkeys. I want yaks, they can travel further and quicker. I'll pay the going rate: twenty-five dollars a day per animal.'

Malang shook his head. 'He doesn't care about money. What good is it to him? He says he needs his animals here, and all we can have are donkeys.'

'Okay, fine. How much?'

Ir Ali Bhai understood this and butted in. 'Ten thousand dollars.' For the first time he laughed out loud. Malang dared to laugh too, but the chief had wriggled close enough to pick up his stick and jabbed it right into Malang's ribs.

Fortunately he was joking. So there we were, resigned to a few skinny donkeys to help carry our gear, despite the presence of more yaks than I could count grazing outside the yurts. I suspected it was all just done for his own amusement.

I bought a sheep from the chief which we slaughtered by the river and shared with our hosts, who naturally saved up all the best bits for later and tried to convince us that they were treating us to a delicacy by serving up the brains and eyeballs. Funny how the chief didn't bother with them and gorged instead on a prime bit of mutton.

In the afternoon we watched as the horsemen played Buzkashi. Afghanistan's national sport resembles polo but involves a decapitated goat and, as far as I could tell, very few rules. Vicious-looking men on horses thrashed and galloped across the steppe, attempting to keep hold of the carcass for as long as possible.

'They learn to ride when they are three years old,' said Malang.

Whips flailed, fur hats were trampled and horses reared up into the clear blue sky. The sound of forty hooves crashed around the stony escarpment and the whoops of the men echoed across the empty valley late into the evening. It was a lonely, bleak existence, I thought, where only the hardest survive. There was no room for the weak here.

That night we stayed with the Kyrgyz, setting up our nice new tents next to age old yurts. Malang played the game, and even blew up his air mattress for form, but I was hardly surprised when I saw him sneaking out of a yurt at dawn the next day. He'd already had a fresh cup of salty tea and had slumbered comfortably under a cosy blanket. Completely at home in the mountains, he'd slept like a baby; struggling to acclimatise and suffering from the cold, I hadn't managed a wink. Despite being June, and sunny in the day, at night it had sunk to below zero and a thin sprinkling of snow covered all of our gear.

As we packed up and the first rays of sunlight emerged from beyond the domes of the glistening Pamir, the chief came to see us off. He cackled out loud as a donkey made a run for it. He knew full well that with these obstinate and temperamental beasts in tow, covering more than fifteen kilometres a day would be a struggle. By ensuring we moved slowly we had to rent the animals for a longer period and he got more money overall. He also knew we'd have to send these animals back and purchase new ones when we reached Wakhi territory fifty miles to the west, beyond Lake Chaqmaqtin, and why should they get more? I knew it and he knew it, but we all smiled and after shaking hands with the shrewd businessman, we left the Kyrgyz behind us.

We walked west, sandwiched between the high Pamir and the Hindu Kush, towards a narrow valley that would lead us up over the Irshad Pass. A five-thousand-metre dent in the mountains, the pass was a centuries-old smuggling route, and even in June was still covered in snow.

We got to Lake Chaqmaqtin and plotted a course along the banks of the Oxus and soon found ourselves in Wakhi territory.

Or, as Malang called it, 'Wakhistan', of which one day, he assured me, he would become president.

For days we walked into the setting sun, sometimes it was hot, sometimes it rained, sometimes it was freezing. It was impossible to predict. At night we'd camp under a billion stars or if it snowed, in the sanctuary of a cave. Some days we passed curious shepherds, itinerant boys, and a few families migrating to the higher pastures with their sheep. Other days we saw no one at all. The Wakhi were herdsmen but they too rode yaks and we managed to find a small camp where another chief agreed to rent us the furry beasts until we reached the Pakistan border. The two Kyrgyz handlers who'd come with us had been complaining for days anyway and we were hardly sad to see them go. Malang was just happy to be back on home turf and to be speaking his native language. He was famous around these parts and everywhere we went, the Wakhi greeted him like a returning hero.

As we progressed west, yurts gave way to huts – basic stone and mud sheds that provided temporary accommodation for those hardy shepherds who wandered up from the lower Wakhan to wherever it was possible to grow potatoes and even wheat. There were still no trees here though, so the Wakhi were reliant upon the yaks for their dung which they burnt as fuel. We lived on the army rations we were carrying, and the occasional goat we could buy from the nomads – usually at extortionate prices. Sometimes we saw wild onions and rhubarb – the only fresh vegetables for two hundred miles in any direction – and hurried to dig them up before the yaks beat us to it.

After a week we reached the Irshad valley. We walked south and the trail was now no more than a treacherous narrow path barely two feet across, that somehow clung to the shale and loose scree. The mountainsides became bare and scraggy and we left the last of the Wakhi villages behind. With us came three Wakhi men. The first was another village chief called Mirza, an ex-policeman in his fifties, and two of his subordinate yak handlers. They sometimes walked and sometimes rode, and found it impossible to comprehend why we didn't want to ride with them.

One evening, we made a campfire with nothing but dung and a few small twigs that the men had brought from the village – valuable stuff. They must have known they were in for a cold night but hadn't brought any tents or sleeping bags.

'How will they get any sleep?' I asked Malang, feeling sorry for them, and guilty for not being able to provide.

'They are Wakhi, it's what they do. Cold, warm, rain, snow, what to do?' He laughed. While they huddled together around the tiny flickers, I wrapped my scarf tight around my neck, pulled my *Pakol* down over my ears and shuddered at the thought of sleeping rough. These were hard men. They walked around in holey leather shoes and no socks, their ragged trousers exposing frostbitten knees, and for warmth, just a waistcoat or an old woollen greatcoat. No Gore-Tex or goosedown for the Wakhi. I remembered that I had a full bottle of whisky in my bag, that I'd smuggled in on the plane. It was a good single malt but it had to be drunk before getting to Pakistan and I decided that tonight was the perfect time. I opened my bag and nudged Malang while our guides threw more dung on the flames.

'Will they mind?'

Malang whooped with joy. 'Mind?' He laughed again. 'They love a good drink. We are Ismaili here. We're not like those Sunni Muslims. We don't do Ramadan and look around – do you see any mosques?'

I knew that Malang would be up for some whisky but you

can never be too careful offering it to complete strangers in an Islamic country – especially a policeman.

Malang asked them if they'd like a drink. I've never seen eyes light up quicker.

I half filled my metal army mug with some of the golden liquid and offered it to the nearest pair of hands. It was dark now and all that could be seen among the dancing shadows were flickering red faces, half concealed by turbans. It was a clear night and up above the stars appeared in light smudges against an infinite darkness. The mountains could only be made out where their own blackness interrupted the Milky Way. I shivered as an icy chill bore down the valley and for the first time since beginning the walk, I realised just how remote we really were.

The chief took my cup and gulped down the lot in one go, smacking his lips in delight.

I poured smaller measures after that, and all the men did the same, along with Malang. The entire bottle was gone in twenty minutes, and only then did they begin to sing. At first it was nothing but a gruff muffled chant but soon enough it became lyrical and Malang joined in.

'What are you singing about?' I asked. A snow coloured yak moved closer to the fire, his shaggy coat seeming to float through the night. He settled against a dirt mound and chewed in silence, presumably enjoying the entertainment.

'Men and mountains. The high Pamir, and women too.'

That night, despite the frosty cold and the burden of altitude weighing like an elephant on my lungs, I slept well.

The Wakhi were already up and fixing the saddles to the beasts before the sun was even above the looming peaks. Breakfast consisted of nothing more than some stale bread and milky chai, suffused with coarse tea leaves. We needed an early start to make the final ascent to the pass. The yak handlers would only come halfway up – to the snowline; even hardy yaks couldn't make it up a glacier. As we rounded the moraine where the river gushed out of a vast block of ice, the chief pointed to a landfall across our path where an avalanche had come down the previous spring, bringing with it tonnes of ice and boulders.

'Three men and ten yaks dead. Be careful.'

It was a horrifying thought to be presented with before making a climb. The scree became steeper as we rose out of the shadows and into the first joyous rays of sun, where we were finally able to take off our thick down jackets. It had been a bitterly cold start to the day but it hadn't stopped us sweating relentlessly as we scrambled ever upwards.

The valley became light and after a couple of breathless hours we finally arrived at the snowline. We had got to an altitude of almost five thousand metres above sea level and I counted that every sixteen steps I had to stop to properly refill my lungs.

'Need to keep moving,' said Malang, with a voice that was unusually serious. He pointed up to an overhang of snow. 'Here is very dangerous place.'

He was right. This was avalanche territory and it was prime summer melt time. However hard it was, we needed to push on up the snowfall and get to the top of the pass, before the sun became too hot and loosened the ice.

We said goodbye to the Wakhi and watched as the yaks plodded off back into the valley. We'd had to offload all but our most essential equipment and had the added burden of needing ice axes and crampons. Not wishing to waste time, we trudged on up through the snow, which was fortunately still hard from the freezing night. The white sheet stretched out as far as the eye could see, interrupted only on its flanks by the unforgiving grey peaks of the Hindu Kush, bearing down on us. For hours, every summit was false, there seemed to be no end to the climb; every inch a victory, every metre a defeat. I was utterly exhausted and now couldn't go more than five steps without stopping. The glacier was steep – almost vertical in places. We had to kick in steps and use all of our power to cling on to the axes and keep pushing forwards. Every bit of me wanted to give up and turn around and go back down to the safety of the Wakhan, but I was spurred on by Malang's almost superhuman endurance and sense of humour.

As we reached the relative safety of a flat build of snow, away from the hazardous cliffs, I thought I could see the top. It was only a few hundred feet above but I knew it was still almost an hour away at the rate we were going, so decided to sit down and cool off for a while. The sun was beating down now and despite being surrounded by a brilliant blinding white, it was hot and sweaty work.

It occurred to me that I still didn't know how old my guide actually was. I'd observed his weathered face and glinting eyes, but they gave nothing away. I informed him that he looked fifty, and he pretended to be hurt and told me that he was actually only forty one. 'If you lived here and didn't have any food, you'd look fifty too. If you ever meet my wife, you'd think she was a hundred,' said Malang with a laugh that boomed across the valley.

We pushed on. Ahead, at a sharp steep angle was the Irshad pass. I could hardly imagine that people actually came this way to trade. Only in the month of August – still many weeks away – did the snow finally clear, and even then, for just a brief inter-lude. What we were doing was madness, but it was too late to turn back now. Malang raced ahead, eager to see what lay beyond the mountain we were climbing, and I lumbered on at my own slow pace. With the sun beating down and the glare reflected off the crystal path underfoot, there was no escape from the relentless environment all around.

Finally, I reached the summit. Malang was waiting for me with a smile on his face and an ice axe raised to the heavens. 'Wakhistan!' he shouted, and there it was. If I thought the view back down the Irshad valley had been impressive, nothing could have prepared me for what lay over the ridge. Standing on the crest of what felt like a gigantic tsunami, about to crash at any moment, I straddled one of the most infamous borders in the world. Behind me stretched out the brown scree of Afghanistan, and unfolding before me was a glistening sea of white peaks and black valleys. One step forward. I was inside Pakistan.

7

Karakorum

The trucks were painted like Wedgwood china vases with vibrant, miniature scenes of paradise covering the rusting hulks. Greens and reds and blues brought a beauty to an otherwise monstrous vehicle; intricate patterns and flowers; art of a juvenile and feminine kind, which you might expect of a little girl asked to decorate a doll's house. It was a stark contrast to the ferocious-looking drivers, bearded and filthy dirty, who jumped down from the cabins.

'It's Pashtu tradition from Peshawar, that's where they paint them,' explained Malang. 'They have artists whose job is to make them beautiful. The owners fight with each other over who has the best design.' Dozens of them were parked by the dusty roadside and yet more rumbled down the highway out of town.

'Isn't it unislamic to draw pictures of living beings?' I asked, wondering how the tribesmen of the North West Frontier, the wildest men in Asia – supplier of recruits to the Taliban and supposed religious fanatics – reconciled this art with their version of Islam.

'They were drawing pictures much before Islam came. These Pashtuns have a very long history, and good art.' Malang nodded earnestly while he admired a picture of an enormous fish eagle emblazoned on the back of a lorry as it jingled down the highway. There was no difference, except perhaps in style, to the way in which proud lorry drivers in England or America covered their trucks in flashing lights and bull bars.

Sost reminded me of one of those Wild West frontier towns you'd see in the films. Rather than the whisky saloons, doorways led into smoky little tea shops, filled with weary Punjabi lorry drivers and Chinese prospectors, although I was assured by Malang that if we wanted alcohol we could get it.

In spite of the fact that Ramadan had begun just a few days before, nobody seemed to be paying the slightest attention to it.

'What about you?' I asked.

Malang burst into laughter. 'I am Wakhi, you have seen how we live, *we* do Ramadan all year round, just drinking salty tea and eating bread. We don't need to fast any more to show we are good people. And anyway I am Ismaili, and the Aga Khan has shown us that these Sunni ideas are just stupid. Those Muslims in the south are bad people and fasting won't change that.'

After the Irshad pass we had walked the length of the Chapursan valley, downhill in an easterly direction, where all the people were also Wakhi. Descendants of migrants from Afghanistan and Persia, their ancestors had crossed the Irshad pass many generations ago, in search, presumably, of a land that wasn't quite as barren as the Pamir, and one where trees might grow. At each house we passed we were invited for numerous cups of tea, made even more hospitable when Malang told them where he was from. They all embraced him like a long-lost brother and he revelled in the attention. Some of them had even heard of him – the first Afghan to climb Noshaq – and I gladly sat in the shadows as he regaled them with tales of his mountaineering prowess.

The Chapursan immediately felt warm and welcoming. While the Pamir had been bleak and windswept, here the environment seemed benign. We didn't need ice axes any more – there were paths. The vast brown escarpments were interrupted by lush green oases where villagers tended expansive fields, and clusters of elegant poplar trees punctuated the landscape. Tiny stone and mud houses were joined by elevated walkways in between the potato and wheat fields. Unlike in the Wakhan, here there were the first signs of development; electricity pylons were strung across the landscape and wires linked every settlement so that each mud hut had its own TV. Rather than turban-clad men working outside, it was the women, dressed in bright clothing and unveiled, who were pulling in the day's produce. The men on the other hand, were loitering on the walkways, discussing 'business', according to Malang. And instead of the Afghan salwar kameez, they all wore Western clothes and were clean-shaven.

'You look like a Taliban,' Malang said, gently gripping my beard, 'the people here will be scared of you.' He put an arm around me as we trod carefully around the edge of a field so as not to crush the crops.

'This is the route Bin Laden came when he escaped Afghanistan. They were scared of him too and he had to keep going till he found the Pashtuns who would hide him.'

We were walking south now, away from the Hindu Kush and into the Karakorum range. These spiny and jagged peaks, so markedly different from the dome-like Pamir, are the mightiest of all the western Himalayas, with three of the six tallest mountains in the world jutting from their midst. I imagined for a moment being able to stand still for a few million years and witness their formation; the constant turmoil and folding of the earth; the crumbling of cliffs and upthrust of granite as these thrones were moulded out of a slow yet deliberate convergence. The mountains here looked restless and aggressive, with a savage beauty that was both alluring and utterly terrifying. Glaciers thirty miles long and a quarter of a mile deep filled the valleys, and around them, an environment so harsh as to be uninhabited. In fact, until just thirty years ago the entire region was so isolated and off limits that it was barely mapped, and even now there's only one way through and that is the KKH.

We had joined the Karakorum Highway at Sost, and I had immediately been impressed at the first sight of a proper road since leaving Kabul. In some ways it was a welcome relief. The highway starts in China, goes over the highest border crossing in the world – the Khunjerab Pass – runs into Pakistan and then winds its way south for hundreds of miles, almost all the way to the capital Islamabad. The flat tarmac proved much easier going than the rough shale and scree on the hills around it. And so we plodded on with the road beneath our feet, like a couple of tramps. Trucks roared past, blaring horns that echoed down the gorges. The road snaked its way along the Hunza river, above which dangled remarkable feats of homemade engineering: hanging bridges three hundred metres wide spanned the valley, high above the roaring water, like horizontal step ladders suspended in the sky. Gnarled and twisted wooden rungs, some not even secured, were the only footholds. Between these precipitous gaps of two, three, four feet were unwanted views into the freezing glacial runoff below.

The valley finally emerged out of the gorge and became wide and green. Behind us were some of the most incredible mountains I'd ever seen.

'They're called the Passu cathedral,' said Malang, and I could see why; a vast pile of needle-like peaks that resemble a hundred snow-capped holy spires rose up into an endless blue sky. If the Wakhan Pamir was the roof of the world, this place was its window into heaven.

'This is where I learnt to climb,' said Malang as we followed the road past the tongue of the Passu glacier. I'd never seen anything like it up close. Malang came here before his famous ascent of Noshaq in 2003, funded by the Italian expedition and supported by a Wakhi teacher. It was the first time he'd ever left his village. Behind a wall of black ice a hundred metres high lay a jagged rug of broken blocks of frozen white crystalline that rose up the valley, two miles into the distance. Looking across from the moraine it looked benign but I was assured of its deadliness soon enough.

'We spent weeks climbing in there. It moves.' He said.

Suddenly there was an ear-cracking explosion, and I ducked instinctively. Perhaps too much time in war zones had instilled in me certain paranoia when it came to loud bangs, but I couldn't help it.

Malang chuckled. 'It's the ice.' I looked down to see a faint cloud of ice dust where another twenty-tonne block had fallen free – all part of the glacier's inexorable retreat.

'One day it will be gone,' Malang said ruefully. 'Only ten years ago it went all the way down to the river. But at least the Chinese will be happy.'

'Why?'

'They used to have to rebuild the highway every few years. There's still one glacier downstream that is going forward which keeps smashing up the road, but that will probably start to go home too. What to do? You know what Karakorum means?'

I didn't.

'It's Turkish for crumbling rock.'

Following almost precisely a branch of the ancient Silk Road, the KKH was built as a joint project by the Pakistan and Chinese governments. By connecting this route to the Asian highway, not only did the Chinese facilitate trade with Pakistan but also gained an overland route to the Arabian Sea, bypassing India.

Unlike India, which regards China as a sworn enemy and threat to its sovereignty, Pakistan has embraced Chinese economic expansionism.

The road was started in 1959 – shortly after the Chinese invasion of Tibet – and took twenty years to complete. Hundreds of Pakistani workers and untold numbers of Chinese lost their lives during the construction, and monuments to individuals and groups lined the roadside. Entire labour gangs were sometimes buried alive when the explosives triggered landslides and avalanches – perils that remain to this day when stretches of the highway, which is maintained by Chinese construction teams, have to be rebuilt. The road carves its way through the mountains, weaving between some of the highest peaks in the world and through impressive tunnels hewn out of the rock. It clings to the cliffs, running alongside cascading rivers, just inches from a sheer drop into the valley below. It is no wonder it is considered one of the most dangerous roads on the planet or why it's known as the eighth wonder of the world.

A few miles south of Passu we reached the village of Gulmit. Up until then the weather had been bright and pleasant in Pakistan and we'd been treated to spectacular views of the mountains, but this morning droplets of rain began to splash on the road. Malang pulled a plastic poncho out of his bag, and wrapped it around himself like a blanket taking on the appearance of a tourist at a theme park. I'd given him plenty of proper trekking gear right from the start but he'd given most of it away in the Wakhan, to his shepherd friends and to complete strangers. I warned him that he'd need it but I couldn't help but be charmed by his selflessness and generosity. The rain wasn't heavy but the air looked full and the dark clouds cast shadows on the surrounding grey hills. People were staying in their houses; we hadn't seen a car in hours. For a while, we tried to take a shortcut by following a footpath that had been cut into the side of the cliff.

'This is the Silk Road,' Malang announced.

'I know it is – the KKH follows the old route.'

'No, I mean, this is the *real* Silk Road.' Malang stooped down to pick up a rock in his hand. 'The actual one. The new road follows the river, but this is the original track that people and donkeys took to get to China.'

I looked ahead to the ancient, narrow footpath, barely three feet wide, and imagined Marco Polo traipsing along with a yak in tow. We continued on the stony trail, occasionally peering over the precipice into the valley below, which was now engulfed in a thick, creeping mist.

Suddenly it started to hail. Dink, dink, dink ... tiny stones were falling from the sky onto the path in front of me. I could see them bouncing like marbles and stood in wonder for a second. I couldn't work out how it could be raining and hailing at the same time.

'Run,' shouted Malang with uncharacteristic nervousness, and with that he pelted away ahead of us as fast as he could, his poncho flailing out behind him. Without a word, I followed as quickly as I could, with no idea what was happening.

'Landslide,' he said breathlessly at a sprint, not stopping to turn around. When we'd finally reached a flatter area, Malang came to a standstill and pointed back. I looked at the path. It wasn't hail at all but small stones bouncing down the hillside. They were followed seconds later by bigger ones, now fully rolling and then a couple of head-sized rocks, which somehow seemed to glide gracefully on top of the moving debris. It wasn't a big landslide by any means but within ten seconds half the track was covered in rubble, before the deep, grinding noise ceased.

Malang shook his head. 'Very dangerous. It happens all the time here. Many people die.'

I could only imagine how easy it would be for a few bigger boulders to come loose and for the entire hillside to come down on our heads. We walked on, but not without one eye fixed to the escarpment that towered over us. I decided it was best to get back onto the main road where it would be easier to avoid rockfall.

It turned out that we couldn't have been more wrong. As we walked down into Gulmit, with the Hunza river on our left, we encountered a spectacular sight. A turquoise expanse of still, milky water stretched out before us; the road had disappeared. Flanked by steep cliffs, which were chiselled from the mountains above, the lake filled the entire valley.

A group of men loitered at the water's edge. Some jingly trucks were parked up, laden with Chinese goods. Bundles of clothes, cement, electronics, shoes, motorcycle parts, children's toys – all bursting out of sacks waiting to be offloaded.

'What happened here?' Malang asked one of the drivers.

A Pashtun with a bright-orange hennaed beard stood wrapped in a blanket over his salwar kameez.

'This is Attabad lake. It's been here for five years after a land-slide downstream blocked the Hunza river.'

'Five years?' I asked. Up to here the Hunza river had been a narrow tumult of white water and I was astonished that the surge hadn't broken through in all that time.

'It broke through after five months and now the river carries on, but it's still only draining slowly. Now we have no road for twenty kilometres.'

'How do you pass?' asked Malang.

'You'll see,' said the man.

After a while, a speck appeared on the horizon of the lake. It was a boat, a small wooden vessel, not more than thirty feet long, powered by a pair of motors attached to metal poles. It pulled up alongside the shore. The captain was steering from what looked like a sawn-off tuk-tuk or rickshaw, which had been welded onto the deck – multicoloured windshield and all; it looked ridiculous. The group of lorry drivers frantically rushed into action; they formed a human chain and loaded the cargo onto the hull, which caused the thing to sink down, leaving the sides just inches out of the water.

The front half of the boat had thick wooden planks that stuck out at right angles to the bow, which I had presumed were for balance. I was soon proved wrong, when a jeep, equally as overloaded with cases and bundles as the wobbly little boat, drove down the banks, across some timber beams and onto the deck. It took great skill not to overbalance and cause everything to capsize, but the driver managed it. His friends whooped and cheered from the waterside and some of them, in their turbans and *pakols,* filmed the manoeuvre on their mobile phones.

The Pashtun seemed unfazed and was laughing. 'Sometimes they fall in and we have lots of fun.'

'It doesn't look like fun. It looks bloody dangerous. That boat is going to sink any second,' I said, flabbergasted at the ingenuity of this improvised nautical engineering and struggling to believe what I was seeing.

'Well, it's going all the way to Attabad and it's the only way to get there so I suggest you get on, before you miss it.'

'We're walking,' I said.

He laughed again. 'No you're not. There is no footpath.'

I looked at the sides of the lake and he was right – completely impassable vertical cliffs rose out of the water all around the lake.

'Until the Chinese finish the new road we have to use the boats.'

We walked up the gangplank onto the deck and perched ourselves next to the precariously balanced 4x4. The driver turned the key and the tuk-tuk ferry convertible spluttered into life.

Off we went, gliding quietly through the cold water. We passed the crests of boulders and the spines of skeletal, dead trees that broke the surface – a reminder that this was no ordinary lake, but one caused by a violent flood. The captain told us that thousands of people had been forced to flee their homes as the floodwater rose. Staring into the depths it was hard to imagine that entire villages were down there somewhere, submerged by the wrath of nature.

The rain had subsided, but the sky was overcast and brooding, giving the water an eerie pale emerald glow. Where the lake narrowed, the canyon rose on both sides to unfathomable heights. I imagined Odysseus as he navigated between Scylla and Charybdis, as we passed swirling eddies on the one side and threatening overhangs on the other.

Somehow the boat didn't sink and forty minutes later we arrived at the remains of Attabad. Half the village had been swept away during the 2010 landslide and even five years later, the rubble and debris were piled hundreds of feet high, yet somehow people had cleared enough of it away to begin work in reconstructing the road. Like at Gulmit, there were jingly trucks waiting to receive the cargo, and more boats too. One even had a lorry balanced on its deck.

I was glad to be leaving the lake behind and enter a region that I had read so much about. From Attabad, the river flows west in a sweeping arc for almost a hundred miles to Gilgit, through the Hunza valley. As the clouds cleared, we were greeted by a scene of unrivalled beauty.

The Hunza valley was the basis for James Hilton's 1933 novel *Lost Horizon*, the inspiration for *Shangri-La* – paradise on earth. Along this stretch, the Karakorum Highway is as quiet as a

country lane, thanks to the landslide, and the peace was undisturbed as we followed footpaths through neatly planted fields of
spinach and cabbage and orchards of apricots, cherries and
walnuts. Malang helped himself to dangling peaches, pears and
plums as we walked, waving at pale-faced farmers in knitted
woollen jumpers. Aside from the majestic 7,800-metre white
face of Rakaposhi, which Wilfred Thesiger described as one of
the finest mountains he'd ever seen, it was easy to imagine you
were in a Cotswold village on a summer's day.

We'd left the Wakhi behind now, more or less, although
Malang still spotted a few villagers along the way who greeted
him in his native tongue. Here the people were from the Burusho
tribe among whom, like in Afghanistan, they liked to claim
descent from the soldiers of Alexander the Great. Their dialect is
unlike any other in the world, bearing no relation to the neighbouring Pashtun, Urdu and Persian languages and has left
anthropologists bewildered for centuries.

'We're actually part gypsy and part Central Asian. Although
there is perhaps some European blood in our veins,' said Sher
Ali, a university professor from Hunza who'd worked in Lahore
university teaching politics.

The balding man with a neat moustache and thick glasses had
greeted us as we arrived in Karimabad, the old capital of the
Hunza valley. He didn't look like the average academic in a
baseball cap and tight jeans, let alone a Pakistani.

'We're different here. We are the *Hunzakut* – the people of
Hunza. For centuries we have defended this valley against invaders – even the Muslims didn't reach us until a hundred years ago.
Now we are Ismaili, like your Wakhi friend here.' He put an arm
around Malang.

Sher Ali had agreed to show us around the central Hunza
regions, and with his background in history and politics, he

was a useful guide to have. Malang had now reached the limits of his knowledge and was outside his own language territory and was fairly redundant as a guide, having never been here before. But I had grown to like him and agreed to let him come along until we reached the Indian border, more for company than anything else.

The Baltit fort sits above Karimabad. It used to be the royal residence where the King or *Mir* of the valley would sit in regal isolation, commanding the splendid scene of perfection below. It reminded me of a Tolkienesque citadel, constructed entirely of mud and wooden beams and surrounded by cobbled streets with medieval houses below. We made our way through the narrow passageways where poplars and willow and rose bushes filled the dreamy gardens. Nowhere else on earth had I seen such idyllic and civilised Arcadian beauty amid such remorseless and seemingly unconquerable nature.

'We're well aware of how lucky we are to live here,' Sher Ali said. 'Of course the road changed everything. It brought electricity and concrete and the Chinese, but nature has a way of screwing things up. Look what happened with the landslide.'

I was intrigued that he blamed nature rather than God. Everywhere else I had been in Pakistan and Afghanistan, and the rest of the Muslim world for that matter, the explanation offered was '*Inshallah*' – 'It is God's will' – the catch-all phrase for that which is unknown or undefined.

'Well, me personally, I'm an atheist,' he said. 'I have nothing against religion *per se*, but Islam is backward. It keeps idiots in the seventh century – just look at what's going on in Syria and Iraq. If those monkeys want to grow their beards and throw stones at women, well that's their problem but we don't want it here in the Hunza.

'It's only because we're so liberal here that we've managed to thrive. Do you know what the literacy rate is for Pakistan?' said Sher Ali, his eyes squinting through the thick glasses. 'The country average is sixty-three per cent. If you think that is shocking, in some tribal regions it's only twenty per cent, and for women, ten.'

I glanced at Malang. He looked away. I hadn't actually realised until we reached Pakistan that he was illiterate himself. He'd done a great job of hiding the fact, until we were required to fill in a customs form at the immigration desk, whereupon he asked me for his help, clearly embarrassed. I should have guessed; that's why he always used to ask what was in the ration packs. He couldn't read the labels.

'It's a stain on the nation,' the professor continued. 'How will we ever become first world if we don't let our women read?'

'But things are better in the Hunza?' I asked.

'Yes, of course,' he replied. 'We have ninety-five per cent. All the kids go to school and we send hundreds to university. All the best surgeons and pilots come from Hunza. And all because we aren't like those Sunni barbarians. Imagine, having to do Ramadan, and giving all your money to the bloody Saudis, just so they can build more mosques.'

He shook his head. He looked like a serious man and wasn't joking about any of it.

'Mind you, before we became Ismaili we were pretty savage ourselves. We prayed to trees and rocks and birds and stuff like that. We were animists and Shamans. Actually we still have Shamans.'

'Really? What do they do?'

'Magic,' he said, the squint altogether more severe now. And then the seriousness crinkled up as he let out a bellowing chuckle. 'Not really. They're just mad, probably a bit mentally ill. Would you like to meet one?'

I said that I would. I'd never met a Shaman before.

Malang and I followed the professor out of town along a country road to a small village called Haiderabad where we found a family waiting for us. They were Sher Ali's cousins. Men and women mixed freely, the women unveiled and happily engaged in conversations with their neighbours; until now I'd almost forgotten it was Ramadan but it didn't seem to make any difference here anyway. Platters of curried chicken and rice were brought out alongside dried apricots and yoghurt.

'You know that we have the longest lifespan in the world here because we are so healthy. No processed food, we grow it all ourselves, and we drink clean water from the mountains. Do you know it actually sells in America on eBay for ninety-nine dollars a bottle? And we just go and get it from the stream! It's full of gold you see.'

Sher Ali held up a recycled Pepsi bottle and a tin plate full of flat bread.

'Help yourself to chapati. And have some of this to wash it down.'

The professor handed me a small glass and proceeded to pour a clear white liquid from the bottle. 'We call it Hunza water. See what you think.'

I gulped down the liquid in one. It was a fiery homebrew made from fermented apricot juice mixed with glacial melt from a nearby ice floe. It burnt my throat as it went down.

Glasses were passed around and everyone had their fill. Malang had just a small sip, but Sher Ali swigged almost a quarter of the bottle himself.

It was getting dark as we finished off the last of the food. 'Come, let's go outside.' I noticed the flicker of a campfire burning in a courtyard in the centre of the village. As we got closer the flames illuminated the faces of a few dozen villagers who'd crowded around for warmth. Men young and old sat side by side on a wooden bench and a few women waited nearby. Skinny dogs limped in between the shadows and more people sat under the branches of a sprawling willow tree.

A few of the men had musical instruments: out-of-tune flutes and drums, which they were tinkering with, oblivious to the chatter around them. Malang and I stood by the fire and it was only then that I realised the gathering was for my benefit. Sher Ali had called ahead to request an audience with the Shaman, and the mystic needed the appropriate atmosphere to perform.

The professor whispered in my ear, 'That's him there'. He pointed beyond the crowd to a solitary figure in a white kameez with long black hair and a pencil-thin moustache. He seemed dazed. I couldn't tell if he was staring at the campfire or me, but his gaze didn't shift from my direction for a solid minute.

The drummer began a slow, methodical beat using a birch stick. A flute player joined in with a high-pitched whistle and then another, and then finally a man with a pair of smaller finger drums, until the noise was calamitous. The rhythm started to get faster and faster and more sophisticated. Everyone in the crowd was tapping their feet to the beat and clapping along.

'They say his great-grandfather slayed a giant,' Sher Ali said with a wink, 'and that he can predict the future. Three generations ago there was a Shaman from this same village who predicted that men would be able to fly inside machines, and also that a big landslide would one day destroy the Hunza river ... all of it has come true. He also said that the Mongol hordes would rise again – maybe he's talking about the Chinese.'

'What about this one?' I said, nodding my head towards the Shaman who stood rocking on the far side of the fire.

'He was a mad child. His parents didn't know what to do so they gave him away to an old wizard who taught him the ways of Shamanism. I think the wizard was probably also mad.'

'And then?'

'Well, he grew up to become a Shaman. They have proper day jobs too: farmers, teachers and the like. But when called upon, they get high and do Shaman stuff, like exorcise demons or bless marriages. No different to mullahs or priests really, except they talk to the fairies.'

Someone had presented the Shaman with a bowl of burning juniper leaves that he seemed to be inhaling with relish, his sweaty face buried among the hot smoky ashes. Suddenly he erupted into life.

He began to whirl like the Sufi dervishes I'd seen in Sudan, round and round, flailing his arms in the air with wild abandon. The crowd was uproarious and cheered. The music got louder. The Shaman whipped his way around the fire several times before closing in on the flute players, shaking his head about with erratic, grinning delight. He moved down the line of musicians, putting his ear to the end of the instruments and then next to the drums. He evidently didn't like the beat as he slapped the drummer hard in the face. The drummer instantly improved.

A black goat appeared from nowhere, bleating in fear at the sight of the madman. An assistant whipped out a kitchen knife and with a swift slice had the poor beast's head off in one fell swoop, which he then threw at the Shaman. The Shaman caught it in one hand and babbled at the decapitated cranium in a nonsensical drawl, before turning the gruesome thing upside-down and drinking the blood right from its severed jugular. I could hardly believe my eyes. Even Malang was gobsmacked. Sher Ali just smiled.

The Shaman jumped up and down howling; I couldn't tell if it was in pleasure or pain. Whatever the goat had told him must have been quite something because then, in an extraordinary display of acrobatics, the lunatic flung himself right into the flames of the open fire, where he stumbled among the burning woodpile. A shriek of horror erupted through the crowd and two of the nearest men rushed to pull him out of the fire. They doused him with water but the poor man was now sprawled on the floor, drifting in and out of consciousness, covered in black ash and blood.

'Is he okay?' I asked with genuine concern as we pushed through the crowd.

Sher Ali took a rag and wiped the Shaman's brow. 'He's fine; he does this all the time. I told you he was mad.'

8

Line of Control

With the giant Rakaposhi to our left, we followed the river west and then south, leaving the Hunza behind and entering the Nagar valley. If Hunza was spectacular, then the Nagar was sublime. Crystal waterfalls swirled from the cliff-face and poplars rose in perpendicular perfection out of the morning mist. Layers of hills vied for attention in the foreground of the glacial valley, and beyond, the razor-sharp peaks of the Karakorum pierced a cloudless sky.

Nomads sat around on the banks of the river panning for gold, their simple tents open to display earthenware pots, homemade daggers and rustic fishing nets; a scene unchanged in centuries. One morning we were delayed for an hour on the road when we encountered a mile-long traffic jam – of goats. Hundreds, or even thousands, of shaggy Kashmiri horned ruminants, some the size of horses, filled the rough track. Young goatherds howled at them and whistled in unison to keep them moving, but like a plague of hairy locusts the goats hoovered up every bit of grass and plant life in their hungry wake. Malang attempted to ride one and failed, which provided much amusement to the herdsmen. When their fearsome mastiff took it upon himself to teach my guide a lesson for interfering with his flock by biting him on the arse, the goatherds roared with laughter.

Walking was a pleasure, and often it was in silence. Malang and I were content in each other's company and happy to simply

take in the view. I wondered if Malang was envious of the serenity of the scene compared to the bleakness of his homeland, or
if perhaps it was just foreign; a place to be visited and left behind,
before returning to his own people to tell them what he saw. I
asked myself the same question but couldn't decide.

Despite having found my stride, I was nevertheless glad to
reach Gilgit. It was the first real town of any size on my route
since departing from Kabul; a good opportunity to restock on
supplies and get a proper bed for the night.

Gilgit lies just north of the confluence of the Gilgit and
Indus rivers, marking the exact convergence of the Hindu
Kush, Karakorum and Western Himalaya mountains. Due to its
geographical position this deep valley has been a crossroads of
civilisations for thousands of years. In the surrounding ravines,
ancient petroglyphs line the goat tracks, some dating back to
the Stone Age. We saw one enormous boulder near Aliabad
covered with pictures of ibex, some nine hundred years old,
which may have been scrawled by medieval hunters or pagan
witches. Some of the names of the villages, like Ganish and
Gorikot, indicated a Hindu heritage. Other signs clearly showed
Buddhist influence. At Kargah Nalah, a vast image of the living
god is carved into a cliff-face, too high for vandals to desecrate.
It was chiselled in the seventh century, when the whole of
Gilgit-Baltistan was part of greater Tibet, and later China.
Muslim rule came much later when the Shahs of Persia and
Mughal Indians invaded from the south, bringing with them a
new form of worship.

In the nineteenth century, British rule in India viewed
Kashmir and the northern territories of the frontier as a vulnerable point in the Great Game against Russia. Just as the Wakhan
and Afghanistan had always been seen as a buffer zone, the
British considered Gilgit and its surrounding valleys as very

much within their sphere of influence and sought to annex the region through proxy kings and compliant fiefdoms.

After the British victory in the first Anglo-Sikh war in 1846, the whole of Kashmir was allocated to the control of the Maharajas of the Punjab. This placed what was clearly a very distinct Islamic mountain region under the domain of a very distinct Hindu plains authority. It was a recipe for disaster, and although Hindu control under a British mandate lasted for a hundred years, when the opportunity arose, the mountain men rebelled. The Maharaja wanted complete independence, and in doing so, set the conditions for fifty years of conflict.

Gilgit bazaar was heaving with men. Pashtuns, Uighurs, Punjabis and Shina tribals mixed freely in the marketplace selling their wares: silver jewellery, hats, dried fruit and watermelons. The few women to be seen in the streets were dressed in burkhas. Until now, the rural areas had seemed liberal and welcoming. The influence of Ismaili Shia Islam had given the Hunza a progressive and tolerant outlook, and I'd been surprised by the high levels of education, spoken English and gender equality. But here in town there seemed to be undertones of a stricter, less compromising culture going on. For the first time on the journey, there were large mosques and almost everyone wore salwar kameez. There were more turbans too, and the majority of men wore long beards, often with the upper lip shaved – a sure sign of orthodoxy. The beards were dyed with bright-red henna and some men wore kohl around their eyes giving them a sinister appearance.

'They all look like Osama bin Laden,' said Malang. He appeared a little nervous and insisted that we both wore scarves and *pakols*. 'You'll be okay. You look like a Talib,' he said to me, 'but I look more foreign than you do, so I have to be careful.'

I had noticed a tension in the air the moment we crossed the Gilgit river; stares and squinting looks and no smiles. The people weren't hostile, just a lot less friendly than we'd become accustomed to and perhaps that skewed my views. Maybe we'd been spoilt by the hospitality of the Wakhi and Hunzakut. Either way, I was happy to follow Malang's advice. We did our best to blend in and not draw attention to ourselves.

In truth we were heading into a notorious area. To the south of Gilgit there had been a resurgence in support for the Pakistani Taliban and tribal factions were happy to fight for whoever paid the most. I was told that as a result, all along the Karakorum Highway to almost the outskirts of Islamabad, security was 'fluid'. The areas around the town of Chilas and Diamer were particularly bad. Revenge killings, sectarian mob riots, bus shoot-outs and stonings were all a frequent occurrence. According to the police commander in Gilgit, there was an army operation going on right at this moment along the N15 road in the mountains, to 'sweep out the undesirables'.

I got out the map. It didn't look good. To the south was an area of wild lawlessness run by tribal gangsters, and to the east, the impenetrable Karakorum mountains, beyond which lay the still undefined border with Chinese-occupied Tibet. The only way I could continue was towards another border, one so infamous that its very name has become synonymous with violence.

Two hundred kilometres to the south lay the infamous 'line of control' separating Pakistan from Indian-controlled Kashmir. The border has been officially closed since 1947, so I only had one option – to try and reach one of the passes and see if it was possible to enter 'semi-officially'. If not, I would be forced to make a thousand-mile detour, all the way to Lahore and the Punjab. I decided it was a risk worth taking.

The Punjab used to extend the whole way across the scorching, verdant plains to the south of the Himalayan foothills of Kashmir. The ruling British officers could gallop freely across and nomads, villagers and pilgrims could walk from the banks of the Indus down to Delhi if they chose.

But by the early twentieth century, dissent was brewing: the Indian independence movement was calling for an overthrow of the British Raj government. Encouraged by the great strategist of nationalist sensibilities, Gandhi, and after years of rioting and mutinies, the campaign had gathered enough momentum to be offered dominion status by the British.

On 15 August 1947, Lord Mountbatten, Viceroy of India, relinquished the region from the control of the British Empire, but not before drawing a line on a map to create India and Pakistan. This partition did bear existing religious populations in mind – a Hindu majority in India, and a Muslim majority in what was now Pakistan – but creating two nations out of what had formerly been 650 princely states was an impossible task.

Partition divided families, tribes, villages and fields. Both sides were soon overrun with refugees, desperately fleeing across the border in the hope of religious majority; an estimated fourteen million people were displaced in the largest human exodus in history.

With its location, north of the Punjabi plains, Kashmir was now in a critical position. The Maharaja – a Hindu whose subjects were chiefly Muslim – voted to remain independent of both Pakistan and India. His attempts at neutrality were soon scuppered though, when Pakistan sent fanatical tribesmen to invade the capital, Srinagar, to reclaim what they regarded as their own.

The terrified Maharaja fled to Delhi, where he appealed for military support and signed away the state to Indian control.

During the war that followed in 1948, the Pakistanis seized back land. A heavily militarised line of control was established, wherein the Indians held approximately 65 per cent of the land, and the Pakistanis the rest. The barbed wire that went up, guarded by countless AK-47-wielding soldiers, has forcibly segregated the two sides ever since.

In 1965 war broke out again. Tank battles raged and aircraft took to the skies.

As bombs rained down on both sides of the valley, whole tribes were forced to escape their homes and hide out in caves, the only place where they could be safe from the sky falling in. War came and went and came again. In the summer of 1998, heavy artillery fire broke out across the line of control, with huge numbers of civilians caught in the crossfire; the death toll was an estimated 30,000. Both nations were atomic powers and there was talk of a nuclear war. Luckily it never came but the fighting raged on until the snow fell. The following spring, after the annual winter ceasefire, the Indian army returned to their territory in Kargil to find that numerous outposts had been infiltrated and occupied. The Pakistanis blamed it on rebel 'freedom fighters', and so the hostilities escalated and yet again, missiles were fired on the mountains below.

For sixty-eight years, the people of these mountains and valleys have been subjected to continuous fighting. Mysterious disappearances and torture have become all too common and militants force children to act as spies and messengers. Separatist protests descend into lawless riots, with disillusioned teens pelting stones at each other. Landmines planted along these borders have killed hundreds of innocent people. As recently as 2014, Pakistani and Indian troops opened fire on each other along the line of control, violating the most recent ceasefire agreements.

Thousands were forced to run from their homes and there were more fatalities on both sides of the border.

The line of control was intended to be a temporary measure, but it was still there; a razor-wire fence separating two nations and one people.

~^~

We plodded on in uncertainty following the Indus river south. The stares grew longer with each village we passed, and so did the beards. At Jutal there was chalk graffiti all over the road and walls: DOWN WITH USA, proclaimed one. ENEMY OF MUSLIMS, said another. AMERICA & ISRAEL KILLER NUMBER 1.

An underlying tension added to the feeling that perhaps foreigners weren't welcome here.

Just south of the village of Bunjii, at the confluence of the Astore and Indus rivers, we were treated to our first view of Nanga Parbat, our first eight-thousand-metre peak. It's the ninth highest mountain in the world and the western anchor of the Himalayas. A scruffy brown sign was propped up at the side of the road giving a summarised history of the mountain. The words at the top had been roughly painted over but I could still make out the outlines. It read 'Nanga Parbat – Killer Mountain'.

The nickname was lent by the early mountaineers. Dozens of men died in the 1930s trying to climb the soaring peak – mainly Germans. They saw the mountain as their best attempt to demonstrate Aryan superiority, as only the British were allowed access to Everest at that time. Before it was finally conquered in 1953, by an Austrian-German team, thirty-one people had already paid the ultimate price for glory.

I wondered why the name had been painted over.

'It's because of the massacre,' Malang explained. 'The Taliban killed eleven climbers at base camp in 2013.'

He was right. I remembered reading about it in the news. Local terrorists had dressed up in the uniform of the Gilgit Scouts – a government paramilitary force – and crept up on the unsuspecting mountaineers in the dead of night, murdering ten foreigners and one Pakistani guide. Why? Nobody seemed to know, except that there were dark forces at play.

'The Pakistanis blame the Indians,' said Malang. 'They say the spies paid criminals to do it, so it looks bad on the government.'

It was obvious that the name 'killer mountain' was no longer politically correct.

'But,' I persisted, 'it must have been an inside job. There are so many police checkpoints around here. How could the terrorists get all the way to base camp and escape without the police knowing?'

I wondered for a moment if perhaps it was an attempt by one of the numerous 'agencies' to increase their spending budget. Cynical yes, but I'd already lost track of the myriad of army units, paramilitary groups, police services and security departments that all vie for control of the mountains. Most of them amounted to little more than a modern-day version of the tribal warriors and bearded gangs that used to roam around brutalising the population during the Great Game. Except now they did it with an ID card and an AK-47.

We walked against the flow of the Astore river, getting closer to the line of control with each day. The terrain was hard going and sometime we'd try and take a shortcut across the river's meanders using whatever means we could. On occasion we'd come across death-defying contraptions that the locals relied upon to get across the gushing white water. I looked in horror one day as Malang pointed out a pulley basket.

Local merchants made their morning commute crouched in a wooden pallet the size of a picnic hamper, comprised of just a single thin wire fastened to a wooden A-frame, heaving on a rope to drag the thing across. At the sight of one such construction, we stopped to ask a man who'd just crossed whether he thought it was safe.

'It's dangerous,' he said. 'But I do it twice a day.'

I couldn't resist and had a go. In what was perhaps the most terrifying stunt I'd let myself do, I got into the basket and pulled myself to the other side, convinced all the while that I was about to fall to my death. I sent the empty basket back to Malang and shouted across the gorge for him to come. By crossing the river we could make a shortcut that would save us a few miles.

I saw Malang freeze. The man who'd climbed Noshaq, the Tiger of the Wakhan, unperturbed even in Paris, simply stood there and shook his head. 'I'm not doing it,' he said.

And so I had to return, making the same perilous journey back across.

'What's up?'

'I can't swim.'

The local man who'd been looking on, bewildered at why we found his rope pulley so fascinating, was about to leave when Malang asked him if anyone had ever fallen in.

'No, not for a while. Oh, hang on, no, there was a boy last year from another village. They never found his body.'

We decided to keep our feet on solid ground.

As we gained height, the hills, which had previously been barren and rocky, were now populated with evergreens, giving the scene an alpine look. Fir and cedar covered the mountains in an emerald blanket and pine needles provided us with a cushioned footpath. Higher still we encountered glades, trellised rice fields and grassy meadows that looked identical to the pictures of paradise drawn on the jingly trucks that plied the Karakorum Highway. We were on the borderlands of Kashmir now and it was every inch as beautiful as I had imagined. It is only a one-day walk that separates the Karakorum from the Himalayas, but those few miles heralded a new world – one that was less harsh on the eyes, less craggy. At first glance it seemed altogether more settled; a landscape with confidence, less subject to change.

But of course, it was all an optical illusion. I was just unused to seeing so much greenery. But something sinister remained, both in the nature and in the people that lived there. Behind the idyllic façade there seemed to be an uneasiness that comes from living in proximity to violence, which no amount of wildflowers could dissolve.

I could tell Malang was getting restless too. The further south we pushed, the more he spoke of home.

'What will you do when you get back?' I asked him, knowing that in just a few days we'd have to say goodbye.

'Walk, of course.' He smiled, with a silver glint in his eye. 'You carry on walking around the world, and I will walk only in the Pamir.'

'What about your children?'

'They will walk too. My boy is already helping as a porter on an expedition; maybe he will be a famous mountain man too, like his father. One day we will climb Everest together. That is my dream – to be the first Afghan on the top of the world.'

His stick, a long piece of willow that he'd cut from a tree, stabbed the ground in unison with his right foot as we walked along the stony road.

'But first I must go home and make some money. I can't come with you to India so I go back to my sheep. Maybe I will sell them and then climb my mountain.'

He looked remarkably happy at the thought.

'What will your wife say?' I asked.

'I like my wife to come too but she is old. So maybe I find a new one.'

As we reached Gorikot, the sky became dark; I could sense that a storm was brewing. With every kink in the road, there was another army or police checkpoint manned by steely-eyed, bearded gunmen. They always waved us through, because we told them we were headed for the Deosai plains – a little white lie – but it kept them from asking too many questions. The Deosai national park is a high plateau just north of the line of control. It's a desolate moonscape that resembles the Peak District. Overlooking Kashmir, it is populated only by bears, wolves and marmot. It used to be a popular tourist spot before 9/11 and I wondered whether the soldiers had been briefed to be nice to foreigners and let us through.

There were very few other travellers on the road. It seemed that no one needed to come this way. There were some *Bakhawal* – nomadic Gujar shepherds – with their colourful tents and decorated horses. They passed us on the opposite side of the road, hardly even bothering to acknowledge us. They reminded me of the Kyrgyz whom we had met in the Wakhan. Perhaps there was something about nomads that made them so aloof, or maybe a restless life instilled wariness of anyone else not of one's own stock.

Apart from the nomads, the occasional army truck sped past, laden with soldiers. They looked like mummies, wrapped up in olive rags to protect against the cold of the high altitude. They too ignored us and drove on to the border, presumably to resupply the troops stationed ahead.

It was the first of July and we'd been walking for almost a month now and had covered two hundred and fifty miles.

The Wakhan Corridor, North Eastern Afghanistan, known locally
as Bam-I-Dunyan, the roof of the world.

Malang Darya, first Afghan to climb Mt. Noshaq – his country's highest peak – walked with me through Afghanistan and Pakistan.

Born horsemen, Kyrgyz tribesmen are descended from the Mongols, and still live a nomadic life in the Wakhan Corridor.

Author and guide, on top of the Irshad Pass bordering Afghanistan and Pakistan, 5000m above sea level.

'Jingly Trucks' carry goods along the Karakorum Highway. The ancient Silk Road remains an important trade route between China and the Indian Subcontinent.

The Hanging Bridge of Passu, one of the few old rope bridges that survived recent heavy flooding of the Hunza river.

A young girl from a family of nomadic Kutchi gold panners on the Hunza-Nagar river.

A major landslide in 2010 blocked the Hunza river at Karimabad causing a new lake to form.

The Hunza–Nagar valley;
inspiration for generations
of explorers and the fabled
'Shangri La'.

Mr Mashruf, the village shaman.
Shamanism is still prevalent in the
remote Hunza and Nagar Valleys.

Astore Valley: towards
the Line of Control.

The Gurez valley, Kashmir. Only recently opened to outsiders,
this is the front line between India and Pakistan.

Mohammed Latif and his family of Gujar nomads. Until partition his family was able to
roam with their sheep across Kashmir, now razor wire and minefields block his route.

Kashmir, trekking up a two mile icefall from the Gurez valley,
a militarised area near to the Pakistani frontier.

Author with Ashwin Bhardwaj at an army checkpoint, Kashmir.

Hundreds of houseboats fill Lake Dal, many are ornately decorated
and have served as floating hotels for generations.

Every August the mountains of northern India are filled with gurus, hermits and wandering ascetics.

Himachal Pradesh, where the foothills become fertile jungle with treacherous roads.

With His Holiness the Dalai Lama at his home in Dharamsala. This is the seat of the Tibetan government in exile.

The gravel road continued for another twenty-six miles to the foot of a mountain. We were both exhausted by the end of the day, having eaten little but a few dried apricots, and I slept badly due to the presence of a rather large scorpion rummaging around the outside of my tent. It had been drizzling for most of the afternoon, and it was chilly too. Neither of us was looking forward to saying goodbye but we knew the inevitable would have to happen today regardless of what occurred at the border.

Chilam Chowki appeared at the bottom of the hill, a couple of miles distant. The small collection of huts was different from most of the ones in the valley behind us, in that they had tin roofs. Most village houses were made entirely of earth and wood, but these glinted even through the grey mist.

'It must be army,' said Malang. 'Nobody else has metal roofs.'

As we got closer, Malang's prediction seemed accurate. I spotted a couple of drab khaki-coloured lorries parked up, and nearby a big green water container and a watchtower. The drizzle gradually got heavier and we were soon soaked through. In silence, we picked up the pace. The road seemed to come to an abrupt end as it reached the settlement. There was a weighted wooden barrier, painted red and white, but no people to be seen. It looked like a ghost town. We walked on towards the barrier. On the far side, I could see a concrete pillbox with a slit in the top where a machine gun poked out menacingly. Before we even reached the gate though, a voice shouted from an alleyway.

'Stop.'

A man on a motorbike came roaring up the track and pulled up alongside us.

'Stop,' he said again.

I looked at Malang.

'Who are you?' said the man, who wore civilian clothes.

Malang said we were tourists. Before we could explain, more people gathered. Uniformed soldiers had emerged from the pillbox and surrounded us. I had been filming with my camera and a guard ordered me to stop.

'This is a military area. This is a barracks. You cannot proceed.'

I tried to protest. According to my map, the road carried on a further few miles to the frontier at Minimarg, which is where I had hoped to be able to convince the border guards to let me pass.

'It is impossible,' said the man on the bike. 'This is the end of the road. Nobody is allowed to cross.'

I looked up the valley where the green hills were half obscured by fog. Just a few miles ahead was India – or rather, contested Kashmir – where for months I had dreamt of going. And here I was, teetering on the border, quarrelling with a barely literate corporal in the rain. A razor-wire entanglement straddled the side of the jeep track. Globules of water dripped from the rusty blades into sad looking puddles.

'Nobody is allowed to cross,' he repeated slowly. 'This is the line of control. Our enemy is there and we cannot let you go. It is too dangerous.'

'Why is it too dangerous?' I asked, wanting to understand his logic.

'For a start there's a big minefield.'

He had me there. I had been in enough minefields to know that I did not want to mess around with them. So that was that. This was the end of the road. I was barely in the Himalayas and I'd already been stopped, not by nature but by politics.

'This is where we say goodbye,' said Malang. He had not lost his smile the entire way. He was never going to come to India anyway, but was insistent on seeing me to the border, or as close to it as we could get; he'd fulfilled his duty admirably. I had known from the start that I would like him. We promised to stay friends and keep in touch.

He hugged me like a brother as we parted, and although the blowing kisses bit was a bit far-fetched, I was sad to see him go. He took a car all the way back to Islamabad, flew to Kabul and then on to Ishkashim to be reunited with his sheep and wife and children.

9

Kashmir

I had last seen Ashwin Bhardwaj the day before I flew to Kabul; he'd seen me off with a bottle of whisky and a promise to join me in the mountains. I knew he had a habit of turning up in the most unlikely places without much notice. When I was walking the length of the Nile, a car had screeched up alongside me in the middle of the Sahara and Ash piled out, all smiles and shiny boots. We walked together for a fortnight across the desert.

This time we had spoken at length about where he might be able to join me and it seemed that India would be the natural choice. He had considered coming to meet me in Pakistan but had been denied a journalist visa without explanation; I presumed it was down to his Indian heritage. Even now it is downright difficult for Indians to visit Pakistan and vice versa, even if they weren't born in either country.

Ash's father was born in the Punjab into the Brahmin caste of Hindus – Pandit exiles from Kashmir. He was the son of a railway engineer whose cousin fought alongside Gandhi and Nehru in the bid for independence, but was arrested for acquiring ammunition and explosives. After arriving in England in the 1960s he set himself up in the restaurant business in Windsor, where he married Ash's mother Dianne, an English woman.

I had originally met Ash at university but hadn't known him very well and it wasn't until after his father died that we met again.

'It's part of the Hindu culture to take your father's ashes back home,' Ash had explained three years before. 'I've been putting it off for so long but I really need to just do it.'

Ash had fulfilled his duties to his father in 2012 by returning the ashes to India and throwing them into the Ganges at one of the holiest sites – Haridwar – where the river emerges from the Himalayas onto the plains on its route to the Bay of Bengal.

'The whole ritual part was a bit of a let-down, to be honest,' he'd said resignedly. 'I was midway through the ceremony when the bloody priest started haggling for a bigger fee. Not exactly all that spiritual.'

Having been to India several times before I was hardly surprised; some pandits and holy men have a reputation for being rather business-like.

'But what I did learn came as a bit of a surprise,' he continued. 'I found the place where my entire family history had been written down on scrolls dating back four hundred years. I'd presumed my family were all Punjabis but it turns out they were originally from Kashmir.'

Since then, we'd discussed travelling in India some more and ever since our conversation in Gordon's five months before, I had known he would find a way to come out and join me.

I found the man sitting on the deck of a houseboat in the capital of Kashmir, Srinagar. It was almost dusk and the lake was shimmering gold. He was in a sleeveless Rolling Stones vest and shorts that belonged in a 1980s porn film.

'What on earth do you look like?' I said, as I pulled up along-side him in a motorised canoe.

He grinned wildly. 'What do you mean? I'm Indian, I can dress how I like. This is my home.' He spread his naked arms out to indicate the surrounding lake and mountains. The hot sun dipped low and red in the evening sky.

'You'll be shot by the Mullahs,' I said, to wind him up. 'And in their defence, it's not like you can speak a word of Hindi or Kashmiri for that matter, to explain your horrendous dress sense.'

'Bollocks!' he said. '*Namaste. Salaam. Dhanyabad. Shukriya.* What more do I need?'

It had taken me six days after leaving Malang to travel around via the official border crosssing at Wagah, between the cities of Lahore and Amritsar, as this was the only way of getting into India. I'd driven down the Karakorum Highway and passed Abbottabad – where Osama bin Laden met his end – then through Islamabad. I crossed the five rivers of the Punjab and saw where Alexander the Great finally turned his back on world domination. On entering India I made my way north for two more days all the way to Kashmir, where Ash awaited my arrival in Srinagar.

'When you get dressed properly, let's get back into the hills,' I said, eager to return to where I'd been forced to stop, and get on with the walk. 'We're heading to the line of control.'

The next morning we drove north from Srinagar for fifteen hours over some of the worst roads I'd ever seen, to the Gurez valley, which runs parallel to the border with Pakistan. At a village called Dawar the track ran right next to the razor-wire and the hill rose up to our left.

'This is where we get out,' I said, and we unloaded the bags from the jeep.

I looked up the steep incline. I was just a couple of miles away from where I'd left off in Pakistan, yet it felt odd that I had arrived here from the other side. In between where I was now and Chilam Chowki lay the minefield that we'd been warned of. This was as close as we were going to get.

'Well, this looks a bit more pleasant than the Sudan,' said Ash, as he stretched his legs.

In many ways the landscape was similar to that of the Pakistan side: alpine-like green meadows, crystal clear springs and pink-and-yellow wildflowers that emanated a surreal sense of peace. It was fractured by the ominous presence of barbed wire and military checkpoints. It reminded me of the scene in the movie *The Great Escape* where Steve McQueen jumps the border on his motorbike. The glistening Himalayas formed a resolute back-drop and rolling hills of pine forests stretched out as far as the eye could see. In the valley, wooden log chalets with smoke pirouetting from the chimneys enhanced the Swiss appearance. It was hard to imagine this was the most heavily militarised zone in the world, where in some parts the occupying troops outnum-bered the residents ten to one.

I looked up and down the road. Over the crest of the hill an old lady trundled past us, her face so creased I could barely see her eyes. She was wearing the traditional dress of the Kashmiri Chinar people and looked at least a hundred. On her back she was carrying a bundle of logs that was bigger than she was.

A few shepherds sat on a drystone wall a hundred metres away, keeping half an eye on their flock and the other on the new curiosity. The driver said goodbye and left us at the roadside with a pile of bags and our rations for the next week. According to my map we would have to walk due south from here, over a range of high passes that no foreigner had been allowed to cross since partition in 1947.

'Why is it that you keep bringing us to places where the last English folk they saw wore pith helmets?' said Ash, half jokingly.

'I'm pretty sure they will have fond memories,' I said, not entirely convinced.

'Well, now's your chance to find out.' Ash pointed to a man in uniform ambling down the road towards us swinging a rifle in one hand.

'*Salaam Alaikum*,' he said with a considered smile. He looked our age, was clean-shaven and rather tall compared to the Gujar nomads and shepherds that ogled us from afar.

'*Walaikum Salaam*,' we replied together.

He squinted and looked a little confused, flicking a wrist in the air. '*Tum kahan se ho?*' asked the soldier in Hindi. 'Where are you from?'

I told him.

'Angreez,' he said thoughtfully to me. He meant 'English' which was the general term used for any white-skinned foreigner. Then he looked at Ash. 'But you are Indian?'

'My father was Indian.'

'You are Punjabi?'

'Yes. Half.'

The soldier broke into a smile. 'My father also Punjabi. Where are you going?'

We explained that we wanted to walk south to Srinagar, over the Satsar pass.

'Come with me,' he said, patting Ash on the back.

We picked up our bags and followed the swinging gun.

The hill was decorated with barbed-wire entanglements that stretched out along the contour for as far as I could see. Occasionally a footpath and a gate marked a break in the wire, where shepherds and colourfully dressed women carrying bundles of firewood could pass. The native Kashmiris were pale-skinned with bright eyes – no different to their cousins just over the hill in Pakistan. Cousins they hadn't seen in sixty years.

The road was potholed and cratered, a result of years of neglect and isolation – not to mention being on the frontline of a sixty-year cold war. Ten years ago this was a battlefield and the craters of artillery shells littered the hillside. The Gurez valley had been closed to foreigners since partition and only opened in 2007, and even then, just the western end.

'Here we are. Come inside,' said the soldier, leading us off the main track.

We ducked underneath a road checkpoint barrier and entered a military barracks. It was surrounded by sandbags and wooden pickets and looked like it had been hastily built. Indians in camouflage trousers and string vests loitered around their mess tents as chickens shuffled about, pecking up the crumbs from leftover chapatis. Wooden boardwalks joined the canvas tents in anticipation of the rains that were due any day. Soon enough these men would be subjected to the Indian monsoon and the camp would become a mudbath. But for now at least, it was dry. Soil embankments had been built to protect against incoming mortar fire. A group of young soldiers sat on a rug underneath a tarpaulin, cleaning their rifles and listening to MP3 players. It was a scene I was all too familiar with.

We went into a tent where an officer was sitting at a wooden table. He too looked smart and wore a beret.

'You are the first foreigners we have had here. And I've been here for eighteen months. Where are you going?'

I repeated our plans to the major. 'We want to walk to Srinagar, over the Satsar Pass.'

'Impossible,' he said in perfect English. 'Don't you know how dangerous it is here?'

'It looks perfectly safe,' said Ash.

'The Pakistanis could attack at any time.'

'They haven't attacked since 1999,' I said.

'Yes. But they could. We are at high readiness.'

He wasn't joking. Despite the peaceful atmosphere his men were indeed ready for war. They drilled, marched, went on patrol and kept their weapons clean.

'Nobody goes into those hills,' he continued. 'There are bears and wolves up there in the woods. And leopards, too. We've had nine locals eaten in the past fortnight, all women. Poor ladies, they go out and fetch the firewood at first light and the leopards get them.' He shook his head.

'We'll be fine,' I said.

'And the path is rough and tough.' He carried on in a language not used in England since the fifties. 'You'd need to be fit and fine, tip-top.' He looked at the pair of us, clearly not convinced that we were up to the challenge.

'We'll be fine,' I said again.

'And if my men see you they will think you are *Pakis* and shoot you. You in particular.' He stared at Ash. 'Are you sure you're not a terrorist?' He raised his eyebrows knowingly.

'I'm pretty sure,' said Ash.

'Look here.' The major pulled out his smartphone and began flicking through photographs. He had a makeshift dossier of India's most wanted – Islamic militants with long beards in camouflage jackets brandishing AK-47s and swords. Pakistani Taliban, Al-Qaeda and Kashmiri separatists. Most of the images looked like they had been downloaded from Facebook but the major seemed to want to show off his detective skills. 'Here, this one, it's you.'

He showed us a photograph of a man sitting cross-legged in a salwar kameez and khaki waistcoat with a black flag draped on the wall behind him. It was the spitting image of Ash. 'Bloody hell, you're right,' I said.

'Bugger off. I'd never wear such a terrible outfit,' Ash protested.

The major grinned. 'Cup of tea?' he offered, adding, 'So who are you? CIA? Mossad? MI6?'

'Just tourists,' I said, explaining our route to him.

He shook his head again. 'Well, I'm afraid I can't let any old tourists just roam about in my hills. The colonel won't be happy about that.'

I insisted that we had all the right documentation and showed him our papers, but to no avail.

I had discovered over years of travelling that sometimes the best way to solve situations like this was to play to the vanities of officials and allow them to believe that they know more than they do. Ash looked at me. We were both thinking the same thing – there was only one way to get out of this spot.

I repeated the words slowly. 'We're tourists.' And then winked as I showed him my British army ID card.

The major glanced at it and leant back in his chair tapping his fingers together in a triangle shape.

'Brigade has been informed,' I lied. 'We have two-star approval. I'm just shocked word hasn't got down to you.'

The major looked nervous for a second but hid it well and looked down his nose. 'I was testing you. Well done, you have passed. Of course I knew about you, we were waiting for you. In fact, I have a friend who went to Sandhurst. Colonel Bob – Cavalry chap. Do you know him? You probably do. He's a fine fellow. '

I nodded with authority. 'Colonel Bob. Yes, of course.' I tried hard not to show my relief.

'Stay here tonight. There's a free building over there. Get some horses from the natives and you can set off tomorrow. In the meantime, enjoy your tea.'

We thanked him and made our way to the empty house down by the river.

'I hope he doesn't actually check up that we don't have permission,' said Ash. 'That was a massive bluff. He'll arrest us immediately if he finds out.'

'I know,' I said. 'But luckily there's no mobile signal down here, so let's hope the radio doesn't work either. Let's get out of the valley ASAP.'

So that's what we did. We woke at dawn and went to a nearby village where we found a Kashmiri called Mehraj to come with us as far as Srinagar. He spoke very good English, having studied in the city, and apart from being woefully underdressed for a five-day walk, made a good local guide.

Kitted out in a pair of jeans, trainers and a knitted jumper he found us three mules to help carry the bags and rations for the fifty-mile journey.

The mountains ahead rose like an enormous green wall. It looked almost vertical from afar and our mules fizzled into tiny dots on the trail ahead. With our backs to the razor-wire we left the line of control and walked south, deeper into Kashmir.

As we climbed the steep slopes into the pine forest I felt glad that Ash was with me. Malang had been a guide, a translator and a good companion, but Ash was a long-standing friend, which makes a huge difference. I had realised by going on long walks that it was futile to try to go it alone. I had been there and done that. When I was twenty-two I hitchhiked from England to India and spent a rewarding and interesting five months learning a lot about Asia and the Islamic world, but ultimately it was a lonely and isolating experience. My best memories had come from the times I had travelled with friends and when I had shared the dangers and exhilarations with someone else. When I walked the Nile I spent a lot of time on my own, but the highlights of my journey were when friends had walked with me. Since last year, Ash had completed his army training and was now a fully fledged reservist officer, qualified in navigation, fieldcraft and survival. He'd come a long way since our ill-fated trek across Africa, and I was glad that he was accompanying me through such a notorious stretch of the Himalayas.

The trail wound upwards for several hours, and at times was so steep that even the mules stumbled. I was relieved that I didn't suffer from vertigo, though I did wonder whether these sheer drops weren't enough to make it start at any time. Below the valley sprawled east to west, its bottom no longer visible. To the north, the direction we had come from, we could now look back and see the white peaks of Pakistan. A month had passed already and although my body was getting used to the rigours of daily trekking, steep climbs like this were still hard going. It made me think back to my chat with Ash in the pub.

'Remind me why we're doing this again,' I said, coughing.

'Because we love it,' said Ash unconvincingly, kicking steps in the crumbling soil.

We stopped to rest on a boulder under the shade of a fir tree. Pretty pink flowers littered the grassy meadow and a clear spring trickled out of the rocks nearby. I looked around and realised that if there were a heaven it would probably look something like this. I did love it really. Views like this made it all worthwhile.

'It is beautiful, isn't it?'

Ash didn't say anything. He just smiled, still breathing heavily.

Mehraj came back down the hill.

'I thought you'd got lost. Are you okay?'

'Yes, we're just taking a rest.'

Mehraj knelt down by the spring and cupping his hands, drank from the clear, cool water. He looked fit and healthy, and had a kind smile. He sat down on the grass next to us.

'What makes you come to my mountains?' he asked with the curiosity of a child.

'Views like that.' I pointed to the summit of a mountain across the valley.

'It's just a mountain,' he said, the smile not leaving his face. 'The Indians come here to occupy us,' he went on. 'I can understand that. They come because they are scared of China and of Pakistan.'

'What do you mean, Indians?' Ash asked.

'Indians. We are not Indians.' Mehraj put a hand on Ash's shoulder. 'Don't be offended, sir. We are Kashmiris. We want our independence back, like we have always had. We don't want Indian soldiers here. But I can understand why *they* come – they are told to come. Why do you come?'

'Because we like the mountains and the views,' I said again.

Mehraj looked at me with a considered gaze.

'You come all this way to see the views and get out of breath? What a strange people you are.'

By nightfall we had made it halfway up the mountain, almost to the snow line where last winter's snowfall had not yet melted. It filled the valley and looked like a glacier. We spent the night in a small village populated by Gujar nomads who had built some huts out of stones. The roofs were covered in soil and grass grew from them, for added insulation. As we pitched our tents, the whole family emerged and watched us in silence. Hundreds of goats descended from the mountain as the sun went down and before long we were surrounded by the bleating beasts, and the noise carried on all night.

'What do these people think of the Indians?' I asked Mehraj.

'They like the soldiers because they give them medicines and sometimes food, but they are from Jammu. They walk here with their sheep and it takes them six or seven weeks. They are not Kashmiri like me, so it doesn't matter what they think.'

Like many of his countrymen, Mehraj wanted to see an independent Kashmir. Or at the very least, some sort of Islamic rule, away from the Hindu domination that had been in place in the disputed area since the 1840s. It was a pipe dream that never seemed to go away.

The nomads gave us fresh goat's milk, which was still warm. Mohammed Latif, the eldest of the tribe, introduced his nine young daughters and countless sons who were still at school. They didn't like coming to the mountains and all wanted to be professionals. One of the boys wanted to become a doctor and showed me his school books – excerpts from *Alice in Wonderland*, *Macbeth* and a government advisory called *Tobacco: The Silent Killer*.

Mohammed told me that their nomadic way of life would probably die out after a generation and that he was glad it would because it was a hard life and he would rather his children were educated.

'We are very poor here,' he said.' I have goats and sheep and even some yaks, but no house. We have three metres of snow here in the winter and so we have to walk all the way back to Jammu to escape the weather.'

He looked at me and then at Ash and smiled. 'Are you a nomad?'

Ash smiled back. 'I suppose we are. No house and we travel to escape the weather. But I don't have any sheep.'

'No sheep at all?'

'Not one.'

'Then you are very poor. What can I give you?'

We declined Mohammed's offer. I ended up giving him my head torch to demonstrate that we were not completely destitute, and to save him some face that he didn't have anything to offer us except a cup of tea. It was a humble reminder of just how relative people's ideas of poverty were.

The next morning we continued the climb, following Mehraj and the mules up the snowfall and beyond the treeline, to where the rock face became bare and windswept. The thermometer plummeted, it began to drizzle and our feet were wet. It is amazing how your mood can swing with the elements in the mountains. With a beautiful view, a kind face and a cup of tea, you can be in heaven one minute, but with blustery winds and rain – hell the next. Today was hell, and only a reminder of what was to come.

The path wound between scraggy rocks and deep pools of grey ice water as we ascended a high pass. The mist came in and it was difficult to see the pack animals ahead. Often Mehraj would be a mile ahead and would have to wait for us. In his thin jeans and knitted jumper, I wondered how he kept his morale up when he must have been freezing. We camped high that night and a biting wind roared through the camp, bringing with it a fine dusting of snow and forcing the pools to freeze over. I was just glad we had tents.

The next night we weren't so lucky.

We followed a ridge for most of the day before descending into a prehistoric forest with enormous ferns and oversized mushrooms. I expected to stumble upon a Stegosaurus at any moment. It had warmed up again and I chatted with Ash about how nice it was to be walking downhill after the debilitating climb yesterday. We loaded our rucksacks onto the mules and just carried our cameras and water bottles to make things easier.

We had last seen Mehraj a couple of hours before. He was looking after the mules so told Ash and me to go on ahead. We could wait for him at the top of the ridge above Naranag where we'd find an open meadow. Apparently we couldn't miss it.

I led the way, following a path that took us deeper into the forest. A thick layer of pine needles covered the track and lightning had felled several fir trees so we kept losing the way. It looked as if no one had been here in months, if not years, so there was no way of knowing which of the myriad of trails was the right one. We tried to stay at the same height but soon enough the path would diverge and then disappear altogether. We would go back and rejoin it and follow another one and then the same thing would happen. The afternoon wore on and both of us were getting frustrated. There was no phone signal to contact Mehraj and it was becoming more and more apparent that we were lost.

'For God's sake, Lev,' said Ash. 'Do you know where you're going?'

I showed him my map. It was simple enough to work out where we were and where we needed to be – the only small problem was how to get there. To our left the hill fell away to an almost vertical drop into a valley where a gushing river chiselled its way through a gorge. To the right the forest was thick; twelve feet high thorn bushes blocked our way. The village we were aiming for was just five miles away – as the crow flies – but it may as well have been on another planet. I looked at my watch; it was already five p.m. and Mehraj would have been waiting for us on the ridge for at least an hour.

'What do you reckon? Up or down?' I said. Both looked equally appalling.

'Let's go down to the river and follow it round,' Ash said. I could tell he was exhausted and in no mood to climb again.

'You heard what Mehraj said. There are no bridges – what if we need to cross?'

I looked down into the valley. It must have been half a mile down, perhaps more. We had two options – a thorny scramble up or a slippery descent.

'Okay,' I conceded, 'lets go down.' I figured that it couldn't be too hard and at least would be easier than going up again.

We slipped and slid on our backsides down through the Jurassic-sized ferns. A huge deer darted out of the bushes and seemed to fly into the pine forest below. I wished for a moment that I were an animal – they never seemed to tire. An adder slithered from under a rock, its diamond ridges flashing in the undergrowth. I reconsidered my aspirations of reincarnation.

At the bottom of the cliff we emerged onto a narrow beach. It was almost quarter past six. My heart sank; we had less than an hour of daylight left. The river was a torrent of freezing glacial melt crashing through the gorge like an icy bolt of lightning. There was absolutely no way of crossing, and on our side, the cliffs up and down the river were sheer faces of crumbling rock.

I was exhausted. I hadn't felt like this at all on the journey so far but now I felt responsible for leading Ash down the wrong route. Fortunately, he seemed to get a second wind.

'Come on, get a grip, let's get out of here,' Ash said.

'But there's no way round,' I pointed out.

'We'll have to climb back up.'

So that's what we tried. Following a gulley, we tried to scramble out of the valley but the soil was wet and the grass fell away in clumps in our hands. It was too dangerous; one false move and we would fall to certain death in the swirling eddies below.

Suddenly a rock came loose above my head and tumbled out of the undergrowth, going straight for Ash's head.

'Watch out,' I yelled.

I stretched my hands out and caught the boulder; it was a miracle I didn't fall myself. I managed to divert it between my legs and let it go, safely past Ash and crashing down into the river. We clung to the cliff, both of us shaking with horror, before slowly crawling back down.

Perhaps we had underestimated the power of nature in the mountains. We had taken them for granted and forgotten that the price of indescribable beauty from afar, could mean horrific deadliness up close.

It had taken us an hour to slide down half a mile. There was no way we'd get back out before dark and I told Ash this.

The realisation set in.

'Shit.'

'Exactly.'

We both sat slumped in silence, side by side on a rock, wondering what to do. It was almost dark and the clouds were black. I was so physically done for that I began gasping for air and vomiting, although there was nothing to throw up – we hadn't eaten all day.

'We need shelter,' Ash said.

It was the first rule of survival – especially in the mountains where the weather could change at any moment, and I was grateful that Ash had done his army training.

He helped me to my feet and we stumbled through the undergrowth back along the narrow strip of rocks to the way we had come down. A hundred and fifty metres away, almost imperceptible were it not for one angular beam, was the frame of an old poacher's hut. There is no such thing as a straight line in nature, and when you're in the forest, little things like that tend to stick out like a sore thumb.

The roof had caved in and the whole thing was overgrown with wild cannabis and vicious brambles, but it was the nearest thing to shelter we could see. Up close I could see that the only way in was through a gap in the bushes and so we pushed through, getting covered in scratches in the process.

'That was lucky,' said Ash.

'A miracle,' I agreed.

Just as we entered there was a loud crack and a flash of light. The rain came down in sheets.

'Sod's law,' said Ash. 'The one time we load the bloody bags onto the mules you get us lost.'

'Me?' I protested. 'It was your idea to come down the valley.'

'Piss off. You agreed.'

He was right. I should have insisted we carry on climbing instead of taking the easy road. Now we were stuck in a ravine in the rain overnight with no sleeping bags, no food and no way of contacting Mehraj. We were cold, wet and hungry, but at least we had a collapsed roof over our heads and a lighter.

'Fine. Let's just forget it and make a fire,' I said.

For the next eight hours we took it in turns to collect twigs and bits of moss to keep the campfire alight. I was grateful we did have a lighter because I didn't fancy my chances of doing a Bear Grylls impression in those conditions. The mere fact that we had a roof above our heads (however leaky) was probably the only reason we didn't die of hypothermia that night. We curled up, shivering around the embers, moving in disgust as the floor crawled with insects around us.

Despite sharing the hut with some hairy spiders and milli-pedes the size of eels, we made it through till dawn. At last the rain abated and a chorus of birds heralded a new day. One in which we were alive. Weak with hunger we climbed back out of the valley, following our trampled course from the day before, hoping to retrace our steps and find Mehraj.

Fortunately our Kashmiri guide had the initiative to send out a search party. After just an hour we heard shouts from the woods up above. I looked up to discover an old shepherd wielding an enormous axe and waiting for us on top of a boulder. I had never been so relieved to see anyone.

'I've been sent to find you,' he said, handing us a soggy piece of chapati before turning around and motioning for us to follow him. He bounded off with the speed of a stag and we lolled behind like a pair of zombies all the way to Naranag, where, four hours later, Mehraj was waiting with a cup of tea and a warm blanket.

'We thought you were dead,' he said with a look of genuine concern.

The Vale of Kashmir unfolded as a welcome sight in front of us. Glistening below was the famous Dal Lake, surrounded by the infamous city of Srinigar and brimming with thousands of *shikaras*, and houseboats, painted as colourfully as the jingly trucks of Pakistan. Bejewelled and dazzling with fairy lights, the wooden verandas made them look like levitating Mughal palaces. Chandeliers hung behind lace curtains and delicate vases promised visitors a world of luxury from within. Vast water lilies guarded the magical kingdom and parted for the long, narrow-tailed boats as they were slowly punted through.

Sikhs in blue and orange turbans cycled through the lakeside bazaar, waving to the Indian soldiers in their bulletproof vests and camouflaged helmets. Machine-gun emplacements were incongruously sandwiched between luxury hotels and hawkers selling pashmina shawls. Gilded minarets towered out of the crumbling bazaar and the gleaming dome of a *gurdwara* shared the horizon with the steeple of a Roman Catholic church.

Endless carpet shops lined the embankment and cycle rickshaws weaved through the traffic, conducting plump Indian tourists to their floating retreats as deformed beggars crawled along the pavements in search of a rupee. Boatmen sold beer, whisky and rogan josh to couples on *shikaras* while the sound of the muezzin echoed across the still water.

After the hardship of the mountains it was completely surreal. Ash led the way as we tramped down the street towards the boulevard, the gushing torrents and horizontal rain pushed to the back of our minds for now. All we wanted was a bed and some food.

It seemed that in the Himalayas of Kashmir there was a fine line between heaven and hell.

10

The Holy Man of the Mountain

We stayed in Srinagar for two days on a houseboat called *The Star of Kashmir*.

India had been experiencing a terrible heatwave over the summer and hundreds of people had died. It should have come as no surprise then to find Dal Lake packed with Indian tourists, desperate to escape the heat of the plains. Families from the Punjab and Delhi flocked to Kashmir and the hill states in droves. What's more we found ourselves in the midst of pilgrimage season. The road south from Kashmir into Himachal Pradesh was filled with Hindus travelling on a *yatra* – a journey – to visit a holy cave in the mountains where it was said that Lord Shiva explained the secret of life and eternity to his wife Parvati.

Pilgrimages are an integral part of Indian culture. For thousands of years Hindus and Buddhists have embarked on journeys to show their devotion to God.

In many places I'd travelled, the concept of walking would raise eyebrows and protests of disbelief. In Africa the locals would laugh at me or ask if my car had broken down. 'Only a poor man travels on foot,' they'd say. Or they would just shake their heads and tut and tell me that I must be quite stupid. I found it easier to say I was just walking to the next village than that I was on a journey of several thousand miles.

In India it was different. Walking is so deeply ingrained in the national psyche that nobody batted an eyelid. There was no question of my motivation; of course I was on a pilgrimage. It didn't matter which god I worshipped, or where I was going – there was just a simple understanding that I was a traveller. Nothing more, just another walker with my own mission, and that was something to be respected.

Ash and I walked south out of the Vale of Kashmir and over a range of mountains into Himachal Pradesh. It was at once an India I knew and loved. Where Kashmir had been wild and unpopulated in parts, this was a region I was more familiar with. We stayed on the roads more or less, and there was no longer any need to camp. We'd sleep in small hotels and guesthouses and eat delicious curries and breakfasts of *aloo paratha*. People assumed we were Indian – having Ash there helped of course. They greeted him in Punjabi and he took great pleasure in reeling off the few words he remembered from his childhood.

Sometimes one village would merge with the next so that we would barely leave habitation at all. It meant that we could pick up porters with ease and had none of the trouble of having to get bothersome horses. Walking on tarmac meant that we didn't have to watch our step all the time and there was less risk of spraining an ankle or stepping on a cobra. It was altogether less challenging underfoot and meant I could relax a little and just enjoy the view. Ash and I chatted about life and travel and shared stories and memories.

We passed shrines to Shiva, Brahma and Vishnu, and sometimes Hanuman, the monkey god. We'd left the Islamic world behind now, although there were still mosques in some of the villages. We'd entered a new world where spirituality was more tangible, more colourful and generally a bit more fun. Purple-faced goddesses and metal snakes wrapped around stone lingams peered out of bushy lairs. Red powder, burning incense and luminous paint denoted holiness here. Nothing was too bright or vulgar; plastic and concrete were just as suitable a medium for the gods as wood and stone.

We were in the foothills now. In the distance the snow-capped Dhauladhar Mountains rose out of the jungle like a cresting wave in an ocean of green. Parrots and hornbills squawked from the canopy and langur monkeys barked as we passed.

The road spiralled around the mountains through forests of pine and rhododendron, and what looked like a journey of one mile in a straight line could easily be five or six, by the time we weaved around the hairpin bends. Sometimes we contemplated making shortcuts but we had learnt our lesson in Kashmir; usually it was easier to stick to the path.

Road signs warned motorists of the dangers of the Himalayas in a language that would have bordered on hilarious, were it not for the content. They read like a dark comedy with bad English.

'Follow traffic rules, avoid blood pools.'

'If married, divorce speed.'

'After whisky, driving risky.'

'This is a highway not a runway'.

And my personal favourite: 'Better mister late than late mister.'

A certain fatalism prevails on the roads in India. Nobody wears seat belts, the buses are overloaded and drivers tear around the lanes at high speeds, overtaking on blind bends with sheer drops into the jungles below. I was just glad I was walking rather than driving, especially on the occasions when we saw the rusting hulks of mini-buses, overgrown with weeds at the bottom of cliffs. As we trudged on through the foothills, with their burgeoning population, it became an all too common sight. It was hard not to wonder how many people had died in a moment of negligence. I tried to put it to the back of my mind but it was a stark reminder of the frailty of life in the mountains. Of all the dangers in the Himalayas, it was always going to be gravity that was the most deadly.

One day Ash and I were walking up the Kangra valley towards Dharamsala when we saw a small white car on its roof, thirty feet below us in a small gulley off the road. The driver had clearly taken the bend at speed and misjudged the turn. He must have rolled a couple of times before coming to a halt when he hit a tree. We looked down to see a couple of men rummaging inside the car.

'Is everyone okay?' I shouted down to them.

One of the men looked up and shook his head.

'No. It was this morning. They all died.'

It was a sobering thought. These tragedies happen all the time in the hills and I thought back to the landslides in Pakistan and getting lost in Kashmir. It could all too easily happen to us.

Perhaps it was a defence mechanism, or maybe just the fact that it had been the first few weeks of the journey, but until I reached India I hadn't really contemplated the scale of my undertaking. I suppose at the back of my mind I knew what I was letting myself in for, and I was well aware of the dangers, but I hadn't allowed myself to dwell on them too much. Before I set off I'd been so preoccupied, planning and preparing for the walk, but it was impossible to compute the true dangers when they were on paper, and I'd given scant thought to what could happen.

The army had taught me to assess risk, mitigate danger and implement operating procedures. You become inured to failure and assure yourself you are invincible. What it doesn't teach you, is how to deal with disaster. You cannot tolerate defeat; it simply isn't an option.

Part of the appeal of going on an expedition is the fact that you can't avoid risk. It is part and parcel of the adventure, and without it a journey would be dull, without reward. I'd learnt to embrace risk, to accept it gladly. And by doing so, I'd been able to face my fears and overcome them. I'd discovered my own limitations – both physical and mental – and then surpassed them through a combination of sheer doggedness, tenacity and perhaps a spot of luck.

I'd learnt about human nature and kindness and put the utmost faith in my own instincts and intuition. Over years of travelling I'd developed a sense of who could be counted on, and who wasn't to be trusted. I took pride in having good judgement, and despite making a few mistakes along the way, it had generally seen me through all right.

But the deeper I went into the mountains the more I began to question myself; why was I doing this and was it worth the risk? I'd been lucky so far, but luck has to run out sooner or later; something told me that I was walking on a tightrope.

'It's probably just the altitude addling your brain,' said Ash. 'But you have had a few near misses on your adventures.'

'I think it's more than that. I'm having doubts I've never had before. Seeing that car down there has made me think. Can you imagine if we'd slipped into that river in Kashmir? Nobody would've found us.'

'True,' Ash agreed. 'And imagine how embarrassing would it be if we ended up on page twenty-seven of the *Daily Mail* under the headline "Explorers lost in the mountains".'

Maybe it *was* just the altitude, or the result of one spicy curry too many, but the thought stayed with me. Perhaps I needed a rest, and I was glad when I saw the first road sign for Dharamsala.

Out of the Kangra valley, the road wound up again, into a wave of deodar pines where macaques howled from invisible hides. Dharamsala is nestled halfway up the ridge but the place I was aiming for was McLeod Ganj, a smaller town five miles up the mountain. It used to be a British hill station, dating back to the 1840s. Soldiers would come to escape the heat of the plains, and soon enough it became a major headquarters for the Gurkhas. Nowadays the British legacy is confined to the eerie building of St John in the Wilderness, a mock Norman church that looked like it had been transplanted from a village in Surrey.

Stone graves covered in ivy and moss lay undisturbed in the quiet churchyard and a grand bell sat outside. The windows were stained glass and a cobbled path led to a thick medieval-looking wooden door. Inside, the cold stone floor suddenly reminded me of home, and the wooden pews filled me with nostalgia for a time I wish I'd witnessed. I imagined the bejewelled Viceroy pulling up in his carriage, horses braying, and ladies in hats and long white frocks gossiping. Officers in red uniforms with bushy whiskers formed a regal procession as they popped in for the Sunday service. The walls were covered with wreaths and brass plaques commemorating past vicars and donations from eminent Victorians. Only the memorial to Sir Thomas William Knowles who had been mauled to death by a bear in 1898 signified that we were not in rural Victorian England. Outside, Ash prodded me to point out a humpbacked cow munching away on a rogue cannabis plant. A wicked-looking monkey sat on a gravestone, scowling. We were still very much in the Himalayas.

A grimy bus station heralded the entrance to the town, and with it, hundreds of people. There was a queue of cars filling the road all honking their horns to no apparent avail. Punjabi Sikh tourists mingled with Kashmiri carpet sellers and monks in flowing orange robes. Backpackers and hippies with matted dreadlocks sat in cafés drinking banana lassi and rolling joints. As we got closer to the centre the buildings closed in around us – great monstrosities of half-built hotels covered in ramshackle bamboo scaffolding. McLeod Ganj is affectionately known as 'little Lhasa' because of its big Tibetan population. A massive neon sign advertised Pizza Hut above the main square and a five-storey restaurant offered cold beer and music. Next door a basement suggested the promise of girls and dancing. Little Las Vegas more like.

The throng of activity was a bit overwhelming at first and for a moment Ash and I just stood still, getting barged out of the way by busy hawkers and young men on scooters. I remembered coming here as a young traveller myself in 2004 when it was still quiet; when the only residents were Tibetan exiles and a few intrepid backpackers. What used to be a quaint cantonment had transformed into a heaving hub of commercial tourism for the domestic market. Shopkeepers sold plastic keyrings of Ganesh and Shiva and a myriad of market stalls offered polyester prayer flags, henna tattoos, Bob Marley wall hangings and shiny mobile-phone cases. Shoe shiners sat on every corner and beggars fought feral dogs for scraps of food.

Ash looked shocked. 'It's . . . It's full of Indians.'

I'd wanted to return to McLeod Ganj for eleven years after finishing a five-month hitchhike here in 2004. I remembered in flashback visions of a sleepy little hostel, walks through the forest to magical shrines and long conversations with wise Tibetan oracles. It had seemed an appropriate place to finish the journey – in the foot-hills of the Himalayas. And here I was again, imagining I was twenty-two and yet consumed with an overwhelming sense of disappointment. Nostalgia, it seems, ain't what it used to be.

We sat opposite each other in a grungy café next to some young Buddhist monks in orange robes which barely concealed top-of-the-range running trainers. They were laughing at something on a computer tablet. In the background a speaker blared out a remix of Tibetan chants with a modern twist.

As Ash was reading the laminated menu card I noticed something written on the reverse and read it to myself silently.

We have bigger houses, but smaller families;
More conveniences, but less time;
We have more degrees, but less sense;
More knowledge, but less judgement;
More experts, but more problems;
More medicines, but less healthiness;

We've been all the way to the moon and back.
But we have trouble crossing the street to meet the new
  neighbour.
We built more computers to hold more information, to
  produce more copies than ever, but have less communication.
We have become long on quantity, but short on quality.
These are the times of fast food
But slow digestion;
Tall men but short character;
Steep profits but shallow relationships.
It is a time when there is much in the window, but nothing in
  the room.
Their lives have become easier and that has spoilt them.
They expect more, they constantly compare themselves to
  others and they have too much choice – which brings no
  real freedom.

Wise words, I thought. They sounded familiar and I seemed to remember that I'd read them before somewhere. Yes! It was when I was last here in the Himalayas. I knew then whose words they were.

There was one compelling reason to stay in Dharamsala, if only for a couple of days. I'd missed seeing perhaps the most famous individual to hail from the Himalayas by a week the last time I was here, and I wasn't going to miss the opportunity again. The author of this tale of caution was of course non other than His Holiness the 14th Dalai Lama, and I'd heard he was in residence. He'd just returned to his home in McLeod Ganj, from England of all places, where he had attended the Glastonbury festival, and I wanted to try and see him.

Not being a Buddhist myself, or particularly into hero worship, I had no preconceptions about the man who is perhaps the most well-known spiritual leader in the world today. I'd been given Heinrich Harrer's book *Seven Years in Tibet* when I was younger and had been fascinated with the concept of a human reincarnation of God. I also thought that perhaps by meeting a man who had completed an epic walk himself, I would better be able to examine my own motivations and maybe thin out a few of my recent doubts. I was simply curious to find out more about the man I'd heard and read so much about.

In 1959 the people of Tibet attempted to rise up against the Chinese communist invaders. The Chinese suppressed the rebellion and took over Tibet, forcing the young Dalai Lama to flee across the mountains to India to seek refuge. The monastery at McLeod Ganj became the new home for the Tibetan government in exile and since then has been the base for His Holiness who has never been able to return to his homeland. With him came thousands of people: monks, nuns and ordinary Tibetans fleeing Chinese rule. In a brave gesture of solidarity the Indian Prime Minister Nehru offered the refugees sanctuary and a permanent home in Dharamsala.

It was a wet and soggy morning and the monastery was still shrouded with a low mist. The weather hadn't put off hundreds of Buddhist pilgrims from making the journey to Dharamsala though, and we waited patiently in the queue to enter.

'It's to say thank you to our leader. We call it the long-life *puja* [devotion].' A young man barely out of his teens stood next to Ash in the queue. He wore the saffron robes of a monk, and his head was clean-shaven. I couldn't help notice a pair of Nike trainers on his feet and a mobile phone in his hand like many of the other monks. I don't know why, but I didn't expect a monk to have such things.

'Tenzin Nyima.'

The boy put out his hand confidently. He spoke perfect English with a good accent.

'We do ten hours of languages a week,' he said. 'I enjoy it. Are you here for to meet him?'

'We'd like to,' I said, hopefully.

'Maybe I can speak with his private secretary. Sometimes he likes to speak with foreigners, especially if he thinks you can help Tibet,' said the young monk.

The monastery itself is a pretty plain modern building, part of the old governor's compound. Inside though, *stupas* fill the courtyard, with relics and paintings and golden statues of a myriad of gods. The image of the Buddha is everywhere. Tenzin showed us round, walking clockwise around the holy shrines as he span the prayer wheels.

'Why do you spin them clockwise?' Ash asked.

Tenzin looked puzzled and then broke into a smile. 'That's a very good question. I have no idea.'

He was very much a monk in training, and even though he joined the monastic order at the age of thirteen he was still only twenty-one and had a lot to learn.

The monastery began to fill up with visitors. Hundreds of monks took their places, sitting cross-legged on the terrace. Nuns did the same, all of them reciting mantras in a deep continuous chant. There was a faint aroma of wood smoke, burning juniper and incense, and then cannabis was poured onto the flame and overpowered all the other smells. The pillars and walls were covered in fragrant orange marigolds and prayer flags fluttered from the balconies. The rain drizzled down onto the open-air courtyard below and a crowd of Tibetan onlookers unfurled colourful umbrellas. These were not monks but ordinary citizens, here to get a glimpse of their spiritual leader. All of them had brought gifts.

'They come from all over,' Tenzin explained. 'Many are second-generation exiles, born here in Dharamsala, but others have travelled many hundreds of miles.' He pointed at one group of round-faced men bearing small golden Buddhas and silk shawls. 'They are from Mongolia. It is their life fulfilment to be here.'

His hand waved towards some teenagers holding prayer scrolls and what appeared to be baskets of fruit. 'They are from Bhutan, like me.'

'You're from Bhutan?' asked Ash. 'I thought you were Tibetan.'

'Yes I was born in Bhutan, but we are all Tibetan. We are one people, the children of the Himalayas. The borders make no difference.' He smiled like a wise old man, in spite of his young years. 'Wait at the side of the temple – you'll get a good view.'

There were groups of men and women from all over India, Sri Lanka, Nepal, Central Asia and beyond. There were even some that had sneaked over the mountains from Tibet itself. They had come in disguise, travelling at night – just as the Dalai Lama himself did in 1959. They too wanted an audience with His Holiness before making the perilous journey back to their occupied homeland.

A bell was rung and the gates to the adjoining residence were opened. A procession of high-ranking abbots and monks spread out along a red carpet leading into the temple and the hushed crowd all peered for a better view. Tibetan courtiers in traditional dress bowed before the entourage, either side of the carpet. Next came Indian security officials in civilian suits carrying Uzi submachine guns. And then came the holy man himself.

The Dalai Lama emerged from behind the tall gates. He cut a familiar bespectacled figure. Wearing the red and saffron robes of a simple monk, it was hard to believe that this was the same man Heinrich Harrer had tutored in the 1940s, or indeed that he was a direct incarnation of the Buddha; in fact a living god. He wobbled in a slightly ungainly manner, but not one that indicated frailty – more a vivacious enthusiasm to get about in spite of the ageing of his eighty-year-old body. The cheeky grin and creased eyes told of a lifetime of laughter. He stopped to wave and shake hands with whomever he pleased.

Every eye was on him as he walked through the yard and up the steps to the temple where he sat down on a golden throne. The ceremony was a modest affair and quite informal. People came and went, some ate *tsampo* and drank salty tea. Groups chatted outside and children played and tugged on the robes of monks. An enormous black dog wearing a red feather boa strutted about as if he were sniffing out the pious. We watched from a side door less than twenty feet away from him, as he recited the mantras and stopped occasionally to ring a little bell. He barely moved except in devout swaying as he prayed.

Then his voice boomed out. It was the voice of a thirty-year-old, young and authoritative with a clarity I could hardly believe. He cracked jokes that must have been funny because the whole audience roared with laughter when he spoke. We were lucky enough to find ourselves sitting next to a Frenchman who was dictating the sermon to a journalist in English, so we got the gist of what he was saying.

He spoke of happiness and the need for simple things in life, highlighting the fact that people in smaller villages are generally happier than those in cities. 'Suicide rates are on the up in Delhi,' he said.

He urged Tibetans to feel confident in their heritage, telling them that they are not a 'backward people' but the inheritors of an ancient legacy of teaching, medicine and science. Medicine, he said, works better when you are happy. So inner fulfilment is just as important as drugs.

He reminded the rapt audience of the need for obedience but also of every man's obligation to learn and acquire new knowledge. He said that knowledge is power and that if you are powerful and learned, then you are better equipped to confront life's problems. There is no such thing as evil knowledge. The only evil is misuse of it. Religion is a choice, but if you choose to adopt it, you need to understand it.

The Dalai Lama encouraged people to set an example to each other. He spoke of the fact that despite the Tibetan exiles being a small refugee community, by keeping their traditions and cultural consistency, as well as a non-violent struggle they set a positive example to the world and keep the flame of independence alive. If you neglect your traditions, you neglect yourself. He spoke of hospitality and compassion – not for their own sake, but for more practical purposes. He reminded the audience of the important work done by Tibetan monks during the recent Nepal earthquake. Despite being a small and fairly poor community, doing such work gives Tibetans a good international standing. Basically he implied that it was all good PR for the Tibetan fight for freedom.

It was a sober, intelligent and pragmatic message. He stated that the past was in the past; in order to succeed – and Tibet must succeed – they would need to be armed with every tool in the box: be knowledgeable, learn Chinese, work the internet, prove that Buddhism is compatible with science, and market themselves to the world with determination and energy.

He left the audience with one final point: 'If you are unhappy, it's not because of external factors. It's nobody else's fault or problem. It's not because you're poor or live in a small house, or even because you are ill. It's because you have an inner emptiness that needs to be filled with light, and only you can do that. It is every person's responsibility to seek that light. Happiness is not a right; it's an obligation, because without happiness you have nothing to give back to humanity.'

The sermon came to an end and as the Dalai Lama stood, the assembly rose, keeping their heads bowed as the master left. His face had changed from devout and serious back to humble and smiling. Yet again he waved to his followers as he waddled back to his house.

Before we left, Tenzin found us again.

'I have spoken to the private secretary. His Holiness will see you tomorrow.'

Public relations are important to Tibetans. Dharamsala is more than just a monastery and a residence – it's the headquarters of a global brand. Everywhere about town there are signs offering traditional Tibetan massages, herbal remedies and traditional paintings called *thangkas*. Well-dressed young men in the street do a great job of convincing foreign backpackers and Indian tourists alike to have their future read by astrologers hidden in mystical-looking booths.

But this is no mere quaint ideology. It is the flourishing home to several business enterprises, charities and political movements all designed to further the chances of Tibetan recognition and keep the hope alive of an independent Tibet. Tibetan flags, banned in China, flutter freely here and murals offer prayers of hope and peace. Just outside the monastery posters show gruesome images of self-immolating monks, a reminder of the gravity of the struggle. Statistics are emblazoned on pamphlets: 'A million killed. 6,000 monasteries destroyed. Thousands of political prisoners still in jail. FREE TIBET.'

The living monks – young intelligent men – may look benign but their aspirations are fearsome. They want independence and some are willing to fight for it. They may walk around in the robes of their forefathers but in their hands they hold smartphones and iPads to keep abreast of the news, relay information back to relatives around the world and fight a cyber war against their Chinese enemies. But it remains a virtual fight and one that they aren't going to win any time soon. It was very much in their interest to gain foreign support and keep Tibet in the public imagination.

The following day we reported to the monastery at 0745 as instructed. A queue of over a hundred people was waiting outside the residence. We went through a security gate and metal detector where a stocky Indian security official searched us.

'You. Wait here, back of queue.' A tall Tibetan in a suit brushed past us, a walkie talkie constantly to his mouth. It was the private secretary.

We resigned ourselves to the prospect of a thirty-second bow and a handshake. There was no way the Dalai Lama would have time for us after greeting all these people.

We stood and waited with everyone else in the gardens. At least this morning the weather had cleared up and if nothing else, it was pleasant to smell the roses and watch the excitement on the faces of those lucky enough to meet the famous man in person. The tension was palpable. Monks shuffled their feet nervously, and previously chatty nuns stood in silence, waiting for him to come out of the house.

'No photo of monk,' said the secretary, eyeballing Ash's camera, as he inspected the waiting crowd. He glared at Ash and looked serious. 'They go back Tibet in secret. If Chinese know, they go prison. Maybe die. No photo.'

His Holiness arrived with his familiar smile and began walking down the line, shaking everyone's hand and receiving gifts. We were each holding white silk *khatas*, or scarves, that Ash had purchased from the bazaar.

But before the Dalai Lama had passed halfway along the line, the secretary approached us again, looking even more serious.

'You, come with me.' He grabbed me by the arm and pulled me out of the queue.

I nudged Ash in annoyance.

'See what you've done now. Taking photos. We're gonna get thrown out before we've even met him.'

Ash looked sullen and followed on.

But we didn't get thrown out. Instead the secretary led us around the back of the line of pilgrims, up the steps into the Dalai Lama's house and into a reception room.

'Wait here,' we were told.

The secretary left the room and we stood there, bewildered.

'We're in the bloody Dalai Lama's living room,' said Ash, with a nervous smile.

'I know,' I said.

The room was basic. A few shelves with Buddha statues on them, simple chairs and a little coffee table in the middle.

I suddenly realised I had no idea what I was going to ask the incarnation of Buddha. Questions buzzed around my head. 'What's the meaning of life?' Too generic. 'How do we find happiness?' He'd tell me to read his book. 'Do you like walking?' Oh, God, this was disastrous.

'Ask him if he's ever worn trousers,' Ash whispered with a wry smile.

But before I could reply the doors opened and in walked the Dalai Lama without fuss or fanfare.

The three of us lowered our heads slightly in respect and offered the *khatas* in open palms but I kept my eyes firmly fixed on his.

He was tall with a good complexion and held his head high. He gave the impression that he was scanning the room with his small black eyes. His arms were bare and bald, and with them he waved the scarves away in a gesture of dismissal, as if to say you're not Buddhist, don't bother. Instead he grasped my hand and shook it, but he didn't let go. He pulled me further into the room, closer to his chair but we didn't sit down.

'So you're walking to Lhasa?' He looked right into my eyes. It felt like he was examining my soul.

Before I could even answer, and tell him that I was hoping to get to Bhutan because I'd been told it was unlikely we would be given a Chinese visa for Tibet, he continued:

'Do you have a Chinese visa?' he asked.

'No, not yet,' I told him.

He was quiet for a moment and surveyed the room. He looked at Ash, and then back at me.

'Okay, you go to Chinese mission in Kathmandu. You tell them you go to Mount Kailash. Then you go quietly, and relax, and then you get permission from local authorities to go Lhasa.'

He continued to stare at me through the thick glasses and I noticed that his mesmerising black eyes had a humorous glint.

'When we have success, you come back. We have big welcome, I would like that. Then ...' He paused for effect. 'Maximum publicity. Till then, silent!'

So that was it. No meaning of life. Just some travel advice. I think he must have noticed my disappointment.

'This is not out of negative emotion, negative motivation. Because you adopt hard work by walk, not easy. Because you do such wonderful work, should be successful. That's my view.' I think he was trying to say that I should not risk getting barred by the Chinese by being seen with their arch-enemy. I wanted to reassure him that it was okay, but figured he probably knew best.

I nodded and asked if he had a message for the people of Tibet. I wanted to ask at least one useful question and knew that in Nepal and Bhutan I'd be likely to meet lots of Tibetan exiles. He thought for a moment and shook his head.

'No.' He paused again thoughtfully. 'I don't think you should mention to Tibetans that you visit Dharamsala and meet Dalai

Lama. For time being, no mention, or you'll risk your work. Your work should be successful. Then after,' he added, 'we are quite free.' He winked in a conspiratorial fashion.

'Like on seventeenth March 1959, I decide to escape from Kamalinga in morning. But in secret.' He laughed and slapped me on the back. 'We learn such secrecy from China: from Chinese communist. To the Tibetans, you simply say from outside world: there are many people who feel a sense of concern about their fate. That, you can say. Then also, you can say, they are interested in the rich Buddhist culture and tradition that we kept, originally came from Nalinder; so a lot of knowledge about human mind; human emotion. What I call science of the mind – very rich. That now, even in the West, even some scientists are also showing interest. And *that*, you can tell them, is their *own* culture, that's *their* knowledge. The communists in the past say: "Tibet, Tibetans very backward, Tibetan culture can be eliminated." So that, I think you simply, casually, mention those things. And even Chinese you mention it. That's true, isn't it? Then I am awaiting your own return. Thank you.'

All the while he never let go of my hand. He insisted we take a photograph and at that, he let go. The secretary nodded sternly and we knew it was our cue to leave.

As I said, I'm not into hero worship and knew little about Buddhism, but I will remember that morning for the rest of my life. I met a truly great man, whose genius lay not in his birthright, nor religious standing, nor even in his philosophical opinions. I think his genius was in his understanding of change in the modern world and the power of people to create change. I walked away feeling elated and more than ready to carry on my own journey.

II

Saddhus and Shadows

Before I left Dharamsala, there was one other person I had planned to meet, and to me he was just as important as the Dalai Lama. It was here that I was to be finally reunited with my old Nepali friend Binod Pariyar.

I hadn't seen Binod for over five years. We had last said our goodbyes in Kathmandu when I'd been mountaineering in Nepal with the army, and I had promised to return one day. We had stayed in touch of course. I'd even convinced him to get an email address so that I didn't have to wait six months for a reply to a letter. I mentioned to Binod that I was thinking of walking the length of the Himalayas soon after I'd chatted to Ash about it months ago in the pub. He replied straight away:

Hi Brother Levinson

We all are well in here. And how about you? it is so long time that we are not in tuch but how was your travelling to niel river I hope must be verry nice.

So brother Leve, whin do you like to come to Nepal? Of curse I am verry happy to wark with you brother across the Himalayas. But can you tell where and whin. Please write. This time I do have my Trekking Guide Licenses to do trekking, so is no any problems to do any trek. We rally like to see you.

Binod and family.

His email was confirmation enough. I took that to mean he was keen to come and so sent him a message along with some money, instructing him to make his way to India and meet me in Dharamsala. He had never been to India before and was excited at the thought of travelling in a foreign land. He wasn't so much coming as a guide but as a friend, and with Ash leaving very soon, I thought it would be good to have another companion.

The following afternoon I received a message from my 'brother', asking me to meet him in the central square. He had just arrived. I found him standing outside the Western Union moneychangers. He was smaller than I remembered but also more muscular and lean. His hair was short and he was clean-shaven and didn't look at all his thirty-four years. He broke into a wide smile as we embraced and I introduced him to Ash.

'How was your journey?' I asked.

'Twenty hours on a train,' he said beaming.

'Oh dear, that must have been pretty draining,' said Ash.

'No, it was wonderful. I've never been on a train before. I stayed awake the whole time to see the countryside. It's so beautiful. I can't believe I'm actually in India. I'm looking forward to walking.'

And so together, the three of us walked east.

An old soldier with a twirling moustache and moth-eaten olive-green pullover stood to attention and saluted as we arrived in Shimla. His beret was faded by years of rain and sunshine and his faced showed no trace of emotion. His boots were gleaming though and despite not being a day under sixty, he stood ramrod straight.

'What is this place?' said Binod looking up at the white towers of the Woodville Palace.

'This is the British legacy,' said Ash. 'It's everything my great uncle fought to get rid of.'

'It's a bloody comfy bed, that's what it is,' I chipped in, giving Ash a punch on the shoulder. 'I thought we should enjoy a bit of luxury while we're here.'

We walked up the steps, through the manicured gardens and into another world. A pair of cannons guarded the veranda. A butler bowed as the doors were opened and we entered the reception. Wood panelling was decked with tiger's heads. Black-and-white photographs of Hollywood starlets and European statesmen lined the walls. Looking down from above a grand-father clock was a vast painting of an Indian prince. He wore a turban and a sword and his steely eyes bore down on the guests to remind them of a bygone age.

A man was waiting for us in the hallway. He looked very casual in a pair of corduroy trousers and a simple white shirt, over which he wore a blue felt waistcoat. He was about my age and had a confident, friendly demeanour.

'Welcome sirs,' he said, shaking our hands. 'Come through to the Imperial dining room.' We wiped our feet on the mat and followed him, feeling rather scruffy amid all the opulence of the hotel. As he handed us each a gin and tonic he introduced himself.

'Raja Divraj Singh Jubbal. This is my home. It was built by a British general in the 1860s but my family took over in 1926 and we like to share it with guests. Make yourselves comfortable and don't hesitate to let my men know if you need anything.'

'Thank you, your highness,' said Binod.

He tilted his head graciously in the Indian affirmative and then left.

'He's a prince,' said Binod. 'One of the last royals.'

He took a sip of the gin and spluttered. 'I can see why they have blue blood if they drink this.'

It was Ash's last day. It had taken us a week to walk from Dharamsala to Shimla as we followed the twisting forest road from the north-west. It skirted the mountains but for the first time we caught sight of the Great Plains to the south. Here we were on the very edge of the Himalayas and the snow-capped mountains disappeared into a distant blur far to the north.

Ash had to get back to work but first was going on ahead: back to Haridwar to meet the family pandit, the priest who submerged his father's ashes. He wanted to find out more about his heritage and try to discover why the family had fled Kashmir. There were so many unanswered questions, and his was a journey back in time.

I was more concerned about the future.

'I'm glad we got to see a bit of India together finally,' Ash said. 'Be careful from here on in. The monsoon is late. We've been lucky so far but when it comes you'll know about it.'

He opened up a newspaper that was laid on the table. 'Look here.' He pointed at an article. Torrential rain and floods had been ravaging the hills to the east and all across northern India. Hundreds of people had been killed. It had been a miracle that we'd escaped with only a few days' drizzle thus far. But even then, as I looked out of the window across the lawn, storm clouds were brewing.

'It's already begun in Pokhara,' said Binod. 'I spoke to my wife last night. She says it's big rain. Very big rain.'

'It's not the rain you've got to worry about. It's the landslides,' Ash said. 'I have to say, I'm glad to be leaving. I don't envy you boys.' He raised his eyebrows. 'The roads will just turn into mush and disappear, and half the hills will come crumbling down. Keep an eye on those roads. I want you back in one piece, otherwise who will I write about?' He winked and patted me on the back.

That evening we walked along the mall in Shimla. The fog had gathered on the ridge, shrouding the mock-Tudor mansions in a white cloud, which only added to their mystique. Binod was enraptured, asking all sorts of questions. I could see why – the whole town looked like a film set from a period drama: the cathedral, the crumbling library, the Viceregal lodge and the terraced high street with its post office and toy railway.

'Is this what England looks like?' said Binod, taking photographs of the church on a cheap digital camera.

'I guess if you mixed up Birmingham, Blackpool and Brighton, with a bit of Lake District, then perhaps.' Ash chuckled as a crowd of noisy Punjabis whipped out a selfie stick and asked to get a group shot. Binod just smiled vacantly.

Shimla used to be the British summer capital before independence. The whole Raj government would decamp from Delhi and make their way to the foothills of the Himalayas in order to avoid the sweltering heat of the north Indian plains. Grand colonial buildings, now falling into disrepair, sat alongside modern multistorey hotels. Nowadays, in place of the British ruling classes, the paymasters of Shimla are the wealthy Delhi tourists who amble along the mall, paying to hold rabbits and sit on horses, wielding designer handbags. The macaques perch on the railings waiting to ambush unsuspecting children and deprive them of a bag of nuts or corn on the cob.

⌒⌒⌒

The last I saw of Ash, he was waving goodbye the next morning from the open door of the Kalka narrow gauge train as it pulled off into the woods. It links the mountains with the plains below and was the same railway that his grandfather helped to run sixty years ago.

163

Now it was just Binod and me. It was sad to see Ash leave, especially knowing that what lay ahead was potentially going to be the hardest part of the journey. It had been good to have the company of a friend, and one who knew India so well. But I was glad too to be reunited with Binod, who I think had been a little shy in Ash's presence. Now that we were alone it would be good to catch up.

We left the ghosts of history behind and walked out into the dewy, bright morning. The path wound downhill, further away from the mountains. The eucalyptus trees created a blue haze across the rolling hills. We were heading for Nepal and the only border open to us was in the Terai – the steamy, hot plains below the foothills. It was a long diversion away from the mountains, but if we were to walk all the way then it was the only option.

For days our route meandered through thick forest, where pines grew strangely alongside palm trees, and wild cannabis and cacti stuck out into our path. Pink rhododendron flowers basked in the sunlight and the petals of wild purple and orange flowers littered the ground. As we followed a ridge, we spotted a massive vulture soaring over the tops of the gnarly Banyan trees.

With every step we were moving further into the spiritual heartland of India.

Every so often we would see a little shrine, marked by the red ribbons and orange paint of Hinduism, set as an offering at the foot of a tree or the base of a rock. A deep sense of reverence for nature prevailed. Everything was holy.

'The locals tie little red strings on them, and say a prayer to Shiva or Kali,' said Binod, explaining that there are thousands, if not millions of incarnations of God. 'Each village will have its own. Sometimes each house. It's up to you who you worship.'

It seemed a world away from the strict doctrines of Islam that I'd encountered in the Muslim world.

Descending from Shimla we had finally reached the watershed of the Ganges. Until now, every drop of rainfall had flowed via the Indus into the Arabian Sea, but now the Gangetic plain was but a stone's throw away. What that meant was that we were getting closer to the biggest challenge yet. Looking down from the ridges of Himachal Pradesh, the next Indian state on our journey, Uttarakhand, was a boundless blanket of undulating green. It appeared as a patchwork of agricultural land interspersed with thick tropical rainforest. The landscape was changing fast. If the brass-tacked railings and pretty little rose gardens of Shimla had given me cause to forget where I was, then the sight of an elephant being ridden down the road by a wizened Gujarati brought me very much back into India.

The closer we got to the plains, the more scorching hot it became. One afternoon, as we realised that the clouds were not going to burst that day, I became set on having a swim in the cool waters of the Giri river. We made our way down through the narrow jungle paths towards the water and eventually reached a small river beach with pristine white sand. It was beautiful and inviting. Gigantic boulders lined the water's edge and a small eddy provided the perfect spot for a safe dip.

'Stop,' I heard Binod yell.

He came running up behind me and pointed to a dead cow, half-submerged, floating by the shore.

'A dead cow is very bad. You mustn't go in,' Binod warned me.

In India a cow embodies all of the Hindu gods and goddesses. By the look on Binod's face, he was definitely not going near it.

'It's a very bad omen. It's unlucky,' he said in all seriousness. Until now I'd almost forgotten that Binod, while being very bright, hadn't had any education after his early teens; like many rural villagers, he wasn't immune to superstition.

I'd discovered on previous trips to India that it's bad news to be associated with the death of a cow. I'd watched as whole streets mobbed drivers for accidentally knocking one of the bovine creatures down, a catastrophic insult to the gods. I decided that I didn't fancy testing our luck with the Hindu deities.

I put my shoes and socks back on and we traipsed upriver to find a more suitable – and less tainted – spot. A sliver of sunlight made it through the steep rocks and shone down onto a little beach. The water was brown, but cool, refreshing and just what I needed. After two months of walking at high altitude in the crisp air, the mugginess of the lowlands was draining. I looked up through the small window of the gorge to the sky above. Cloudy, but still no rain. The gods seemed to be teasing us. Only the chirp of cicadas broke the sound of water crashing over the rocks. On the beach, Binod had been joined by some curious langur monkeys, and was feeding a banana to one of their babies.

We walked east, following a group of singing pilgrims down into Rishikesh, where orange temples hovered on the banks of the river and the clang of bells chimed out over the mountains. This was where the mighty Ganga emerged from the Himalayas. Descending from a misty jungle ridge we found ourselves scrambling down a rocky scree slope towards the river. The sight of fossilised shell encased by stone took me aback. It was a living reminder of the ancient days when the Indian subcontinent, adrift on the earth's mantle, pushed north to collide with the great landmass of Asia, driving the sea bed inch by inch, five miles into the sky. But the rise of the Himalayas, which began fifty million years ago and continues to this day, hasn't managed to stop the inexorable flow of the great rivers, which flow south from the Tibetan plateau. The Indus, the Brahmaputra, the

Cremations line the banks of the Ganges river in Haridwar.

Millions of Shiva worshippers dressed in orange descend on Haridwar for the Kavad Yatri.

Binod Pariyar, about to take his first dip in the Ganges.

Entering Nepal to find the roads almost empty because of strikes that last for weeks at a time.

Tiger footprints in the Bardia National Park.

On patrol with the Nepalese army to counter poaching in Bardia.

Our transport was still there 50 days after
it crashed off a 150m cliff.

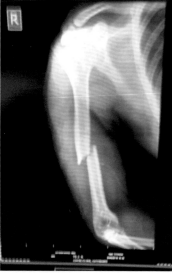

I was lucky to escape the
crash with a broken arm
and shoulder.

Reunited with Binod's
family at their home in
Sarangkot after 14 years.

Machhapuchchhre, the fishtail mountain seen from Sarangkot, Pokhara.

Ash Bahadaur Gurung – veteran honey hunter – leading the youngsters
to the precarious cliff hives near Annapurna.

Earthquake damage in Kathmandu.

The army sacrifices hundreds of goats and buffalo in Kathmandu's
Durbar Square during Dashain Celebrations.

Holy men, 'saddhus', play an important part in Hindu culture throughout the Himalayas.

The Stupas overlooking Kathmandu are places of prayer and pilgrimage.

A special moment: seeing Mt. Everest from Kala Pattar.

Jamyang Dorji in front of The Tiger's Nest monastery in the Paro Valley of Bhutan.

Setting up at Gangkhar Puensum base camp, close to the Tibetan border.

On Snow Leopard mountain with Gangkhar Puensum in the background.

Mekong and the Ganges are all much older than the mountains that have risen around them, forging the great chasms that I was traversing.

I'd been looking forward to reaching Rishikesh just so that I could see Binod's reaction. He had never seen the Ganges before, and as a Hindu, this was an important moment – second only to Haridwar. We walked through the bustling town down to the *ghats*, where steps led to the water's edge. Binod knelt to say a prayer and trailed his hand in the holy waters.

'Thank you, brother,' he said, with an emotion I hadn't seen in him before. 'I never imagined that one day I could see this river.'

From my spot by the footbridge, I could watch the eclectic mix of travellers who found themselves in this little town. While scantily clad backpackers roared by on Royal Enfield motorbikes, hordes of Shiva devotees, all dressed in bright orange T-shirts, came down to the river to offer their prayers to the god of the Himalayas. Housewives wrung their laundry out and thwacked it down on the banks of the Ganges before laying it out to dry, as their infant children frolicked in the shallows. Monkeys made mischief on the bridge, holding up the tide of pilgrims.

Rishikesh has always brought in the crowds – an old favourite with the hippies since the 1960s for its laid-back vibe and cheap marijuana. Even The Beatles came here in their attempt to find Nirvana. But the town also attracts serious and disciplined seekers of enlightenment trying to fathom the reason for their existence. Its position on the Ganges and proximity to the holy Shivalik hills makes it doubly sacred. It's said in Hinduism that saints and yogis have meditated in tranquillity on the banks of the Ganges since antiquity. Naturally, therefore, Rishikesh is also a haven for yoga practitioners – people come from all over the globe to meditate, offer their sun salutes and learn from the gurus who teach here.

The most devout of the Hindu religious gurus are the swamis. These are the preachers who set aside worldly pursuits to dedicate themselves to the service of God.

Of course, as Ash had found out halfway through scattering his father's mortal remains, not all of these holy men have honest intentions. Every week the Indian newspapers report another fraudulent sadhu who has staged a fake miracle or absconded with great sums of money. I just sighed with resignation nowadays at the stories I heard from female travellers in India, who'd gone off to find themselves by doing yoga in an ashram. Lo and behold, it turned out the guru's sermon was mainly about free love and the spiritual benefits of orgies. Usually involving him.

However, through an Indian friend from university, I'd heard about one man based near here who did have a clean reputation. His name was Swami Chidanand Saraswatiji, or, less of a mouthful, just Swamiji to foreigners like me. He lived in an ashram on the banks of the river a couple of miles away. Having met the Dalai Lama and received some words of Buddhist wisdom, I thought it only right to get some Hindu guidance too. In doing so I also hoped to learn more about Binod's faith, and get more of an understanding of just why this river, and the mountains it comes from, are so important to the millions of Indians who travel here each year.

I was ushered into the room by a tall man dressed in black, one of an entourage of stern-looking security guards. Swamiji sat in the middle of the floor, cross-legged with a serene look on his face. Well, what I could see of his face. He had an enormous shock of black hair, which was greying at the front, and a long frizzy beard that reached his chest. He looked like an Indian Moses.

'*Namaste*,' he said quietly, and motioned for me to sit down next to him.

I glanced around the room and he must have noticed my perplexed look. It had been decorated to resemble a cave, complete with plastic flowers and imitation rocks.

'Yes, reminds me of my days of silence in the forest. I used to live in a cave.' His arms floated around when he spoke and his delicate, feminine hands hung in the air when he stopped for long dramatic pauses. I could tell he was used to performing. On the walls I noticed framed photographs of him holding hands with the Dalai Lama and Prince Charles.

'I spent many years in prayer,' he whispered. 'I left my family when I was seven, and roamed into the mountains. I found a cave and decided to stay. I meditated. There are too many distractions in this modern India – big cities and fast life – but here I could just sit. And all around me was the natural glory of the Himalayas, the Ganga. The mountains have watched over mankind. They have been here since eternity and have seen every incarnation of every living thing.' He stared at me with deep brown eyes. I couldn't decide if it was sinister or not.

'And then when I was eighteen I came back. I walked down, the same way you have, I hear. From the very same mountains, maybe you passed by my cave?' He looked straight at me. I couldn't tell whether it was appropriate to smile.

'What made you come back?' I asked him.

'I realised that it was time to help. *Swami* means master, and after I had done self-mastery, I knew it was time to guide others. We look after many young orphans at the ashram, children who had no teacher, children who had nothing. The best way to honour God in our lives is through serving humanity. My ashram has space for over six thousand pilgrims and people come from all across the world to hear my teachings.'

'Do you have any advice for my walk?' I asked, wanting to come away from this meeting with more than just some visa tips.

He smiled. 'It is easy to find peace in a cave, in the forests, in the jungle. When you are isolated you can start on the path to renunciation very easily. Walking can help, 'For contemplation and calm.' He nodded at me.

'But harder, much more of a challenge,' he continued, 'is finding peace in the cities. One should be at peace always, not in pieces.' He laughed at his own joke. 'But it is hard amid the hustle and the bustle. Once, when I was in London Heathrow it was busy, so very busy. People were shoving and one man was so preoccupied and distracted, that he pushed me and I fell over and broke my wrist. I could have complained, or – what do the Americans call it? – sued him, but there is no good that can come from that. I was calm and I forgave him. Gandhiji said that we must be the change we wish to see in the world and forgiveness is a lot more effective than grumbling. If we set this divine example, of kindness and sacrifice, others will follow.'

He smiled a triumphant grin. His message was simple and benign. I still had some doubts but I could see why so many hundreds of thousands followed him. He preached inner peace, and in the modern world, that's hard to find.

'Do not wait for miracles to come to you, you *are* the miracle,' were his last words to me as I left.

On the way out I was escorted by Swamiji's personal assistant, who led us through to an office where she handed me a piece of paper.

'Don't forget to like us on Facebook,' she said with a straight face.

I smiled, but she wasn't joking. I looked down at the paper. It was a list of tick box questions asking me to rate the quality of service at the ashram and the level of spirituality I had attained. It was an actual feedback form.

It was almost dusk and the PA invited me to join in the *Aarti*, the evening prayer ritual on the banks of the Ganges. Outside, I found a throng of young boys all dressed in orange and sitting in lines on the steps of the *ghats*. I waited at the edge of the ashram and walked with Swamiji as he made his grand entrance. Silence fell and he took his place in the middle of the crowd with hundreds of rapturous faces gazing up at him. He patted the floor next to him and I sat down. He immediately began to sing.

Everyone quickly joined in and I clapped along awkwardly at first, slightly cringing at the gaudiness of it all. I looked over to Binod for moral support, but he was fully immersed, singing away too. There was no escape. I couldn't do anything but join in the sing-song. Soon the whole crowd had become absorbed in their praise, and I saw how unselfconscious his devotees were. One girl, dressed all in white amid the sea of saffron, was in a deep trance. Her eyes were closed and she had a look of unashamed contentment on her face. Swamiji sat in awesome serenity in the middle his followers, legs crossed with his palms facing up to the sky. He was intensely charismatic and his message of peace seemed harmless enough, inspiring even. The heady aroma of sandalwood wafted over the crowd. One by one, each person advanced to the river, and once everybody had made an offering, the Ganges was alight with floating candles, like glistening stars in the night sky. The congregation continued to sing and clap in unison as the water lapped against the *ghats* and the sun set behind the Himalayas.

The trail of pilgrims continued south, fifteen miles to Haridwar. We joined the throng of orange leaving Rishikesh and followed the Ganges down onto the more open and accessible plains.

'It's called the *Kavad Yatra*,' said Binod, noticing me staring, wide-eyed, at the pandemonium below. I could barely believe what I was seeing.

Hundreds of thousands of tents, shacks and huts packed the bustling fields along the banks of the river and the entire city seemed to be alive with action. It felt like we'd just arrived at a massive pop festival – minus the alcohol.

'Each year they come to collect the water of Mother Ganga. Then they take it back to their village, to offer to Lord Shiva.'

'How do they get the water home?' I asked him.

'In those *kanwars*.' He pointed to a luminous orange construction that was passing us. A pilgrim in saffron robes and no shoes was carrying the bamboo pole, which had a water pot attached to either end, decorated elaborately with silk, tinsel and marigolds.

'The pilgrims are coming from all over India. Sometimes they don't eat for days and days on the way. If they have food they share it with the monkeys – it brings good luck.'

As we walked down through the masses the atmosphere was electric. Carnival floats with multicoloured images of gods and goddesses rolled between the makeshift huts. A woman dressed as the goddess Kali had her face painted blue and long needles pierced through her arm and cheeks. Naked sadhus sat in silent contemplation amid the chaos, as cows and buffaloes munched at cardboard waste. Children were dressed up as deities, adorned in jewellery, wearing crowns and the three stripes of Shiva on their foreheads. Rudimentary tightropes had been assembled and tiny girls wobbled their way across with golden pots on their heads. Touts weaved between the water carriers trying to persuade pilgrims to part with a few rupees in exchange for plastic trinkets or a good old-fashioned ear clean.

As we passed beneath the enormous statue of Shiva and reached the banks of the Ganges, the clamour rose; people jostled for space and the air was thick and hot. Devotees were singing hymns; chanting emanated from nearby temples and children shrieked as they splashed in the river.

I felt a tap on my shoulder. 'You like shave, sir?'

A skinny barber brandishing a cut-throat razor, a towel and some shaving foam was grinning expectantly at Binod and me. My beard – bushy after weeks of trying to blend in across Afghanistan and Pakistan – was definitely in need of a trim, especially considering that here in India, and in Nepal, just across the Ganges, men tended to be clean-shaven. I agreed and was plonked down on the *ghats* while the man got to work.

Cows trotted along the banks, painted in shades of saffron and amber, covered in silver-and-gold jewellery. In front of us, the water was heaving with Shiva worshippers washing away their sins in the water. Elderly men, unable to swim, were grasping iron chains to prevent them from drifting downriver. They plunged their heads beneath the surface and washed their bodies in the filthy water. Women immersed themselves, some fully clothed, some bare-breasted, their red silk saris sparkling in the sunlight. They emerged with looks of faithful serenity and fulfilment, a miracle considering the commotion around them.

'These rituals are the most sacred and spiritual in Hinduism,' said Binod. 'Some people waiting a whole lifetime just to come to the Ganga and take a dip.'

Next to us, a tiny, terrified-looking boy was having his first haircut, a Hindu rite of passage in a child's seventh year and a symbol of purification. The pandit blessed him and then turned to Binod and me. He had overheard Binod's excitement about being next to the holy Ganges for the first time.

He led my friend down to the water's edge and blessed him in the name of Shiva, and then Binod submerged himself in the waters that had run down from the high Himalayas. He placed a banana-leaf basket, brimming with marigolds, into the water as an offering to Ganga and I watched as the camphor flame drifted off downriver.

As I looked on I wondered if all this holiness might just rub off and give us the luck we needed to carry on with the journey. As we'd descended from the hills it was all too easy to think we'd left the hardest parts behind, but I knew deep down that something had to give. I can't explain what it was, except that I felt something ominous looming over the expedition. Maybe it was the thought of the oncoming monsoon, or perhaps it was just that I'd reached the halfway point without incident. The feeling remained that I was tempting fate. I looked at the peaceful joy on Binod's face as he prayed in the river and I felt grateful to have such a good man with me. But I also knew that soon, as we headed north and into Nepal, we were walking into somewhere infinitely more wild and remote. I could only hope that my guide knew what he was doing.

Our day wasn't over yet. Just outside the town we noticed rising plumes of smoke spiralling from the shores of the Ganges.

'Cremations,' said Binod. 'Shall we go and see?'

I wasn't so sure. I didn't like the thought of just turning up at someone's funeral but Binod assured me that it was fine, in fact it was a mark of respect and the families would be glad.

As we walked down to the stony beach, a crowd had gathered around the burning pyres. More were being built, out of wood that had been offloaded from the roofs of buses. The corpses, wrapped in cloth, were unceremoniously carried from the car park and lumped onto the stacks. There were no women to be seen, and male family members piled wood and rubber bicycle tyres on top of the bodies. As it started to drizzle, kerosene was poured on to help ignite the wet wood.

Men looked on. There seemed to be little emotion, and some carried on with conversations on their phones as the bodies sizzled away. It appeared to be a very matter-of-fact affair.

'When we took my father for cremation, we had to wait until his head had exploded. We must make a hole in the skull, to let the spirit go and be sure it goes to the next life,' Binod told me.

I noticed a wooden shack where an old lady watched the proceedings from afar. The rain was getting heavier now and I suggested to Binod that we go and take shelter in the shack. He agreed and we walked over.

The shack was draped with a blue tarpaulin to keep out the rain, but the frame was made of thick wooden poles. Inside the porch were three statues. There was a blue concrete Shiva holding a trident and two of the monkey god Hanuman; one was white and the other red with five heads. The old woman cackled as we approached.

'Let us take shelter, sister,' said Binod.

'Who are you?' asked the woman. She looked like a witch.

There was a distinct smell of shit all around us, and mangy dogs picked through piles of rubbish. A pig scuttled around the waste ground, snuffling among the human excrement. Flies buzzed around the unhealthy air.

We told her who we were.

'He is not here.' Her eyes glinted menacingly in the fading light.

'Who?' I asked.

'The Aghori baba, of course,' she said.

Binod's eyes opened wide. I knew immediately what he was thinking. I'd heard about the Aghori but had assumed they were a myth.

Binod looked at me. 'We should leave. I don't like it here.'

I looked at the woman. Her grey hair was tied back to reveal a wrinkled face that clearly came from the mountains of the north. Withered arms poked out of the faded turquoise sari. They were covered in badly drawn tattoos of various gods. She grinned, revealing terrible yellow stumpy teeth.

The Aghori were a mysterious sect of Shiva worshippers, known for their controversial rituals. Not only do they drink vast amounts of alcohol and smoke marijuana but they are also said to be cannibals; hanging around the cremation grounds waiting for bodies to float past, which they then devour in a bid to bring themselves closer to god.

'They drink from human skulls,' said Binod with a shudder.

The woman cackled again. 'Who are you, sister?' Binod asked her.

'I am his servant,' she replied with a sneer as she crouched down on her haunches, spitting into the mud, seemingly oblivious to the rain. 'He likes to eat the bodies of people. I used to, as well,' she added with a malicious smile.

Binod and I just stood gawping at the self-proclaimed flesh eater. She revelled in the attention.

'I ate an arm, a human one, ten years ago. It tastes like salty chicken.' She laughed.

I glanced at Binod. The Aghori are condemned by most Hindus for their unsavoury practices and I could tell he was uncertain about being here. I think he must have regretted offering to show me the *ghats*.

'Come tomorrow night,' she said. 'He will return. Bring whisky.'

At that we left. All the next day, as we finished our prepara-tions for the next phase of the journey I couldn't help but think of the cannibal. Out of sheer curiosity I wanted to go back.

'Let's not bother,' Binod said, eager to avoid the place.

But I felt compelled. After meeting all sorts of monks and princes, I didn't see what harm one more could do. We returned the following evening, just as the sun was setting, to find the little stretch along the Ganges deserted. The shack looked empty and Binod and I put our heads inside.

'Hello?' I shouted, even though it was obvious nobody was inside. But I noticed the ashes of a fire were still smouldering. Someone was around.

'*Namaste.*'

I looked around to see the monk standing there. He was a fat man in his early forties wearing a dark-maroon toga. His skin was almost black and he looked more African than Indian, espe-cially with the nest of matted dreadlocks that was twisted up in a bun around his skull. On his forehead was painted a bright red *tikka*.

He grinned and walked past us and sat down by the fire. Out of a pouch he handled some powder and threw it into the embers causing flames to magically roar up. With a stick he prodded the fire.

'What do you want?' he said in Hindi. Binod translated nervously.

I sat on a filthy rug opposite him, the flames lapping my bare feet.

I handed him the whisky we'd brought for the occasion, which he took without a word and pocketed. What I really wanted to ask him was what on earth possessed him to eat dead bodies. But I thought it more prudent to see what advice he could offer about my walk and how it might compare to that of the other holy men I'd encountered.

'I am on a journey. I am walking the Himalayas and have reached the halfway point. Do you have any advice?'

He looked at me down his flat, stubby nose and scowled. He reached out and touched my forehead.

'Do you have a brother?' he asked.

'Yes. Why?'

'How many?'

'Just one.'

The Aghori shook his chubby head.

'I think you have three. I can tell by the lines on your forehead.'

'No I'm pretty sure it's just one.'

'Is he dead?' he asked.

'No,' I said, taken aback.

The monk looked confused and shook his head again.

I looked at Binod. 'Ask him why he said that.' But Binod just lowered his eyes.

'You will complete your journey. You are strong-willed. But first you will face something terrible.'

'What is it?'

The monk said no more. He seemed to be uncomfortable and shuffled, and then looked at his watch.

'It's late,' said Binod. 'I don't like this place. Can we go?'

I had so many questions and felt suddenly very uneasy, but thought it best to placate Binod. It was indeed getting late and I knew that with the night would come the rumble of thunder and the threat of rain.

12

On Foot Through Tigerland

I woke up in a pool of sweat in the poky little guesthouse room. The power had cut out and within minutes the dank, sweltering air had stagnated as the ceiling fan slowed to a halt. I was getting used to it now, and in any case it was marginally more pleasant than being in a tent. Outside the rain was coming down in torrents and I knew it was going to be another tough day. I went downstairs to sit and drink *chai* as the tin roof clattered under the pounding water.

After we'd crossed the Ganges and walked east across the plains, the monsoon had finally arrived. Slowly but surely, the sporadic drizzle turned into daily downpours, initially just for an hour a day and then, as we got closer to the Nepal border, sometimes for five or six hours non-stop. Now it came without warning; the sky would blacken in a matter of minutes and people would run for shelter as the heavens opened. The roads turned into quagmires of mud and the paddy fields into filthy brown ponds.

A stream had formed from the bottom of the plastic guttering and the runoff filled the walkway to the main road. Bullfrogs croaked in delight.

'It is almost a month late,' Binod said. 'We need it for the fields, my wife will be happy now. Without the monsoon everything will die.' He was a lot more philosophical about it than I was.

I could also tell he was happy to be back in his homeland. He'd been excited to return to Nepal, and now it was only a matter of a few weeks before we reached Pokhara where he could be reunited with his family. I was happy for him, but at the same time I couldn't help but think of my own family. I'd called my brother immediately after the Aghori's ominous forecast and was relieved when he answered the phone, alive and well – albeit somewhat bewildered at my concern. But even hearing his voice hadn't completely alleviated my worries and the words of the Aghori continued to trouble me.

With the rains came a new challenge. It would mean days on end drenched through, roads in turmoil and the added dangers of flooding and landslides. I looked out from under the tin roof at a poor dog, completely sopping wet, shivering pathetically in his brown shaggy coat. Apart from a couple of brave cyclists wrapped head to toe in plastic ponchos, the roads in Nepal were completely empty.

'Is it because of the rain?' I asked Binod, surprised that it was so quiet.

'Not just the rain. I think there is also a strike. We call it a *bandh*. It means everything is closed.'

'What are they striking about?'

'I don't know. People here are always striking. Striking and rioting, rioting and striking, it's the way of life in Nepal. You remember?'

I did remember. I thought back to 2001 when I first met Binod in Pokhara, it was the reason I was here now: the Maoist riots and the Royal massacre that had caused me to head for the hills where Binod had looked after me all those years ago, as a result of which I'd made the promise to return and repay my debts. It seemed little had changed.

We left the shelter of the guesthouse and went outside to brave the rains. Within minutes we were soaked through. Binod found a plastic poncho which kept his upper half dry, and I wore a waterproof jacket which did the same, but neither of us had waterproof boots and soon enough we were grimacing at the sensation of squelching toes and wet socks.

With the driving horizontal rain it became hard to appreciate the beauty around us. Vibrant green paddy fields stacked row upon row were tended by young girls in *kurtas* for whom the rain was a blessing; their dresses clung sensually to wet bodies. Mothers sat plaiting their daughters' hair on charpoys under canopies, watching with amusement as we stumbled on under the weight of wet rucksacks.

The thatched huts and piles of hay gave the villages the appearance of Saxon England. Little boys played games outside their homes, expertly shooting marbles into rain-filled gulleys and crevices. Buffaloes, coaxed by spindly farmers, lolloped along the road, their leathery hides sparkling in the rain. Women fished in wooden-framed nets in little pools and men cycled along the bumpy roads clutching umbrellas. Soggy dogs sifted for leftovers and oxen looked on, chewing the cud stoically. As we crossed a bridge over a river, children scampered about, naked in the water below us; it was a primeval scene.

Our first sighting of the Nepali Himalayas came into view. They loomed in the distance, the snowy peaks glinting on the occasional breaks in the weather. The lofty reaches of the Annapurna range were just north of here and at this time of year it was not just rainfall that added to the fast-flowing rivers but also mountain meltwater. As the sun burnt through the clouds, whole chunks of ice and snow could thaw in a day, sending torrents of water down into the valleys. Water came crashing down the mountain any way it could, carving out the fastest route to the sea, and annihilating anything in its wake. We rounded a corner to find that last night's onslaught of rain had set the whole hillside free. Loosened by the water, vast boulders had made a bid for freedom into the valley below. Roads here could become blocked in an instant with metre upon metre of unstable debris piled in the way of these mountain routes. A snaking queue of buses and trucks waited for the locals to clear the rockfall – a painstakingly slow process that was being done with shovels. We watched as foolhardy car and minibus drivers mounted the landslide, wobbling next to the precipice and skidding over the mud and silt. Not for the first time on this trip, I was glad to be on foot.

We continued down into the valley where the first signs warning pedestrians of tigers and elephants lined the road. I wanted to get to Bardia National Park, the thick and uninhabited jungle to the east, before nightfall. We slept in a small guesthouse on the outskirts of Bardia that night.

At dawn the following morning, two men waited for us at the entrance to the national park. Both of them were short, stocky figures, Tharu people – descendants of the Indian invaders that took over the Terai plains hundreds of years ago. Binod had told me that we needed local guides to get us through the protected area and that we'd have to seek official permission. These were to be our guides for however long it would take to get through the jungle.

'Good morning, sir,' said a man with shoulder-length black hair and the face of a pirate. He wore an olive-green military shirt and looked like a rebel soldier.

'My name is Umanga, and this is Chandra Oli, our ranger.'

He motioned to the man stood next to him; a skinny lad with a contorted face in an oversized rain mac. He grinned but said nothing.

The road came to a muddy end at the ranger station, and beyond it was a steamy wall of green forest. The seemingly impenetrable mass of bamboo and vines appeared alive with movement. Flickers of motion indicated curious langur monkeys and macaques watching us from their camouflage. There was a flash of brown and I noticed a pair of eyes staring from underneath antlers not more than a hundred metres distant: 'forest deer', said Binod as he pointed. The deer turned and vanished into the undergrowth.

'There are many dangerous beasts in this jungle,' Umanga told us, with an excited glint in his eye. 'If we see a tiger, best thing is, don't turn your back. If you turn your back, tiger will attack. They always come at you from behind.'

Binod nodded solemnly. 'It's true. We used to have them in Pokhara and many women were eaten in the fields.'

Umanga continued with his sombre brief. 'If a rhino is charging, you must climb a tree, but if we see a bear, no climbing the tree. The bears can climb very easily. In this case, you must stand your ground. The leopards are afraid of the humans, so they won't come close. No worrying about the leopards.' He pronounced leopard to rhyme with leotard, and had reeled off the whole thing with a nonchalant smile on his face.

'For the leeches, we can do nothing. Just take them off fast fast.' He added. I'd forgotten about leeches.

Chandra Oli just stood there grinning with a big stick he'd picked up. He looked more like a boy scout than a park ranger.

'Don't we need a gun if we are going into tiger territory, just to be safe?' I asked him, noticing that he looked woefully underprepared for our fifty mile expedition through some of the most dangerous rainforest in the world.

'No, no, sir. All we are needing is a stick.' He grinned but I couldn't have been less reassured. The safety briefing was over before it had even begun and Umanga hadn't even mentioned half of the creatures that I had concerns about. But with that Oli raised his staff, motioned for us to follow on, and we trotted off into the jungle.

We followed narrow paths between grasses that rose up either side of us, some twenty feet high. The going underfoot was thick with mud and the air was humid and sticky. Often it was so dense we couldn't even see the sky and it felt like we were walking through a tunnel of foliage. After a while though, the grasses cleared and we came to the swampy banks of the Babai river. A herd of chital deer, with their distinctive spotted coats and twisted antlers, were drinking from the fast-flowing waters.

Umanga looked out at the wide flood plain and shook his head.

'This one is too fast to cross on foot. The rains have made these waters very high. We will take boat instead.'

I looked around, but there was no sign of any boat. A crane lurked at the water's edge and I wondered how many crocodiles were skulking nearby, camouflaged by the murky water. I was grateful for the promise of a boat to get us across to the far side. That was until I saw what Umanga was referring to. He pulled aside some grass and tugged on a rope. Out of the reeds emerged a long, thin dugout canoe; nothing more than a hollowed-out tree trunk. He dragged it as close to the riverbank as it could get and motioned for us to hop in too. Binod laughed nervously. He'd never been in one before and suddenly I had recollections of the hundreds of river crossings I'd had to do on the Nile, watched by crocodiles all the while.

Sunk low in the water and rocking precariously, we made our way across the river. Binod clung on to the sides of the boat as Oli punted us across with a long bamboo pole.

'There's dolphins in there,' mused Umanga.

'Dolphins?' I said, not sure if he was joking.

'Yes, Gangetic dolphins. They are very blind, very rare creatures.'

'What's a dolphin?' asked Binod.

Umanga laughed. I realised then the stark difference between the people of the plains and those of the mountains. Nepal is almost like two very different countries, and as I was to discover later this was the source of a lot of friction.

We clambered out of the boat and pushed deeper into the forest. Here the canopy was thick, and no breeze permeated the lower layers. At every turn, Umanga identified the shrill call of one of a hundred different birds and pointed out different species of trees. They towered up beside us, their closeness oppressive and threatening. The shriek of a peacock pierced the air and I could hear the far-off call of a parakeet. Streaks of sunlight broke through the branches high above us; a few narrow shafts of light making it down to the forest floor. I had to concentrate not to trip over the criss-crossed patchwork of gnarled roots that hid king cobras and green pit vipers. Every rustle unnerved me; there were rock pythons in this tropical forest so big they were known for swallowing deer whole.

Oli, who was quiet and spoke little English, had been walking along with his eyes on the ground. I wondered how he was going to spot these elusive tigers if he wasn't looking out for them. Suddenly he stopped, forcing us all to come to a halt behind him.

Without a word he pointed at something on the ground. In front of us was the unmistakable paw print of a tiger, marked in the mud. He put a finger to his lips as if to tell us to be silent, but I didn't need to be told. The paw print looked fresh – there was a tiger nearby.

Oli shimmied up into a tree with the ease and agility of a monkey and beckoned to us to follow him.

'We looking tigers. Very near. Fresh tracks,' he whispered.

I borrowed Umanga's binoculars and scanned the green horizon. Despite their relaxed attitude to the big cats of the jungle,

I was grateful that our guides clearly knew their stuff. It was all very well being able to track a tiger, though I did wonder how good they might be at getting away from one.

'Look,' I heard Oli whisper.

I glanced up, excited at the prospect of seeing one of the notorious beasts prowling through the undergrowth. I struggled to focus my eyes on what he was pointing at.

'Elephant,' he said.

On the banks of the river opposite, was a solitary wild elephant, a grey blur against the trees beyond.

'Let's get a better view,' Umanga suggested. With that he bounded down out of the tree and continued off on the path ahead of us.

We came upon a lookout tower half a mile away. It had been built years before by the rangers as a way of tracking the wildlife and conducting surveys and of course for spotting poachers. As we climbed the rickety steps, we were able to see over the grasses and the treetops, and the thick canopy of a myriad of shades of green extended out for miles before us. The curve of the hills was gentle and I thought just how different it was to the steep escarpments where I had spent the last three months. Here in the jungle we had to have our eyes peeled and be constantly alert – the dangers ranging from the sting of a scorpion to being eaten alive by fire ants. Not to mention the prospect of getting squashed by an angry rhino. Up here above the forest, it was a relief to have some respite from the perils of the jungle below.

'Somewhere down there is our tiger,' said Umanga, taking the binoculars out of my hands. 'Actually, there are fifty tigers inside Bardia. We counted last year.

'My father's father used to lead hunting expeditions – tiger hunting was big business. The Indian princes would come and they would ride on their elephants into the deepest parts of the jungle. They took their rifles and from the top of the howdah they could shoot at the tigers.

'But now we care for the tigers instead,' he added. 'This is a conservation area. Now there are not so many. At that time they were breeding well and had to spread out to look for new territory and new prey, so they roamed higher into the hills.'

'But now there are poachers, instead of the royals, that we are worrying about. Tigers are very valuable and many people are wanting to buy their heads, or their furs, especially the Chinese. The poachers are very dangerous. They are carrying guns and hiding in the forests and many villagers have been killed by them in the past.'

Oli had remained silent the whole time Umanga had been talking, his eyes glued to the horizon. I asked him what he was looking at and he pointed out a herd of twenty-two wild elephants that had emerged from the grasses and were now frolicking in the water. The babies played between their mothers' legs, rolling in the shallows and squirting each other. I saw a shimmer of turquoise, as a kingfisher fluttered from its resting place on an elephant's back.

They lolloped about, their long trunks curled up into the sky, unwittingly crushing the high grasses in their wake.

Umanga saw us watching. 'There are elephants everywhere in Terai, but they are tamed, and have a *mahout* who looks after them, and drives them. But here in Bardia we have wild elephants. But they are very dangerous for man. If they get angry, they are running at fifteen miles per hour and crushing everything they see.'

With a feeling of both electrifying excitement and nervous trepidation we descended the lookout tower and set off deeper into the jungle. For days we walked through the forest, sometimes camping, sometimes staying in remote army outposts with the anti-poaching unit that Chandra Oli worked with. Sometimes we'd see nothing for hours on end except the dark green shadows. We tried to stick to the rangers' trails but when it rained they would often disappear into nothing and we found ourselves hacking through the bush with our machetes. We'd try and follow the ridges for the sake of navigation or just walk on a bearing of due east. The problem of course came when we found ourselves at the tops of sheer cliffs with no way down, or faced with raging rivers that were impossible to cross. Then we'd have to backtrack and add miles onto an already exhausting journey. As I'd found on most of my expeditions, guides are usually the first people to get lost. Umunga and Oli were no exception. Neither of them had a GPS or a compass and they relied solely on their instincts and knowledge, but we'd been walking well away from their usual tracking routes and were breaking new ground. More often than not I found myself at the front having to lead the way and 'guide the guides'. I was fine with that as I was used to it from my journeys in Africa but I could tell Binod was becoming more and more frustrated with the two plainsmen. On top of that he was much more at home in the cool mountain air than in the humid jungles of the Terai and I'd noticed he had become increasingly slow and quiet, often trailing at the back and not getting stuck into the usual duties of collecting water or cutting a trail.

On the afternoon of the fifth day we came across a tributary of the Babai. It was a wide but shallow river and the water appeared quite slow.

'We can walk across, I think,' said Umanga. 'Let me check.'

Umanga stepped into the brown depths and immediately plunged to his waist. Still he regained his balance and waded on, out into the middle of the river which was about fifty metres across. He waved at us to follow and so we did.

I stepped down into the river. We'd given up taking our boots off to cross streams on the first day after we realised they were going to get wet regardless but it didn't make the sensation any more pleasant. The cold water gushed down into our boots and swirled in little eddies around us. We started to wade across and aimed for the dark figure of Umanga. We pushed through the water, a silent train of sullen walkers.

I scanned the banks for the gharials – the common narrow-mouthed crocodiles that looked like miniature dinosaurs but are generally pretty harmless, and the far bigger and more dangerous muggers that make their home on the banks of this jungle river. Umanga had been regaling us with stories of one that was three metres long and had snapped up a patrolling soldier. I squinted to focus through the distant vegetation but failed to make out anything apart from a blur of green. We kept trudging, pushing our way through the river using our hands as paddles, as the brown murky water lapped against our stomachs.

Suddenly Umanga put his hand in the air and without stopping, pointed to the banks of the river opposite us. Only a hundred feet away, there at the water's edge, I could make out an enormous crocodile. It was a mugger. We all froze. Its mouth was open as it basked in the sun. Then it suddenly lurched straight into the water, launching its bulky frame into the river. Somewhere beneath the surface the monster was scouring the riverbed and hunting for prey.

If we splashed or caused a commotion it was far more likely to notice us. Umanga and Oli clearly knew this, and we ploughed on without a word, my heart hammering in my chest. With every step I half expected the jaws of a giant reptile to wrap themselves around my leg.

We scrambled up the banks on the far side and once we were at a safe distance, stopped to catch our breath and I heaved a huge sigh of relief.

'I don't want to go on any more,' Binod said to me as he plonked himself down on a fallen tree and removed his pack. 'My feet hurt.' Clouds had begun to form, and the bright morning was threatening to morph into yet another miserable afternoon.

Umanga and Oli looked away, clearly uncomfortable with the apparent dissent. The first drops of rain began to patter down onto our faces.

'We should wait until the rain stops, then keep walking. I am covered in leeches and tired. My legs are smaller than yours.' He pulled up his trouser leg to reveal a dozen fat, slimy beasts feasting on his blood. I helped him pull them off.

'Sorry, mate, we need to press on.' I explained to him where we needed to reach that evening in order to make it through the park within the week. We only had permits to travel and camp for a few days, and there wasn't much room for negotiation when it came to the authorities. On top of that we had to make camp somewhere safe before it got dark.

'We can't let a little rain stop us from crossing the jungle,' I insisted. 'Get your pack back on and let's move.'

I was trying to make light of the situation and encourage Binod, but I could tell he wasn't getting on well with Umanga and was tired and hot.

My own boots were filled with puddles of river water and I too had leeches gorging on my legs. I wanted to rest and I'm sure so did the others but I also knew that the main priority was finding a decent camp before dark. The jungle is no place to be walking around at night.

As we marched on, Binod sulked and I wondered if he was up to the job of walking with me. Perhaps it was just the heat and oppressiveness of the forest but he seemed to be less enthusiastic than I remembered. When we were younger he had been so sprightly and laughed at my snail pace as we climbed the steep paths together. He was always at the front leading the way as a guide should be, but now, as we pressed on, he seemed to be losing interest. I could only hope that when we got out of the Terai and back into the mountains he'd perk up a little.

We made camp by a river that night in a valley leading down to the main channel of the Babai. The sides were steep and thick with undergrowth and the only flat ground we could find was on a raised island in the middle of a riverbed. There was a steady trickle of water flowing down from the hills but it was barely ankle deep, and the island was sufficiently high, just in case the water did rise in the night.

Binod pitched his tent in sullen silence and we all went to sleep early, exhausted and damp. We'd been lucky to get the tents up while it was dry because the moment we got inside it began to pour down. For the past few weeks we had been stopping at roadside guesthouses, by no means luxurious, but certainly bearable. We'd had mattresses, some running water and a solid roof over our heads to defend against the deluge. Now that we were off road again, it was back to the tent, sleeping bag and mattress for me. It felt good to be back in the wilds again initially but after a while the novelty wore off. The pouring rain had left us in a constant state of dampness, and my boots refused to dry out overnight. I was hungry for anything that wasn't *dhal bat*, the Nepali staple of rice and lentils, and I would have killed for a bite of steak. Dengue-ridden mosquitoes buzzed around, annoyingly close to my ears, as I drifted in and out of sleep. Outside the tent a scorpion scuttled around my boots and an army of ants marched for the comforting shelter of my flysheet. I listened to the water tumbling down the river outside and shifted about, struggling to find a comfy position.

Suddenly I heard a scream. As I wriggled out of my sleeping bag I realised that it was Binod's voice and I heard loud swearing in Nepali.

'Lev, Lev, fast, fast,' he yelled out into the blackness of the night.

As I got out of my tent and shone my torch into the pitch black, I realised why. The river had risen by two metres in a matter of just a few hours. The cliff, on which he'd pitched his tent, closest to the water's edge, was crumbling into the abyss, eroded at a ferocious pace by the oncoming flood. The little patch had been metres away from the edge the night before, but now Binod was standing on a perilous overhang and the water was just inches from the ledge. If we didn't act fast we'd be washed away into oblivion. Binod had already torn his tent down and was desperately trying to move everything away from the water as quickly as he could.

'Shit, I'm coming.' I ran to help him drag all of his kit out of the way of the encroaching water and we hurried to pack the rest of our gear up.

Umanga and Oli had woken up in the pandemonium and I'd never seen them move so fast. We gathered all of our kit within the space of just a few minutes and rushed through the thick undergrowth. I could only hope the far side of the island wasn't flooded as well, and luckily the main flow of the water hadn't breached this side. We frantically scrambled over the boulders, slipping and sliding and getting cut to shreds by the thorns and razor-sharp elephant grass. We made it to the side of the valley where we could climb a hill for safety. Binod was visibly shaking and even Oli was looking nervous.

Umanga, ever vigilant, scanned the blackness with his torch. Somewhere down below, visible only in concentrated patches of reflected light, our little island was slowly but surely being destroyed. The rocky fringes and muddy banks were inexorably being sucked into the river; into its powerful swell, which swept everything off downstream. We climbed and climbed, exhausted but spurred on by the alternative prospect of a watery grave. Finally we reached an outcrop high enough to be safe from the clutches of the river and collapsed in a heap.

'Look, quick,' whispered Umanga.

I turned around to where he was pointing the torch, and there, shining like glinting amber was a pair of eyes looking straight at us, not more than a hundred feet away. We froze, staring right back. In the night it was impossible to tell the size or what animal it was.

'What is it?' I whispered back.

I could feel Umanga's breath warm on my cheek as he spoke softly. He paused for effect and I knew he was smiling.

He said just one word.

'Tiger.'

I looked back at the torch beam and the eyes were gone. Nothing remained but the black and green of the jungle.

I looked at my watch – it was four a.m. Perching on the rock in stony silence the adrenalin wore off and it started to get cold as the sweat dried and my pulse slowed. We sat miserably waiting for the dawn in the stillness of the night as raindrops dripped down the backs of our necks.

13

The Perilous Mountain

Binod and I trudged along in silence, drenched through from the pouring rain. We left the jungle behind and found a rough track that led east to a road. Umanga and Oli said goodbye at a turnoff that led back to the west, to the ranger station. We hadn't spoken in hours. The rain came in sideways and we resented even the sound of each other's footsteps as we sloshed through the puddles. A cycle rickshaw passed us and Binod gazed longingly at the multicoloured, rickety vehicle as it chugged off into the distance. We reached a bridge over the Babai river. It was half obscured by mist and a solitary wild elephant stood moodily on the banks below, like a vast grey ghost. Binod sat down on his rucksack and smoked a cigarette. I didn't want to stop. I wanted to carry on and find somewhere to eat.

Everything was wet and Binod sat shivering on the bridge like a child. I was annoyed with him. He was supposed to be the guide and yet here I was, chivvying him along like an angry parent. I was losing my patience. I was wet and cold and hungry too.

'Get up,' I snapped. 'This isn't a holiday. You're my guide, you're getting paid for this.'

'I can't go any more.'

'Yes you can, you're being bloody lazy. Get up and walk.'

I stormed off, hoping to set an example.

Luckily it worked. As I turned round to check, I saw him sulking, a hundred metres or so behind me. I picked up my

194

speed and walked on in silence. The rain was demoralising us. This was becoming thoroughly unpleasant and neither of us was enjoying it any more. I could tell that Binod wanted to be at home, and so did I. The jungle had sapped all our energy and the prospect of walking along a main road for two weeks to get to Pokhara was about as appealing as turning around and going back through the leech-infested forest.

Up ahead an army checkpoint dissected the road. There was a lean-to shelter where young corporals sat in string vests drinking tea. Their sodden shirts were steaming as they dried under the shelter.

I ducked in and sat down without invitation. A soldier laughed at my pathetic figure and handed me a cup of tea. Binod, still sulking, didn't come in and instead went across the road to sit with some local farmers in a shack.

'Where can we get some food?' I asked the soldier.

'Nowhere,' he said. 'Everything is closed because of the strike.'

Having been in the jungle for a week I'd almost forgotten about the strike. That explained why we hadn't seen any cars along the road. The whole country had an eerie, deserted feel.

'What are they striking about?' I asked the soldier, as Binod couldn't give me a clear answer.

'The new constitution. Some like it, some don't. These Tharu people don't. They want more representation in the government,' the soldier told me. 'The Maoists don't like it either – they organise strikes for any reason. At least once a month they are out causing trouble.'

'And why are there no cars?'

'For a start there's no fuel. Also the unions put in pickets. If anyone dares break them then the youths will be out smashing up the cars and the drivers will be beaten – sometimes killed.

They burn the cars to set an example. Whatever you do, don't get in a car.'

I sighed. 'I can't anyway, I'm walking.'

'Good,' he said.

I wondered why the soldiers didn't do anything about it.

'We stay out of politics. Too dangerous. The Maoists got into power a few years ago – imagine if we'd tried to fight them, they would now have us all killed.'

The biggest problem for me though, was the fact that I was running low on local currency. I had US dollars left but nobody would accept them. I needed Nepali rupees, and fast.

'Where's the nearest bank?' I asked.

'You can try Nepalganj.'

I took out my map and stared at the soggy creases. The road we were supposed to take cut through the foothills in a zig-zag pattern for two hundred miles east and Nepalganj was in completely the wrong direction.

'What about Tulsipur?' I asked him.

He shook his head. 'No, it's full of Maoists there. Everything will be closed. You're best going into the hills. Less trouble there.'

Since my first trip to Nepal fourteen years ago I'd learnt a lot more about the Maoists. After I'd escaped the country with Binod's help, the nation descended into a state of emergency as the Nepali government attempted to stop the communist rebels. Years of truces, insurgencies and counter-insurgencies followed, before the Maoists became a mainstream political party in 2007. Since then, there had been less violence but no shortage of these *bandh* – the strikes of which the soldier spoke. Apparently the strikes could last for up to a month at a time and it was the most effective way the Maoists could hold whole villages, towns and cities to ransom with nobody able to function until they got their way.

There seemed to be only one good option: to avoid the main road altogether and get back into the mountains as soon as possible. It would be cheaper there, and there was more chance of finding somewhere to change money with a rogue lender. And maybe, just maybe, we could finally escape the rain and get back into the clear, crisp air of the Himalayas so that Binod and I could get on with the walk without the constant harassment of the weather. I decided that was what we'd do and called out to my guide in an effort at reconciliation.

'Come for some tea Sir,' I said to Binod, knowing that the simple act of calling him Sir would mean that all was forgiven. Nobody calls a low-caste man Sir in Nepal, and it meant the world to him.

As we left the army checkpoint behind and walked on up the road I noticed the universal sign for communism – a red hammer and sickle – painted on an arched gateway into a village; clearly their legacy in this part of the country was still strong.

'They are still popular here in Nepal,' Binod told me. 'Many *bandh*, and rioting, and big protests. There were many deaths before too; they kidnapped school children and murdered men, leaving many widows. But also they did help the poor people, lower caste like me.'

The reality was that even in the twenty-first century, the caste system was still prevalent in South Asia. Not dissimilar to the feudal system of medieval Europe, it follows a strict hierarchy of classes, with the *Brahmin* priests at the top, followed by the warrior *Chetris*. Beneath them are the merchants and traders, the *Vaishyas*. And at the bottom are the *Shudras* – the farmers, labourers and unskilled workers. Binod had been born into the lowest caste, without land and with little opportunity to better himself. The Maoists promised a more egalitarian structure that would do away with the elitism of the caste system and the old monarchy.

'These days things have started to change – the Maoists helped that happen,' he told me. 'When the Britishers first started coming to the Himalayas, they needed guides and sherpas to show them the mountains. The Brahmins and upper castes were educated, so they could speak good English. But they saw these foreigners as impure, unclean and they refused to help them or guide them. For my people, they had no risk, nothing to lose, so they offered to do guiding for the foreigners. Like Sherpa. The Sherpa people used to be very poor, and now they have earned so much money and good reputation from tourism, and the Brahmins have not.'

'So don't they have any power any more?' I asked him.

'Yes, they do, they hold most government jobs,' he replied. 'And some are still priests even now, they still think they are better than us. They won't cross the shadow of an untouchable, an outcast, and they would certainly not shake their hand. I am still a bit uncomfortable if I am going into the house of a Brahmin or entering the temple at the same time as him.' Binod looked slightly ashamed to admit this to me. He continued, 'But slowly, slowly, things are changing. And the Maoists helped the Nepali people to see that equality is important for the future.'

The night we left Bardia I received a welcome surprise. Amid the rain we arrived sodden at a small lodge at the edge of the forest. As we were hanging our wet clothes on the wooden banister under the shelter of a tin roof I heard a familiar voice.

'Ay up.'

I looked across the veranda to find my own brother standing

there with an enormous grin on his face. He must have antici-
pated my reaction.

'What the . . .?'

'Well you sounded worried on the phone when we spoke a
couple of weeks ago, so I thought I'd come and join you for a
few days,' he said. I remembered calling him after the ominous
words of the cannibal Aghori.

'Pete?' shouted Binod, running across the decking and slapping my brother on his back.

'I said I'd come and visit.'

'I didn't think I'd see you again. Not here, not this time. Now
we are all together.' Binod looked genuinely delighted.

I couldn't quite get over it either. I hadn't seen my brother in
months. He rarely visited London, and I rarely visited him in
Nottingham where he lived, but five years back he'd wanted to
travel in Nepal and so I'd introduced him to Binod. Pete had
trekked with him on the Annapurna circuit and stayed at his
home in Sarangkot, as I had done nine years before that. It
almost felt like we had all come full circle, and Binod too was
one of the family.

'How on earth did you find us?' I asked, still in astonishment.

He smiled. 'It wasn't exactly hard. I knew you'd be coming
through Bardia and this is the only place to stay around here for
miles. Plus everyone has heard about the lunatic walking all the
way to Kathmandu, so I thought I'd hang around here till you
arrived.'

'You realise what you've let yourself in for, don't you?'

'Yes, well considering the last time we went on holiday I
almost froze to death. I did say I wouldn't do it again but that
was twelve years ago and by the time I'd booked my flight I'd
forgotten about that. I thought it was about time I joined you
on one of your walks.'

It was good to see him after so long, and I guessed that since relations were a bit strained with Binod, having someone else along for a few days would be no bad thing.

'Here,' he said. 'I thought I better bring something to keep away the mosquitoes.'

He handed me a bottle of decent scotch whisky. Binod went to fetch the glasses.

With a delicate set of heads we finally reached Tulsipur, which had the promise of lunch and shelter from the rain. I still desperately needed to change my US dollars into Nepali rupees, and the strike meant that so far all of the banks had been closed. The further we got from the Indian border, the harder it became to encourage people to take foreign currency. The soldier had been right; I saw plenty of signs for ATMs but every one we tried was closed. The security guards who stood outside with their shotguns simply shook their heads.

'Binod, can you ask the locals for some help?'

Despite the fact we were back on speaking terms, he'd been hesitant to go out of his way since we'd started falling out.

He just shrugged his shoulders.

I was used to being with Ash who is well travelled and organised or Malang who was an experienced guide and knew which side his bread was buttered. Binod on the other hand was altogether more stubborn.

We walked north from Tulsipur, skint and frustrated. It had been difficult to find porters and even when we'd asked auto-rickshaw drivers to help, they refused to come beyond the outskirts of the village. We were laden with our bags and walking became slow and laborious.

I did however count our blessings. In spite of the strike, we'd still managed to find places to stay. I'd been warned that because of the *bandh* all the hotels and guesthouses would be closed. Plenty of them were, but up until now we'd managed to convince hard-up hoteliers to let us have a room for a few rupees. Even if we'd wanted to camp, it would have been impractical. Outside of the jungle and national-park areas, every inch of spare land is farmed – not to mention hilly. Rice trellises make up the majority of the foothills and the issue of property is hotly contested in Nepal – as we'd found out. Even if the Nepalis we'd met were on the whole very hospitable, they weren't likely to let us just camp in their gardens willy nilly.

But we had managed. For all his faults, Binod had begged and pleaded and found us beds every night. It was usually just a filthy mattress in the corner of a room but it was better than nothing. Sometimes if we were lucky there would be a generator and we could pay for a few hours of electricity to charge up our gear and maybe even get the fan working.

As we ascended into the foothills the weather became more pleasant. It had stopped raining and we left the mugginess behind. That evening we reached a small village in the district of Khalanga. It was spread out along the top of a ridge and over-looked the valleys below. It wasn't much more than a high street with a few shops selling second-hand clothes and spare parts for motorbikes.

'Let's see if there's somewhere to stay,' I suggested to Binod.

It was already past five p.m. and the sun was hanging low in the sky. It was red and brilliant, yet somehow foreboding.

Pete and I shoved our rucksacks at the side of a restaurant and I ordered some milky *chai* while Binod went off to have a look around town. Considering its small size the market was bustling with people. Everyone was on foot; even up here it seemed the strike was still in full force. Only ambulances and police jeeps were moving.

Binod came back.

'Good news and bad news,' he said.

'Good news first,' I replied.

'I have managed to change some money for you.' He handed me a wad of notes held together with an elastic band.

'Good work. How did you manage that?' I said, relieved that we weren't destitute any more.

'I found a man who wanted dollars to escape from Nepal.'

'And the bad news?' I asked him.

'The bad news is that there is nowhere to stay here.'

'What? Nothing?'

'Nothing,' said Binod, shrugging. 'There is no guesthouse. It's only a small town and I don't know these people. They are not very friendly – they won't let us stay.'

I wondered for a moment if it was because of his caste.

'What about camping?' I said, before realising the futility of my suggestion. It was already dusk and the light was fading fast. Either side of the street, steep slopes fell away into the valleys and every inch was cultivated with banana, rice and wheat.

There was nowhere to camp here.

'Well, what do you suggest?' I asked.

'There's a bigger town not far from here, just five or six miles away. Maybe we should go there – there should be a guesthouse.'

My legs were aching and the thought of walking another ten kilometres was out of the question. I knew Binod wasn't up to it either. Pete on the other hand was fresh and keen but was happy to go along with our suggestions.

'There's one vehicle,' he said. 'We can drive there and then come back and walk from here in the morning.'

'I thought they weren't allowed to go anywhere,' Pete said, talking about the Maoists and the strike.

'I already spoke to the driver. He said he will drive after sunset, and nobody will ask, they'll just think it's an ambulance and leave him alone.'

It seems like Binod already had it all figured out. I wasn't so sure. The thought of driving at night along these roads was even worse than walking. I'd already seen plenty of accidents in the hills down to negligent drivers and bad brakes, and it went against everything I knew about health and safety.

'It's too dangerous,' I said. 'How do we know the brakes even work?'

'It's fine,' said Binod smiling. 'Just come look.'

Against my better judgement I followed Binod to a small alleyway where an Indian Mahindra SUV was parked. The driver was tinkering away under the wheel arches with a spanner.

'*Namaste*,' said a shadowy figure getting up. It was dark now and I could barely make out his features.

'Hello.'

'I take you Musikot,' he said, grinning. 'Cheap price.'

'It's late and dark. It's too dangerous. Do you know where we can sleep tonight?'

The shadow shook his head. 'Only Musikot. Nothing here. Very safe, no problem, sir.'

I looked at Binod. I could see he was exhausted and so was I. He'd done well to change the money and for the first time in days I could afford to splash out. The prospect of sleeping rough in a muddy car park was suddenly eclipsed by an overbearing desire to get to a real bed. Pete just shrugged.

The driver got into the car and revved the engine.

'Very good motor, sir. Good brakes too.'

'Fine,' I said. 'Let's go to Musikot.'

Binod excitedly loaded the bags into the boot of the car and got into the back next to my brother while I sat in the front passenger seat. With the headlights switched off we rolled out of the market and sneaked out of town. It felt strange to be in a car, and even stranger to be trying to escape like a criminal. As we got out of the village the driver turned on the lights and began to relax.

'No problem, sir. No Maoists this way. We all okay.'

We hadn't gone more than a mile though before we stopped at a police checkpoint. The driver waved at the policemen on the barrier and opened the back door.

'My friend come too.' He grinned.

'It looks like we have company,' I grumbled to Pete and Binod.

Being the only motor on the road, it was clearly in high demand and the driver asked Binod and Pete to squeeze up to make way for an off-duty detective. The cop got in silently without even a smile and just nodded for us to carry on.

The road wound up through the hills, which were obscured by blackness. All I could see of the surroundings was the flash of the headlights against a bush or the wide, flat leaves of a banana tree as we wended around the hairpin bends, up and up over a ridge. The road was narrow. To the right the grassy verge sloped upwards, covered in wild bushes, and to the left was a seemingly sheer drop off into the jungle below. Sometimes I could make out the faint sound of a gushing torrent of a river or waterfall in the blackness, but I couldn't be sure.

There wasn't enough room in the front seat to get my big map out so I had to content myself with checking our location by the GPS on my mobile phone. The blue dot showed a zig-zag of yellow where the road would now descend into the Bheri valley. We should soon be able to see the lights of Musikot. As far as I was concerned, we couldn't be there soon enough. The driver wasn't going particularly fast, or being reckless, but I was still terrified as we swerved to avoid fallen branches and small boulders that had tumbled from the cliffs above.

We must have reached the apex of the ridge as I sensed that we had begun to drive downhill. I was glad as it meant we were halfway there. I looked into the back seat. Pete gazed out of the window as Binod's head was bouncing rhythmically against the window as he tried to doze off. The off-duty police-man was fast asleep with his mouth fully open, snoring loudly. I wanted to sleep too but the road was too bumpy and I was too scared.

There was a grinding noise as the driver tried to go down a gear. I looked over. He was frantically groping the gear stick and pumping the brakes. The car suddenly jolted and we picked up speed. I knew immediately what was happening.

'Hit the wall,' I said, realising the brake cable had snapped. The headlights shone against a neat wall of black on the right-hand side. The road was straight for at least a hundred metres.

'Hit the fucking wall, go right!' This time I shouted at him.

The driver looked at me pathetically. He was trying to drive straight, trying his best to go down the gears, but it was no use. 'Hit the wall, go right now,' I pleaded.

I could see there was a ditch on the right – it was perfect. All he had to do was turn the steering wheel right and go into the ditch. We'd hit the wall and have a crash but it would be all right. But he didn't want to scratch his paintwork, I thought. The selfish bastard. Now it was too late. We were going too fast, the wheels clipped the ditch and the driver must have knocked the tyre left. Whatever happened we started to skid, veering left until the car must have been almost on two wheels as it spun to face up the hill, all the while still careering down the road.

The last thing I saw was the edge of the cliff coming closer and closer. It felt like it was all in slow motion – just like in a movie. The headlights lit up the tops of the trees that poked up above the edge of the road, indicating a small taster of what was to come. I knew right then, in that second, that we were about to go off the edge. I knew I was about to die.

Perhaps I've suggested that there was pandemonium and panic. There wasn't. It all must have happened in a matter of seconds. From that initial crunch of the gears, to speeding up, to the failure to hit the wall to the inevitable plunge off the edge of the cliff.

As we flew off the edge, and I mean flew – we were going at well over forty miles an hour at this point – I felt my body fill with adrenalin. That's what happens when your subconscious mind knows you are about to die. Your veins flood with chemicals and you experience absolute clarity. For the first second or two, I held my breath. I knew there was going to be a crash. I knew it would hurt. There was no 'life flashing before my eyes', only a massive sensation of loss and resignation. The only thing I thought was the word no. NO, no, no. The words seemed to echo through my entire soul. It can't end like this. Not at night with Binod and my brother in the car. They'd die too.

Then came the first bounce. The car must have hit a rock or a tree and we somersaulted. Then there was another, and another. We were rolling down, tumbling to a tragic doom at the bottom of an unholy ravine. It felt like I was inside a tumble dryer, each crash more horrific than the last. But with each bounce I couldn't believe I was still alive. I waited and counted the milliseconds for the next one to come. I knew that with the next one I would hit my head and I'd die. I wondered what it would be like – death. I mean the process of dying. I wondered if it would hurt after death. I hoped it would be painless. I prayed for Pete and Binod. I prayed that mercy might be shown. I didn't pray to survive, I don't think. It was too late for that.

As we rolled, something fell into my hands. I grabbed it and held it tight. It was a head. I didn't know whose head, but all I knew was that I had to protect it come what may. There was no point in trying to save myself at this point. I covered the head with my body, pulling it closer to my chest.

The car came to a crashing halt. I was upside down but couldn't see. It felt like we'd come to a halt, but no. We shunted again and we were off, rolling two, three, four more times. I couldn't hear a thing until there was silence, and then I heard everything.

We really had come to a halt now. I let out a breath. Had I held my breath for the whole time? I couldn't tell. I was dead. The head was gone. I was moving. Not by my own force but some sort of an ethereal motion – propelling me head first through wet grass in slow speed. I think I went through a window, like a worm, utterly flexible and malleable, unrestrained by gravity.

And then I was outside the car with my back to it. I must have been sitting, or kneeling. I still couldn't see. Everything was black and the silence was overwhelming. Was this heaven or purgatory? No, it was almost certainly hell. I couldn't feel any pain. All I knew was that I'd left my arm in the car. I had to go back and get it. I felt back through the opening of the smashed window but I couldn't find the severed limb. I felt at my elbow but no, it was still gone. Yet the oddest thing was that it wasn't wet. There was no blood. I couldn't understand why there was no blood. Yes, this was hell.

The silence was overwhelming until it stopped. There was a faint whimper, a subdued groan. It was a muffled sort of pain that didn't sound at all human. It was pathetic and sordid and I wanted it to stop. And then I realised where I was.

'Who's that?' I shouted, expecting an angel, or the devil perhaps.

I remembered I was with Binod. 'Is that you, Binod?' There was more muffled groaning. 'Oh no.'

Then, suddenly I remembered the words of the cannibal Aghori monk in Haridwar. 'Your brother, is he dead?'

I was overwhelmed with a paralysing fear and dread at the thought of Peter. No. It surely couldn't be true. I was in a nightmare and I just wanted to wake up. I tried to scream, 'Pete. Are you alive?'

And then the pain came.

It was a horrible, evil pain that filled my body with an agony I'd never experienced before. I grasped frantically at my severed arm and realised it wasn't severed at all, just mangled and pointing the wrong way. I grabbed it. The whole lower limb was utterly numb. I twisted it into shape and gave the most almighty yell I've ever given in my life.

'Lev,' Pete shouted. 'I'm here. It's okay. I'm alive.'

'Pete,' I shouted back. Blocking out the pain. 'Come here.'

'I'm in the car. I can't get out. It's dangling off a cliff and we're near the water.'

I don't think I'd ever been so glad to hear anyone's voice in my life. Pete was alive.

'Be careful,' I shouted. The relief of hearing my brother's voice gave me a brief renewed energy.

I used my good arm to grope for the figure next to me, the one who was muttering and moaning. I pulled him towards me. 'What happened?' it said.

I was suddenly elated. He was speaking English. It was Binod and he was alive.

'Binod,' I said.

'Brother? What happened?' He burst into tears.

I did the same. At that moment Pete, my own brother, emerged from the wreckage.

He'd climbed from the front seat. God only knows how he'd got there. He fell out of the windscreen onto the ground beside us. He was alive, and what's more, he could stand.

'Are you okay?' I asked.

'Better than you by the looks of things.' He laughed.

A wave of utter relief and sheer joy came over me. I was alive, and while we were currently in hell, there was at least a chance of salvation.

14

Return to Pokhara

As the realisation that I was still alive dawned on me, the pain got worse. My arm was in indescribable agony and I could barely move. The smallest motion caused me to scream out loud. Binod was dazed and muttering nonsense to himself. There was no sign of the driver or the policeman. Neither of them was in the car. From what I could make out, the vehicle was now nothing more than a twisted hulk of metal. All the windows had been smashed. I still couldn't figure out how I was alive, not to mention how we'd found ourselves outside of the car sitting together. I realised that the head I'd been cradling had been Binod's. He must have been forced over me in the tumble and then we must have been thrown through the windscreen together on the final collision. Either that or a guardian angel had plucked us from the wreckage and put us to one side.

It felt like an eternity, sitting there in anguish. We were at the bottom of a ravine, unable to move. I could tell my arm was broken and goodness knows what else. Binod couldn't move his back or his neck, and was in pain too. Pete was in the best shape. He climbed back into the car and found a torch and was busy flashing it back up towards the road. I couldn't tell how far we'd fallen. It must have been as much as a hundred feet, maybe more.

It began to rain and Binod was sobbing now. And then suddenly there was hope.

'Lights!' shouted Pete.

I was beginning to hallucinate. I'd started to believe that actually I wasn't alive after all, and that this was really damnation. The distant torchlights only made it worse and I recall telling Pete not to bother them. They would never find us. We were destined to stay put in that jungle gulley. Pete luckily took no notice of my rambling and screamed like hell in the direction of the lights. They gradually got louder and closer but my thoughts alternated between resignation and frustration at their seeming lack of urgency. It didn't occur to me that we were at the bottom of a cliff in the middle of the forest and whoever our saviours were, they were having a really shit time of it too, trying to get to us.

It was only when they finally found us half an hour later that I truly believed we'd been saved. There were dozens of them. Farmers in rags, men and women soaked through. It looked like the whole village had come out. God only knows how they'd found us, and why they'd come. Perhaps they'd heard the noise of the crash, or my screams, or Pete's shouts for help. It didn't matter; we'd been saved. The army came after that. My final hazy memories are of some police loading me onto a stretcher and picking me up, and then a hellish twenty-minute scramble through the jungle, being passed around and jolted and almost dropped three times. Every bump was agony but I couldn't feel anything other than gratitude. I remembered my days as a soldier when we'd trained to carry the weight of an injured man five miles off the battlefield. These poor bastards were doing it for real, crossing waist-deep rivers and pushing through dense forest. I knew how hard it was for them so I tried to keep my whimpering to a minimum.

We eventually reached a road and I remember being unceremoniously dumped down. There was the sound of a car engine nearby. Torchlights swirled around like dancing fairies; a bearded face leant down and grinned. Then there was a sharp pain in my arm. I was being injected. I don't know what with. I didn't care – the pain went away after that. Pete helped a soldier pick up the stretcher to load me into the back of the car and off we went. Speeding even faster around the mountain lanes. I closed my eyes and tried not to think about it.

I can barely recall the rest of the night. Flashes of movement come back to me now. A nurse in white, a doctor in red, my brother's smile, Binod with a black eye and his face covered in blood; tubes, needles and pipes; a chicken clucking; the groans of the injured and a dirty bed in a hospital where the lights stayed on all night.

The next day I was more conscious. I don't think I'd actually slept properly at all and I couldn't stay still for more than a few seconds without feeling a shooting pain in my arm. It was bloated and covered in blood. I was on a drip and used needles littered the floor.

I tried to sit up.

'Get back down,' said a familiar voice. It was Pete. 'You're okay. We're all okay.'

'Where's Binod?' I asked.

'He's here. He's asleep, but fine.'

'What about the driver and the cop?'

'I don't know. They were carried out too. They'd been thrown out somewhere on the hill. The last I heard they were alive. It's serious though, they've been taken to a proper hospital in Nepalganj.'

'Where are we?' I asked.

'We're in Rukum. This is the village clinic.'

For someone who hadn't travelled outside of Europe in five years, and had never been in a survival situation, Pete had acted heroically. He'd co-ordinated the rescue while I was high on painkillers. He'd tried to get us extracted to a town where I could be treated, but my arm was too severely broken to be moved by car again.

'I'm trying to arrange a helicopter,' Pete said. 'But the weather is too bad.'

I looked out through the window, where a vast spider's web stretched under the awnings of the roof. The black clouds had gathered again, obscuring the hilltops.

'Maybe tomorrow,' he reassured me.

Every time the painkillers wore off a nurse would come round and inject me again with the unknown drug. I wished she'd come round more often. It was only when I kept perfectly still that I could tolerate the agony. The doctor came and apologised that he had no facilities to treat my arm. It would need surgery as soon as possible, and my gashes required stitching. We all needed X-rays and maybe spinal scans. We had to get out.

It was two full days before a break in the weather meant that we could finally escape. I was indebted to the doctors and nurses and the villagers who had come to my rescue. It was them who'd saved our lives. They'd gone above and beyond too; local policemen had searched the area and gone back to the crash site and recovered all our bags and personal belongings including my camera and my diary. They must have been flung out of a window during the free-fall, and, despite having spent two nights in the monsoon rain, somehow still survived. In a bizarre twist of fate, as I was going through my memory cards to check the data was all okay, I found a blank file, forty minutes long. I played it. It was all black but there was audio, somehow, and it must have been on the first roll – my camera, which was in the bottom of my bag, had turned itself on and recorded the sounds of the crash. Noises only – but it was all there: the screams, the shouts and the cries. I couldn't listen to all of it and to this day I don't think I will ever be able to forget the horrors of that episode.

∿⌃∿

The helicopter came and Binod, Peter and I flew all the way to Kathmandu. My brother had never been in a helicopter and had his eyes closed for the entire flight – particularly as we banked sharply to avoid the streaming clouds and monsoon rain that appeared as shape-shifting black ghouls, creeping over the mountains.

But we landed safe and sound and were all taken to a hospital in the city where I spent a further couple of days until I was finally ordered to go back to England. There was nothing to be done here. X-rays showed a clean fracture of the upper humerus and severe lacerations. The jagged bone had torn my bicep almost in two. It needed to be operated on soon, and it was best done by an orthopaedic surgeon in London. In my dream world I had imagined a couple of days' rest and then cracking on with my arm in a cast, but it was not to be.

I said goodbye to Binod after arranging for him to fly back to his family in Pokhara. Pete decided to stay in Kathmandu for a few more days since his holiday had come to a rather abrupt and dreadful end and he wanted to get over the accident in his own way. So I flew back to London alone. I was naturally shaken up, but at the same time I don't think I'd ever felt so happy. I was in a state of euphoria for days and days, just glad to be alive.

The time went quickly. I kept a low profile and spent my time writing and going on short walks, trying my best to keep fit and active. The doctor filled my arm with metal plates and screws and stitched me up well, and before I knew it I was doing bicep curls and arm stretches with a very patient physiotherapist who tolerated my profanities with a kind smile and gentle words of encouragement. I told her I wanted to be fixed up and able to carry a rucksack within five weeks. She said she'd do her best. In the meantime I did my utmost to avoid feeling sorry for myself, and despite the agony of a limb in repair and not being able to sleep for more than half an hour at a time I reminded myself just how lucky I was.

The physio signed me off after just four weeks, at the point where I had full spectral movement and could just about pick up a bag. And so on the fifth of October – fifty days since I'd gone off the edge of the cliff in Rukum, I set off once again from Heathrow on a flight bound for Nepal.

Binod was waiting for me outside the hotel already dressed in his trekking gear with his rucksack on his back. He was ready to go.

'Welcome back, brother,' he said with a smile on his face, hugging me. It felt like no time at all since I'd waved goodbye to him in Kathmandu amid the pain and morphine-induced haziness of that terrible episode.

'How's your arm?' he asked me.

I rolled up my sleeve to show him my scar, which stretched from the elbow to my shoulder. Apart from a rogue stitch that refused to dissolve, it had almost healed.

'How's your back?' I asked.

'Fine,' he said with a slight pause. 'Just a few bumps here and there.' He told me that he'd been resting in his house in Sarangkot with his family.

'Are you sure you're okay to carry on walking? What did your wife say?'

'Of course I am,' Binod replied. 'Chandra understands it's my job and there are risks but what to do? When it is our time it is our time, only God can decide that.'

'And how's the situation here now? Has the strike finished?' I asked him.

'Oh no, brother. It is much worse now. The Indians have closed the border and no fuel is coming into the country. The economy is very bad and no one is allowed to buy petrol – it is reserved for the government and emergency services only.'

It turned out that in the intervening weeks since I'd left Nepal the situation there had gone from bad to worse. The signing of the new constitution had caused riots and protests across the Terai, mainly as a result of the ethnic Indian Madhesi feeling politically disenfranchised. It was a terrible setback for the poor Nepalese who'd been through hell already this year. It seemed that their misfortune was never-ending. From the expedition's perspective, it wasn't helpful either.

'How are we going to get back to Rukum and carry on with the walk then if we can't drive?' I asked Binod.

'There's only one option. We need to fly.'

My heart sank. If there was one thing that terrified me even more than driving around ghastly mountain roads it was the prospect of a gravity-defying flight.

It was a petrifying journey in the tiny Twin Otter plane back to Rukum. The poky little aircraft bounced and clanked through the skies in a way that convinced me yet again that I would almost certainly die. It weaved and jolted through the storm clouds and every bit of turbulence made me grab my seat till my fingers hurt. To make matters worse, just the thought of where we were heading filled me with horror. The plane skidded to a halt on an obscenely short runway that seemed to balance on a knife-edge ridge in the middle of the green mountains, and here we were again. It was like returning to the scene of a crime.

A huge part of me wanted to skip this bit altogether and just recommence the journey in Pokhara, a hundred miles to the east. But a piece of me knew that if I didn't go back, I might just regret it for the rest of my days. Plus I wanted to see if I could find the people that had saved my life and thank them in person. I knew it was something I just had to do. Binod was as nervous as I was, walking up through the little village of Rukum towards the clinic. Both of us were visibly shaking at the prospect of reliving the memories of that day.

The first person we met was the doctor who'd treated me. He recognised us immediately and came over to shake our hands.

'Did you forget something?' he asked, bewildered at what we were doing back in this remote village.

Binod explained that we'd come to offer our gratitude and make a small donation to the clinic and that brought a smile to his face.

'Thank you, dear,' the doctor said. 'As you can see we don't have much funding here.'

It had occurred to me that was the case, what with the chickens running amok in the wards and an outside long-drop toilet that could be smelt from the airstrip, not to mention the poor breastfeeding mothers outside in the gardens as there was no space in the two wards. It was the least I could do.

A policeman offered to take us to see the crash site and we agreed it was something we should do. My memories of that night were so vague that until then, I had no idea of where it had happened, or exactly how we'd been rescued, and to go back, I hoped, would give me some closure.

The road wound through the verdant forest, which was bright and fresh, past wooden villages where women plucked rice from the fields in the autumn harvest. We drove through shallow fords and around switchback turns; this was the route we must have taken in the ambulance during the extraction, but I remembered none of it. It had been a bumpy, drug-fuelled haze. This time around I asked the driver to go slow, and stay away from the edge. He nodded solemnly.

'Don't worry, brakes are good.'

'That's what the last guy said,' joked Binod.

'It's there,' said the policeman pulling over at the side of the road. It was as I remembered. Getting out of the car I saw the cliff and the ditch we tried to swerve into. There was a pile of logs inside the ditch – what we must have hit in order to bounce and swerve off the edge. The policeman walked over to the precipice and pointed down into the jungle below. I gulped in anticipation and slowly peered over.

I could hardly believe my eyes. It was a vertical sheer drop for the first ten metres. The exact spot where we took off was the only gap in the trees, where a rocky gulley made a natural path through the otherwise dense forest below. Of all the places to go off the road it looked like the worst – no trees to stop our fall. There was no sign of the car.

'It's down there,' said the policeman shaking his head. I strained my eyes but still I couldn't see it. 'Very far,' he said. 'You very lucky.'

'Shall we go and see?' said Binod.

He led the way. I couldn't refuse despite the obvious dangers of trying to climb down the cliff-face with a still broken arm. Curiosity got the better of me.

We scrambled down the rock face and found a narrow trail that led to the ravine. It was steep and I kept slipping on the gravel underfoot. After fifty metres the gulley was covered in trees and we pushed on through the overgrown green tunnel. There was debris from the car everywhere. Pieces of glass were embedded in the trees; parts of the exhaust poked from grassy mounds; the plastic bumper was snapped in two; I found one insole of my shoe, and then the other. The further down we slid, the more we came to appreciate the enormity of the descent. Eighty, ninety, a hundred metres. Still no car. The gorge continued with its ghastly trail of litter.

I wasn't counting exactly but it must have been over a hundred and fifty metres down when we finally encountered the ruined hulk of the jeep. Seeing it in broad daylight, I almost broke down, but I restrained myself for the sake of Binod who I could tell felt the same.

'Thank God,' he said aloud. 'We are blessed. No one should have survived this. Our parents did good karma.'

The car was mangled. Without a shard of glass left in any of the windows, it was as I remembered, and the full horrors came flooding back. I remembered the free fall, the first collision, the rolls and the bumps, grabbing Binod's head and trying to shield it; the imminent sense of death, my wonder of how it would feel; the crash, the silence, the guilt and the agony. It was all real and utterly horrible. The state of the car said it all.

Except now it just looked pathetic. It was just the empty shell of a horrendous memory; the ghost of a lucky escape. It was the kind of place you'd explore as a child and fairy tales would be created. 'This is where they all died,' I imagined future generations of Nepali boys to say. 'Not a one survived.' And nor should they have, I thought.

Binod knelt down and picked up the orange scarf he had bought in Haridwar on the banks of the Ganges. It was filthy and rigid from a month of sitting in monsoon rain, but he took it as a souvenir of his survival.

The jungle was eerily quiet except for the shrill of a lone cicada that echoed through the canopy. Binod and I sat for a while, just looking at the wreckage. There were no words needed, we both knew what a lucky escape we'd had. But as the rays of sunlight that beamed through the trees lost their power, I knew it was getting late. It was time to leave the ghosts behind and carry on with our journey. Following the gulley down to the river, the valley opened up once again to reveal a magical setting sun and the full glory of the lush mountains shining in the evening half-light. The path through the long grass and the paddy fields was the same one I'd been carried out on a stretcher just a few weeks before.

We walked east the following day. It felt like a new beginning. The monsoon was almost at an end and the rain no longer came down in sheets. It was good to be away from the roads and cars and we followed little footpaths over the crests of pine-clad ridges and along the banks of gushing rivers. The white-tipped peaks of the Himalayas loomed in the distance and the further east we trod, the bigger they got. Everywhere we were greeted with friendly smiles and courteous *namastes*. Up here in the hills, the people took on a more Mongolian appearance. These were the Magars and Gurungs. The men wore *kachad* skirts and rubber wellies and homespun woollen waistcoats. In their cummerbunds the older men sported enormous *kukris*, the curved knives made famous by Gurkha soldiers. The women swept along the paths in colourful saris and some had rings made of gold. The younger girls were pretty yet hardened, carrying heavy loads of thatch for roofs and animal fodder.

But it was by no means plain sailing. In fact the area we were traversing was the heartland of the Maoist insurgency that had plagued Nepal for twenty years. Everywhere we went, the archways into villages were inscribed with the hammer and sickle, and graffiti displayed open support for communism. A new Prime Minister – Khadga Prasad Oli – himself a communist, had been elected, much to the dismay of the Indian government. Civil unrest had led to the southern borders being closed. The news reported violent protests in the plains and the strikes were ongoing. There was a widespread fuel shortage too, which meant that prices had rocketed and tensions were high. It hailed back to the ten-year civil war and reminded me of my first time in Nepal in 2001. It seemed that unfortunately little had changed.

I asked Binod what he thought of them.

'I voted for the Maoists myself,' he said after a while.

I was quite shocked. When we were younger, he'd always been an advocate of the monarchy.

'After the King was overthrown, I thought what harm could it do? Things were bad already and at least the communists promised equality and rights for the low-caste people. You know, I have to look after my family.'

'And what about the future?' I asked. 'Will the new Prime Minister succeed in making Nepal better?'

'God only knows. Nepal is a mess, and how can our country improve with all these riots and strikes and border closures? That's the bad thing about the communists – all they do is complain, but we need action, and I hope this man can do something to make it better.'

Binod wasn't too interested in politics, but he was a patriot and it struck me that he, like most people in Nepal, simply wanted peace and to have the opportunity to thrive.

'You see, we're like a small pebble, stuck between two big rocks. To the north we have China who we cannot fight, and to the south we have India who give us all our fuel and all the things we need to buy. What can we do? The communists want us to start making our own things so that we don't need to rely on India but they play games, political games, and if we fight they will crush us, so we have to find a balance. I don't know any more, all we can do is pray and hope.'

It took a week to walk to Baglung, following terrible roads that had succumbed to the monsoon over the past months. The mud was still knee-deep and landslides had wrecked entire portions of the mountain paths. The few trucks that were able to find diesel had their routes blocked for hours, sometimes days. We walked past, helping where we could, but generally just glad that we were on foot. It seemed the government was doing little to fix the devastation.

'Terrible corruption,' said Binod, shaking his head in disgust. 'The local authorities get grants from the government to build bridges and put down tarmac but they never finish the job, and steal most of the money.'

It seemed you could almost speculate on the relative levels of honesty of a particular district authority by how much infra- structure was actually completed. But it was rare to find a bridge that wasn't half built. One exception that did impress me though was the footbridge at Kushma, a 350-metre-long bridge that spanned a vast gorge 150 metres deep over the holy Kali Gandaki river; it had cut down the villagers' commute across the valley from two hours to five minutes. But as I say, it was rare. The earthquake hadn't helped matters either; the closer we got to central Nepal and the epicentre of the deadly quake, the more we saw of the ruins and devastation. Mile-long queues formed at petrol stations as cars and motorbikes waited for days to get their ten-litre allowance. Armed police patrolled the villages in case the unrest down south flared up in the hills. There was a feeling of tension in the air but more than anything it was hard not to feel saddened at the plight these people were going through, over and over again.

But at least we were alive and I was grateful for every new day. Binod seemed to have changed completely. Gone were his complaints about walking, and now that we were back on the road, he seemed to be a transformed man. He was his old self – the Binod I remembered; the trusty guide and faithful friend. He found us porters along the way with a new-found charm and confidence, he'd wake up early every morning to bring me tea and offer to carry my bags. My arm was still weak from the accident and the rogue stitch on my shoulder had become infected, so I wasn't able to carry my rucksack. Binod went above and beyond what I had ever expected of him and he carried my share of the gear.

Perhaps it was the fact we were closing in on Pokhara but Binod seemed happier, more jubilant than ever. I was excited to see his family again but he was ecstatic to be passing by his home for the start of the Dashain festival, and for the chance to spend a few days with his family. And moreover, to share the experience with me.

'My neighbours will be so jealous,' he said with a mischievous wink. 'They all know about my English brother. I have been telling them for years but they never believe me, and now you are coming home. Now they will see.'

I suddenly felt abashed and almost feared what his wife, Chandra, would make of me – the person who'd put Binod's life in danger.

'Don't worry brother, she is happy you are coming. We will all celebrate.'

And so, finally, we rounded the northern road and from the top of of Pauderkot hill I saw Pokhara city and the famous Fewa lake. There, unfolding before us were the looming mounds of Kaskikot and to the north the Seti Gandaki river. And beyond that, marked by its lush green jungle-clad slopes – topped now by a telephone mast – the hill known as Sarangkot. Binod's home, a place I hadn't seen in over fourteen years.

'Remember?' said Binod, pointing down the valley.

'I remember.'

It was hazy and the town was covered in a low-hanging cloud. Nothing whatsoever could be seen of the Himalayas. Annapurna and the fishtail mountain Machhapuchchhre were hidden by an impenetrable wall of grey. But in spite of it I was happy, glad after all these years to have finally fulfilled my promise to return.

15

The Road to Kathmandu

Nothing had changed and everything had changed. We walked down the hill and into the outskirts of Pokhara. At every petrol station queues lined the roads as men waited patiently for their weekly ration of fuel. I'd seen on the news that the strike was getting worse, but the way the Nepalis smiled and joked as they stood for seven hours at a time you'd think they were just hanging around for fun.

The town was much bigger than before. I remembered it as a quiet little place, with sleepy cafés lining the lakeside and just a few hotels for the handful of backpackers. The hippy hangout known for its mountain views and banana lassis seemed bigger and more bustling than I recalled. Now the main street was heaving with people and despite the international bad press caused by the earthquake, it was still popular with the tourists. Israelis sat in the restaurants smoking shishas and American girls roamed in pairs. Bistros served a plethora of international cuisine and there was an Irish bar with a happy hour. Commercialisation had set in, and as I struggled to reconcile my own memories of 2001 I couldn't place exactly where I'd met Binod, or which internet café I'd found myself stuck in as the Maoist riots raged outside. New luxury hotels had sprung up in the place of the grubby guesthouses and you couldn't even see the lake from the high street now for the three-storey shops that had appeared selling everything from Kashmiri carpets to top-of-the-range trekking boots.

But despite my nostalgic reminiscences I was happy to be back. It felt like a homecoming, and after reliving the horrors of Rukum I was looking forward to a cold beer.

Binod couldn't stop smiling. It was already dusk and too late to make the trek up to Sarangkot so we decided to stay in a hotel that evening.

'Tomorrow, brother, we shall go back and you can see my new house,' Binod told me.

So that night we filled up on a buffalo pizza and watched the sun set behind the mountains and afterwards I slept like a child and dreamt of home.

The next afternoon we set off along the main road with the lake to our left and made our way up the steep slopes of Sarangkot hill. Now instead of the grazing buffaloes at the lakeside there were piers offering lake tours in private boats and even paddleboarding. The jungle was thinner than I remembered and instead of thatch, all the houses now had tin roofs. What hadn't changed though was the relentless climb and the clouds looming grey: rain threatened. Even time hadn't flattened the mountains, nor could it improve the weather. But at least nowadays there was a stone and concrete path carved into the mountain. Binod had a spring in his step.

'Come on, brother, they are waiting for you.' He slapped me on the back. It reminded me of the first time we had climbed together. I could hardly believe I was at the point where my Himalayan journey had begun all those years ago.

Soaked through with sweat we finally arrived at Binod's old house. He was renting it out to some of his neighbours now and children were playing in the tiny garden. Gone were the cannabis plants and the wild orchards and in their place stood an enormous mobile phone mast and tourist shops.

Binod was proud of his tin roof and little extension made of concrete blocks. 'This is what you helped me with, brother. The money you sent, now the hailstones can't come through into the kitchen. Thank you.'

We walked a few steps further up the hill, almost to the top, to the viewpoint overlooking the town. Although my memories were skewed by all of this modern development, I could still remember that this was where Binod had led me, aged nineteen, into his village and introduced me to his mother and wife.

At the edge of the path stood a small house, slightly back from the stone steps where a plastic table invited weary trekkers to sit down. Behind it was an opening into a teashop. There in the doorway stood a boy in a T-shirt that was too big for him; he was beaming and I felt like I recognised him. I looked at Binod and back at the boy. Binod just smiled.

'Bishal?'

Binod laughed. 'You see my son. Look how he has grown.'

The teenager walked over confidently and offered his hand. '*Namaste*, uncle.'

I could hardly believe this was the same boy I had held in my hands when I was just a couple of years older than he was now. Of course it was Bishal – he had the same kind and honest face as his father. A little girl came running out of a doorway. She jumped up and grabbed Binod's waist, hugging him lovingly.

'And you must be Binita.'

This was the nine-year-old daughter I'd heard so much about. She smiled shyly and nodded.

'Say *namaste*,' said Binod.

'*Namaste*,' she squeaked, before nestling her face in her father's stomach. And then Bishwas came wobbling out. I thought he was a girl at first as he had long hair tied back in a pink bobble. Binod sensed my confusion.

'It's our tradition; it will be cut off now he's in his third year. We just haven't got around to it yet.'

The boy squealed with delight at the sight of his father and begged to be picked up. Behind them all standing proudly was Chandra. She wasn't the shy girl I'd glimpsed fleetingly years before. Instead she was a noble-looking mother, her hands clasped together.

I bowed my head and returned her *namaste*, remembering that it was culturally inappropriate to shake a woman's hand unless it was offered first. But with Chandra there was no such formality. She came over and embraced me, holding me tightly and sobbing. She was saying something in Nepali I couldn't understand, but I already knew what she meant.

'She welcomes you home, brother. She says that this is your house and she thanks you for everything you have done for us.' He blushed and I blushed too.

'She also says that she is grateful to you for bringing me home safely.'

She patted my arm, motioning for me to show her my scar. I unbuttoned my shirt and pulled down my collar to show her my shoulder. She burst out crying aloud and held me so tightly I could hardly breathe. She was barely four and a half feet tall but was as strong as an ox. Binita came over and held her mother and began to weep too, and then she held my hand.

'Uncle Lev,' she said in English, looking up with wet eyes. 'Come sit down.'

It really was a homecoming, and we had made it to Sarangkot in time for the festival of Dashain.

'Now that you are home, brother, we must celebrate,' Binod announced. 'Bishal, go and fetch the goat.'

We all sat down. Chandra was now smiling and she bustled off to make some tea. I sat on the chair overlooking the lake as the clouds rolled in, covering the town in a blanket of white. It was already dusk and the sun had disappeared into the blackness of the coming thunderstorm.

'Tonight it will rain,' said Binod.

He was right. Just as the sword came down on the goat's neck the first drops of rain pattered on the tin roof. A fork of lightning shattered the greyness of the night above a temple on the far side of the valley. The thunder that followed gave a deafening rumble, causing little Bishwas to cover his ears. We moved inside and sat on the floor to drink tea, eagerly awaiting the goat to be curried. Chandra, unperturbed by the storm, busily butchered the animal and cooked it up in a pot while Bishwas danced and Binita sang. They got used to me after an hour and insisted on me playing with them. Bishwas took hold of my phone and within minutes he'd figured out how to scroll between photos. I showed them the old snaps of their dad and me from 2001 and 2009. Bishal found it very amusing to see pictures of his father only four years older than he was now. The thunder boomed outside and we ate the goat as the lightning lit up the valley in quick flashes and we were all very happy. I didn't want the night to end and so we agreed to all go up to the viewpoint the following morning for sunrise in the vain hope of a clearing in the weather.

I remembered back to fourteen years ago when, as if by magic, Binod had predicted a view of the mountains.

'What do you think, Binod? Will we get the view tomorrow?'

He shrugged as the rain came down in buckets on his tin roof.

'If we are lucky then we will. If the mountains want to be revealed then they will. We should try.'

And so we tried. We woke up at five to the sound of crickets. It had stopped raining now and it seemed to be clear, but there was no way of knowing if the clouds would obscure the ranges to the north. But we made the climb up the hill regardless, past the phone mast, to the same spot that we had stood on when we'd first heard the news of the royal massacre that fateful June.

'If the mountains want to be revealed then they will.' The words echoed in my mind as we crested the final few steps to the top.

We weren't disappointed. There, floating above the haze and the green foothills beyond Pokhara was the majestic panorama of my memory. Dhaulagiri, the Annapurnas, and the towering twin peaks of the fishtail mountain, Machhapuchhre. The peaks shimmered in the dreamlike pink of the morning as the sun rose beyond the Manaslu range. The mountains had chosen to reveal themselves and I was humbly reminded – not for the first time – that we were entirely at their fickle mercy.

Bishal appeared from behind us holding a flask of coffee and poured a welcome brew. Binita sat quietly, innocently contemplating the glorious landscape, as only a child could.

'Brother, we are lucky today,' said Binod.

'That, Binod, we truly are.'

It was sad to say goodbye to the family later that morning, but Chandra bade us farewell in true Nepali style. She placed a red *tikka* made of sticky rice and dye on our foreheads – a blessing and offering to the gods to give us safe passage on our onward journey. She hugged me again and said I must return. The children kissed their father on his forehead and he told them to be good and that he would come back soon. I promised them I'd make sure he was okay and he would come home safe.

'Goodbye, Uncle. *Namaste*,' said the children in unison.

And with that we walked off down the hill and back through the town, east out of Pokhara.

A few days later we were in Gurung country on the southern reaches of the Annapurna conservation area. It was a place of extraordinary beauty, away from the main roads. Only the hardiest of jeeps penetrated this far north and so the valleys were quiet, the villages virtually untouched by modernity. We came across a small settlement called Syange, at the base of an enormous waterfall that seemed to fall from the skies above. Rope-hanging bridges afforded the only way to get across the gushing rivers and Buddhist prayer flags fluttered softly from bamboo poles in the morning breeze. It was a peaceful, serene place where trekkers used to come before the earthquake, but now it was very quiet.

'Let's get closer to the waterfall,' said Binod. 'We can climb up to the next village.'

And so we left the main valley and climbed up a rocky path, through the terraces of millet and corn and patches of wild bamboo to where wild untamed jungle sprouted from the cliffs. There we rounded a path that weaved graciously between glacial boulders and up and up until our legs were tired and our breathing heavy.

'There it is.'

We carried on as the trail flattened out on a plateau of lush greenery. A village called Mipra perched in between the fields. All the houses were made of stone and mud, with slate roofs and pastel-painted walls. Chickens ran wild and enormous dogs kept one eye open as they slept under the shade of firewood sheds. Women plodded the footpaths under the weight of baskets laden with fodder. Some carried seemingly impossible loads of grass on their heads, which made them look like bushes with legs. The monsoon, it seemed, had disappeared, and now there was only glorious sunshine and endless blue heavens. After the months of walking under ominous skies it came as a welcome reward.

An old man was seated on a doorstep and motioned for us to join him. His name was Ash Bahadur Gurung and he was seventy-two years old. He wore the traditional *topi* hat of the hillmen and tattered shorts that revealed gnarly, weather-worn legs, which looked like they were covered in leather.

'Come and sit down and have some tea,' he said through broken teeth. I felt like we'd been transported back to an age where time was of no consequence. As we sat and drank sweet tea he produced a bottle full of yellow liquid. It was honey.

'I used to hunt it myself but now I'm too old.'

'Hunt it?' I asked him.

'Yes, hunt it. We used to go like a war party and fight the bees for it.'

I suddenly had fanciful images dancing round my head of troops of *kukri*-wielding mountain men doing battle with swarms of bees. It turns out my imaginings weren't far from the truth.

'Now it has all changed,' he told us. 'My students go in search of it but they have proper clothes. Hats and things. In the olden days we went in traditional dress.'

'Didn't you get stung?'

He laughed with the vigour of someone much younger.

'Of course we got stung. But we are immune. It hurts for a bit and then just makes you stronger.'

He rolled up his sleeves and showed me scars from years of fighting the bees.

'Would you like to see it?'

How could I resist? He shouted at a young man nearby who nodded and then disappeared.

'Follow me,' said Ash Bahadur.

He got up and raced off along the trail and we followed. I couldn't believe the speed at which he walked, much faster than

Binod and me. Along the way he picked up from a neighbour's shack a basket lined with sheeting. We came to a field where a group of youngsters were unfurling a homemade ladder. It was made of grass rope with wooden rungs and was at least thirty metres long. More men arrived; there must have been twenty-five of them in total. They proceeded to sling the ladder over their shoulders and walk in step out of the village. Ash Bahadur led the way and we followed on. It really did have the feel of a hunt. All the men looked focused, they marched in unison and sang war songs and chanted prayers for the success of their mission.

It was an exhausting trek. We climbed out of the rice paddies and into the bamboo forest, following an ancient trail. The old man never seemed to tire, nor did the youngsters, under the weight of the long ladder. There was no scope for any of them to dawdle; they had to keep up with the man at the front and certainly didn't want to be seen to lose face in the presence of the seventy-two-year-old honey veteran.

I hadn't heard of the honey hunters before, but it transpired this was a traditional way of harvesting the golden syrup. For centuries the men of this particular region of Nepal had risked life and limb climbing down sheer cliffs with nothing more than rope ladders, a bamboo pole and a wicker basket to collect the severed hive.

After a gruelling forty-five-minute ascent up a perilous trail we reached a narrow ledge overgrown with bushes and ferns. Not more than a few metres away was an enormous waterfall, which coursed down into the unknown chasm below. Just peering over the edge was a dangerous affair, as the rocks underfoot crumbled and the grass was wet and slippery from the spray of the cascade. The men all crowded onto the ledge and attached the ladder to the surrounding trees with ropes, before hurling it off the edge.

Ash Bahadur, despite claiming to be retired, was fully in the mix, shouting orders and directing the operation with aplomb. Before anything further happened he lit a torch of grass and waved it around to summon the mercy of the gods.

'You cannot be here,' he said to Binod and me. 'You aren't used to the bees. The immunity isn't in your blood. Go down there.'

He pointed to another ledge a couple of hundred metres below us to the right. I was relieved not to be expected to go down the ladders myself, and from the ledge below we would get a much better view.

So Binod and I climbed down through the undergrowth, grabbing on to thorny bushes to stop us from falling. We emerged at a clearing and looked up to see the full scale of the sheer cliff above us. The old man waved down from his perch, below which the rope ladders dangled freely.

The next moment two men, kitted out in overalls and hats with bee-proof meshing, began climbing down the ladder. In their hands they held two extraordinarily long bamboo poles, sharpened at the end. They descended slowly, one above the other until they reached three-quarters of the way down. And even from where I was watching, I saw their prize.

Three dark-brown blobs drooped from underneath an over-hang – these were the beehives. It only occurred to me that the darkness was just the colour of the bees themselves when they started to fly around, trying to attack the men. The lower of the two was passed the burning torch that hung at the end of a rope. He carefully swung it around the beehives, smoking the fierce insects out from their nest and within a minute the blobs were no longer brown but pure white. Millions of bees buzzed around the men in a frenzied defence, while the two heroes calmly used the poles to prod two holes into the honeycomb. The other man passed down a rope toggle, which was expertly poked into the holes. Then, using the bamboo pole again, the man slowly cut away about the incisions until the hive fell free, held together by just the toggle at the end of the rope. It swung precariously as the top man hauled it up as fast as he could. The bees were still swarming, now on the assault – presumably bent on revenge at the loss of their home.

The men didn't flinch once. Their protective clothes seemed to be working. Either that or they were just as hard as nails. I couldn't even begin to imagine how the old man used to do it in just a pair of shorts. We watched on in disbelief and thought we were at a safe distance but soon discovered that we were wrong. After ten minutes, the bees started to spread out – now they just wanted to attack anyone within range. I covered myself in a thick jacket and put a hat on. Binod was too late. A bee stung him right on the cheek.

The dangling mass of honeycomb finally reached the top where it was lumped into Ash Bahadur's basket amid whoops of congratulation from the ladder men. The whole process was repeated twice, until all that remained were the tops of the hives attached to the cliff. After a few weeks or months the bees could rebuild them and the tradition could be maintained.

It was time to move on before we got stung any more and so we joined the hunters as they retraced their route along the narrow path. When it was wide enough for them to do so they rested, on a clifftop overlooking the village. Ash Bahadur sat smoking a cigarette.

'How was the catch?' I asked.

He shrugged his shoulders and laughed. 'Terrible. Hardly any honey.'

He plucked out a piece of white honeycomb where dying bees writhed in the sticky mass. He was right; there was barely any liquid at all, but the little I did try tasted unlike anything I'd ever tried before.

'If you come at the right season sometimes it gets you high, when the bees have been pollinating the marijuana and the poisonous flowers.'

Alas it wasn't the right season, but it was still magical.

Back at the village we assembled in the garden of the house. The honey hunters sat on thatch mattresses and smoked, while the womenfolk brought out *rakshi* – home made fermented millet 'wine'. It tasted foul but it kept on coming. Just when you thought you'd been polite enough to drink your fill, another young girl would come round and top you up. Before long everyone was drunk and by nightfall someone had produced a drum and the married women began to sing as the children danced. Then the old ladies danced, followed by the old men. There wasn't an eligible girl to be seen, which was just as well considering how inebriated everybody was. Despite the poor harvest the whole community was happy. The hunt had brought people together and was a good excuse for a knees-up, if nothing else.

It was almost six months to the day since the devastating earthquake that ravaged Nepal. Until now we'd seen little evidence of the damage except a few cracked walls, but the closer we got to Gorkha and the epicentre, the more evidence there was that something truly awful had happened. One day we climbed a tall hill to a village called Manakamana just south of Gorkha, overlooking the Trisuli river.

'I came here a few years ago,' said Binod. 'It was a pilgrimage to see the Buddhist shrine.'

'But you're Hindu,' I said, confused.

'It's all the same here in Nepal,' he continued. 'Where you find Hindu temples you'll find Buddhist monasteries and the other way round. Remember in the Dalai Lama monastery? We saw all the statues of Hindu gods. Buddha was a Hindu. We are the same people, we just look at things in different ways.'

If only all religions were so tolerant, I thought to myself.

So we climbed to the top of the hill to be greeted with a very disappointing, and rather tragic sight. There, in the centre of the village, where the shrine used to be, was just a mound of corrugated iron sheeting around a pile of rubble.

Binod tutted. 'Such a shame. People used to come here for blessing and *puja*.'

The entire shrine had collapsed during the April quake, leaving just a few walls and pillars standing. Hundreds of years of history reduced to rubble in just a few minutes. What was remarkable was that all the modern concrete houses that surrounded it were absolutely fine – perhaps saved by their pliable iron supports – whereas all of the ancient brick structures had vanished. But life seemed to be carrying on as normal. There was still a steady stream of pilgrims coming for a blessing from the pandit who put *tikkas* on their forehead and broke coconuts as a symbolic sacrifice.

On the other side of the village we came across an entire street that had been affected by the quake – yet bizarrely it was only the houses on the right-hand side. All the ones on the left were fine.

As we walked down the lane past the piles of bricks and shells of houses an old man waved us over.

'Come and see my house,' he said smiling.

Bhim Bahadur Shrestha was an old soldier of sixty-six.

'I was in the Indian Gurkhas,' he said proudly. 'I fought in Kashmir against the Pakistanis and also the Chinese.' He beamed and pushed out his chest. 'I've been living in the mountains all my life and never seen anything like this earthquake.'

He showed me the remnants of his home. What used to be a four-storey house, made of mud-brick and wood, was now only one. Somehow the bottom floor had survived, and luckily for him, so had Bhim.

I told him he was a lucky man.

'Yes, I am very lucky. My neighbours were even more lucky – the whole wall fell on top of them, the man and his old mother, but they survived by the grace of God.'

He showed me his hand. 'I got away with just a broken finger.'

Inside Bhim pointed out the cracks in the walls and the spot where he'd fallen down, protected it seems by a wooden beam that had stopped the masonry falling directly onto his body. A mangled finger was a small price to pay. Others weren't so lucky.

'It was a Saturday morning, and there were lots of pilgrims,' the old man related. 'Two people died over there near the shrine. They weren't locals. They had just come for a blessing.'

'How many people lived here?' I asked.

'Twenty-one people used to be in this house! My children and their children. I have lots of grandchildren.'

'Where are they now?'

'They had to leave after the house was destroyed. My boys went to work in Kathmandu and abroad and took their children with them. Now I am alone and I must rebuild the place so they can return.'

I felt sorry for the old man, forced into seclusion by the force of nature that had scattered his family. But the smile never left his face.

'Why don't you leave?' I asked.

'Leave? How can I leave, this is my home. I am a soldier. A Gurkha,' he said. 'The earthquake was terrible, but it is not the end. It could be worse and the people of Nepal are strong. We will build our houses and carry on as before.'

Like everywhere else in the Himalayas, it seemed the people of the mountains were made of strong stuff, and I felt very humble to be in the presence of such a stoic breed.

It was a theme I encountered more and more as I got to know the Nepalese. The country had been to hell and back over the past twelve months, and there appeared to be no end in sight to the troubles. The border with India was still closed and the fuel shortage was at critical levels. Every petrol station we walked past had people queuing for miles to get their allocation. But I rarely saw a face that suggested anything other than patience and understanding. I couldn't imagine what scenes of chaos I'd find on the streets of England under similar circumstances.

The road wound east following the river. We were walking along the main highway that connects Nepal's two biggest cities and yet it was like walking along a country lane. Apart from a few overcrowded buses, the road was quiet. It rose up and up, winding through the trellised hills. We plodded on in happiness. Binod told me stories of his time over the last few weeks waiting for me to come back, and how Chandra had nursed him back to full health and how happy his children were at the prospect of their father gaining the respect of the village for coming on this expedition. It made me glad to have repaid my debt to my guide.

As we crested the hills of Naubise the potholed road made its final rise through the pine forests until we found ourselves standing at a junction. We had walked over 1,200 miles to reach this point.

'We made it, brother,' said Binod, excitedly.

There, unfolding beneath us was the open plain in which the historical capital of Nepal erupted. Kathmandu exploded from its valley in passionate, colourful glory. There it was, the biggest city of the Himalayas, ten times as big as I remembered it. The concrete mansions and medieval brickwork of a city emerging from its ashes. Not even an earthquake could stop the inexorable triumph of man, even on the roof of the world.

16

The Wild East

It was dusk by the time we reached the monkey temple. It had taken hours to weave between the endless queues of cars and lorries that were waiting for petrol in the shanties. They all wanted to leave the capital. The festival of Dashain was in full swing and people wanted to go home to their villages and celebrate with their families. We climbed the 365 steps to the top of the wooded hill where an enormous white dome topped with a golden pagoda shone in the sunset. Revered macaques dangled from the shrines and made impious gestures to passing pilgrims. For Binod and me, it marked an important milestone in our journey. Swayumbhunath temple, one of the oldest shrines in Nepal, overlooks Kathmandu, with the watchful eyes of Lord Buddha painted onto the glinting tower. We'd come a long way.

From the ramparts, amid a sea of faithful devotees, we stood in awe of a city defiant. Buddhist prayer flags fluttered in a gentle wind. If the media reports were to be believed then the whole town should have been a big pile of rubble after the earthquake, but it wasn't so. Thamel, the backpacker ghetto, was unaffected and life went on as usual – except there were barely any tourists these days. They'd all been scared off by the Foreign Office advisory that even now, six months on, hadn't been lifted. But as we descended from the viewpoint and found ourselves in a warren of alleyways, where the local Nepalese were seated in the shop doorways, hopeful as ever to make a sale.

'Good price, mister,' said the turquoise bead hawker.

'Best silk, sir,' said the Kashmiri carpet man.

'Very old, won't find anywhere else,' warned the Tibetan antiques vendor.

'You want some stuff?' asked the drug dealer with a wink.

It was all as I remembered. The Irish pubs, the steak houses, the live bands playing traveller classics, the trekking outfitters, the fake North Face gear and the hundreds of tat shops all selling exactly the same thing. The smells of a congested city where cows get right of way, and the oversized rats scurry through the piles of rubbish, all came flooding back with a nostalgic vengeance. The noise of a thousand car horns; the wheels of cycle rickshaws clattering down the potholed roads; the dodgy wiring overhead; the neon signs of a hundred restaurants, all misspelt.

We checked into a hotel and handed over fat piles of laundry to an enthusiastic receptionist, all too glad of the business. We took a couple of days to rest up and I went shopping for trinkets to add to my collection of souvenirs that now lay hidden in a storage box in London.

Now that we'd reached Kathmandu, everything to the east represented the long walk home, even though it was in the opposite direction. The end was almost in sight. My thoughts wandered back to a grey London. It was mid-October and I imagined the sullen raindrops falling on the Thames and the familiar chatter of people on the daily commute. I thought of tea and toast and mulled wine in Gordon's. The parakeets of Putney would be roosting now and the leaves of Fulham Palace park reddening with the onset of the festive season. No doubt the Christmas lights were going up and tourists would be clogging the tube and the price of a sausage roll in the Sand's End had probably surpassed a fiver. I reminded myself that I was lucky to be here in the mountains of Asia rather than stuck on a draughty night bus. But nevertheless I couldn't seem to shake off a longing to make it back before December. I'd been on the road long enough.

'You're going to miss them,' said Binod.

'Miss what?' I replied.

'The mountains. You don't have mountains like this in England, do you?'

'No. Not like this.'

He was probably right. I would miss them. But a mountain – like a seductress – though irresistible, had to be treated with caution; it was wise to know when to walk away, even if deep down, you knew one day you'll return.

The people were getting ready for their own festivities as we rested. It was the eighth day of Dashain, the most popular celebration in Nepal, and a time when families were reunited, gifts given to children and animals sacrificed to the gods. Tomorrow was to be a big day. The ninth day of the festival is when it reaches its peak, where crowds gather at dawn in the great squares of the ancient city and watch as the Goddess Durga – manifested as the bloodthirsty decapitator Kali – is appeased.

We woke early and made our way to Durbar square, the famous medieval courtyard that housed dozens of temples dating back over five hundred years. I was saddened to see that many of them hadn't survived the earthquake. The rubble had been cleared now, but many areas were still fenced off, and just the foundation platforms remained.

'Here many of the towers were just made of mud-brick and carved wood,' said Binod as he showed me round. Some had completely collapsed, whereas others had just fallen over or sustained minor damage. But even this wasn't enough to stop the party. In between the temples, the city folk had already gathered to make offerings to the statues of Durga. A procession of men beat drums and played flutes and Gurkha soldiers marched in step before the sun had even fully risen above the surrounding hills.

The cobbled streets were covered in pools of bright red blood where animals had been killed the night before.

'Let's go and see the sacrifices,' suggested my guide.

We walked to where a group of soldiers were standing in line and a priest was blessing a pile of offerings: coconuts, baskets of flowers and bananas that surrounded regimental flags. One of the men was in a white gym outfit and held a massive *kukri* in his hand. He knelt down and began to sharpen it. Near by two buffalo were tied up next to five bleating goats. One by one they were dragged over and splashed with holy water.

'When the animal shakes it is given as a sign that he approves and accepts that he will be killed,' said Binod solemnly.

'Or perhaps he just doesn't like water thrown in his face?' I suggested.

Binod looked quizzical. 'No, he likes it.' He was convinced.

Then the moment came. A soldier grabbed the hind legs and another the horns, as they held the goat still. The man with the knife raised it above his head and whoosh, down it came, severing the neck in one fell swoop. The body fell to the floor and was dragged in a circle around the shrine leaving a trail of sticky blood. The head was picked up and placed down with the other offerings as it took a minute to actually die; the goat's eyes still moved and the mouth opened quietly until all was still.

It went on and on. The buffaloes were led to a post where the ropes around their necks were pulled tight like a garrotte as two men held the tails and the same was done. Instead of a *kukri* an even bigger sword was used, but the effect was the same. The head was lopped off in one. With each sacrifice the soldiers in line fired their rifles into the air at the moment of death, scattering thousands of pigeons into the sky with each loud bang.

It was gruesome and seemingly barbaric, but no different to what goes on behind closed doors in the abattoirs back home, and, not being a vegetarian, I had no cause for complaint. If anything, the festive atmosphere was welcome and the people of Nepal deserved a good party after what they'd been through this year.

As the blood dried under the morning sun and the shadows of the temples shortened, it was time to leave and carry on east.

Apart from the Terai lowlands, the rest of the country is so mountainous that it is said that if you flattened out Nepal, like pulling on a creased tablecloth, then the surface would amount to an area bigger than the whole of the USA. East of the Kathmandu valley we climbed up towards Sagarmatha National Park. Because the monsoon had arrived late this year, there was still an oppressive humidity and haze that filled the sky. Even though it wasn't cloudy, nothing could be seen of the mountains to the north because of the translucent sheen.

Drinking Everest beer in the backstreets of the old town had made me contemplate. It seemed Binod was thinking the same thing.

'We can't go on a Himalayan journey and not see the highest mountain on earth,' Binod said. 'It would be a shame.'

He was right. We'd come this far, but as I looked at the map I realised just how off course the famous mountain was. It lay far to the north on the border with Tibet – a two-week walk up a one-way valley.

'It's not where we're going. It's completely off route,' I said.

Since Tibet was closed to foreigners, I had set my sights on Bhutan, three hundred miles away. It was a place I knew virtually nothing about. I'd been to all the other countries before, but Bhutan was a mysterious blank on the map, a place only whispered about – isolated by its mountains and a monarchy resistant to outside change. I was immensely excited not only to complete my journey, but also to set foot in one of the least known countries in the world.

But first there was the long road through east Nepal and back into India to contend with. And with the onset of winter and the threat of closed passes, I couldn't afford the time to make the side journey on foot.

We reached the town of Charikot late in the afternoon, five days after leaving Kathmandu. It had been a hard slog uphill, along the main road that leads towards Tibet, and then east again. One day we'd climbed over two thousand metres over the obscenely short distance of ten kilometres. There was a road that zig-zagged up the mountain, weaving between the jungle slopes, but Binod insisted on taking the ancient shortcuts. I always preferred to take the longer and gentler route, but my guide was having none of it.

'Come on, brother, my legs are shorter than yours,' Binod teased me.

It seemed Binod, like all the porters we'd had along the way, had only one gear. He'd dawdle along at a frustratingly slow pace on the flat roads, then come into his own on the hills and rough tracks. I huffed and sweated all the way to the top, and was relieved to reach the town, which was perched on a cloudy narrow ridge. Mount Everest was tantalisingly close now, but blocked by a series of north–south-running valleys. Anyone wanting to climb the fammountain, or even just reach her base camp, opted for a charter flight to the infamous airstrip at Lukla.

'Sod it. Let's fly,' I said to Binod, unable to resist the temptation any longer. We'd come this far and I knew the call of *Chomolungma* – mother of the world, as the Tibetans call her – could not simply be ignored. Even if we couldn't walk there, we simply had to go and pay our respects.

There was no proper airstrip in Charikot so a plane was out of the question. It would have to be a helicopter. Arrangements were made and a hefty sum transferred, but I knew it would be worth it. The next morning we were told to wait on the only flat stretch of land in town – the local recreation area, a scruffy bit of waste ground where goal posts stood rusting after a heavy monsoon. Feral dogs yawned as the cockerels heralded dawn and a few early risers squatted on their haunches, watching with suspicion as Binod and I loitered on the pitch. At seven thirty the unmistakable noise of the chopper broke the quiet and a bright red Eurocopter banked over the forested hillside.

Blasting dust everywhere it landed in the middle of the field and the doors swung open. The pilot, a stout Swede with the head of bull, greeted us as we boarded.

'It's half an hour to get there and then you've got fifteen minutes on Kala Pattar, that's all the fuel I have. I'll keep the blades turning.'

With that he slammed the door shut and we took off, wobbling vertically until we had a clear height and could bank off to the north.

It was a far more pleasant experience than the last time we'd been in a heli on the extraction from Rukum and I meant to enjoy it. Looking down at the shadow of the aircraft as it flitted near and far over the trees and rocky escarpments, we crested the gorges one by one until there we were, in the famous Khumbu valley. The trees suddenly disappeared as we reached four thousand metres and the landscape below became barren. Beneath us was the rocky moraine of the glacier, littered with boulders the size of houses. We were above the haze now and the clouds were nothing but a blanket of white guarding the foothills.

We entered the midst of the mighty Himalayas. The white peaks towered above us and I felt as insignificant as a little fly as we buzzed between them up the valley. Even here though, on a stage of such remote solitude, there was life. Tiny *stupas* stood proudly on grey hilltops, their colourful prayer flags a monument to man's continual insistence of dominance over nature.

Surrounded by a wall of glistening snowy peaks we landed on the brown hill of Kala Pattar, at 5,545 metres, looking down on Everest base camp. I couldn't see any tents at all – there were no climbers this season after the horrors of the earthquake.

Jumping out of the helicopter I looked at my watch.

'Fifteen minutes,' repeated the pilot, shouting above the noise of the rotors. I ran across the scree to clear the blades and found a spot on the edge of the ridge. Up above, the morning sky was a perfect blue. We were so close to the heavens that it was a deep, dark blue that formed a sharp contrast to the sparkling slopes around. Binod pointed them out. To our left, the sheer walls of Pumori with its light grey cliffs looking like a watercolour. In the distance ranged Khumbutse and Changtse, an impenetrable barrage of vertical ice with a serrated edge like shark's teeth. And then to the right, in the foreground, loomed the twisted crown of Nupste, dominating its sister Lhotse which seemed to sit calm and unbothered in the middle distance only a mile away. And there, rising behind her twin guardians was Sagarmatha herself – Everest. She loomed almost black, swept of most of her snow by the ferocious winds, which seemed to provide a halo to the revered summit.

'It's nice,' said Binod, never one for overstatement.

The thrill and awe of looking up at the greatest mountain on earth, I had to admit, was rather nice. I could barely take my eyes off the peak. It looked so cold up there.

'Don't you want to climb it?' said Binod.

'Perhaps one day,' I said. The allure was certainly there and I imagined for a moment the joy that Hillary and Tenzing must have felt at being the first to the top all those years ago. To know, even briefly, that you are at the highest point on earth would surely be an unsurpassable achievement, even in an age when dozens of climbers make it to the top every season.

But I reminded myself that I wasn't here to climb mountains – not this time. I would have to be content to watch her from afar for the few minutes I had left. There at the top of the world, in the silence, I thought back to that fateful night in August when I lay screaming at the bottom of a jungle ravine. I realised that I had truly seen both sides of this mountain range, light and dark, heaven and hell.

The pilot whistled and tapped his watch. It was time to go and carry on walking.

We trekked east through Phaplu into the Solukhumbu region, following the course of the Dudh Koshi river to the south as its milky grey waters gushed from the highest mountains on the planet.

The jungle returned and the landscape took on an altogether wilder, more isolated aspect. Roads simply didn't exist, only overgrown stony paths that weaved through the forests. The shrill whirr of cicadas roared through the canopy and each step was fraught with fear, as whoever was in front faced the threat of walking straight into gigantic spiders' webs. Just touching them accidentally would cause the creatures to rear and dart straight for one's face. Sometimes we'd walk down the streams themselves, in a bid to avoid the spiders, hopping from boulder to boulder as little fish and tadpoles darted in the clear pools. Occasionally we'd come across small villages, cut off from the outside world. Habitation was usually preceded by the sudden appearance of rice paddies in the most unusual of places. Terraces dangled off cliffs; secret gardens in the jungle, and long lost shrines that looked like they should feature in a movie set for Indiana Jones. One day we came across a field with tall rice stalks surrounded by impenetrable jungle.

'Be careful,' said Binod hastily as I walked on its perimeter. 'Don't crush the rice. The people will come and kill us, it's their life and we must respect it.'

I trod carefully at the front, making sure I didn't step on a single grain. Then the field ended. A two-metre drop into a stream gulley was the only way down. I jumped, but in the split second before I landed, I saw something move directly below. It was the thick brown tubular body of a snake, gliding between the grass with a terrifying deliberation. I'm glad I saw it when I did; I had just enough time to part my feet before landing them either side of the slippery beast. It slithered straight between my legs and disappeared into a hole in the bank.

'You're lucky,' Binod said, 'that was a cobra.'

'No shit,' I replied. 'If I had landed on its tail it would have bitten me for sure.'

'No,' he said smiling. 'You're lucky to see one. They're a very holy snake in my religion. We say they hold the world together.'

There was no electricity here, only an existence unchanged in centuries. Old Gurkhas sat on the wooden frames of open shacks getting drunk on homebrew. The people looked more ethnically Tibetan here and Binod often struggled to communicate

with them. Wizened faces contemplated us with mild amusement but usually they'd let us camp in their terraced fields for a
small price. At the village of Shale we camped on a strip of land
less than ten feet wide behind someone's cow shed. Pigs the size
of ponies shuffled around the garden and a shaggy black mastiff
growled at us, fortunately restrained by his thick metal chain.

That night, we asked to a buy a chicken to eat, but when it
came, having been killed by the elder of the village, we were
sorely disappointed.

'Where's the meat?' mumbled Binod to himself under his
breath.

'I was about to say the same.'

'These people have stolen it for themselves. They've saved all
the good bits and just given us the feet and ass.'

I pushed the rubbery colon around my plate as the peasants
grinned through toothless mouths in the darkness. I wanted to
complain but didn't bother.

One lesson this journey had taught me was knowing how to
make do. There was no point in complaining; it wouldn't get
you anywhere. You just had to accept things the way they were
and get on with it.

'It's like when people ask us where we're going,' said Binod.
'It gets boring, the same questions. Having to explain to the
villagers and police and army checkpoints what we are doing.
No point in getting angry, Lev. Just tell them and smile. It
keeps them happy and only wastes five minutes of time. What
to do?'

I liked Binod's philosophical stance. He was content with his
lot, more or less, I thought. There was much I'd learned from my
guide.

Just as we were finishing up the elasticated cockerel there was
a commotion in the blackness.

'*Bagh, Bagh*,' a man shouted in Tamang.

Men ran into the millet fields clattering pots and pans and flashing wind-up torches. The mastiff howled a blood-curdling cry.

'What the bloody hell is going on?' I asked Binod who'd stood up to try and see. Although I have to say the distraction did give me a good excuse to lob the remains of the chicken claws into the bushes.

'It's a tiger!' exclaimed Binod. It's coming for the goats. I jumped up excitedly, more eager to catch a glimpse of the noble beast than worried about our safety. I strained my eyes but could see nothing except the dull torchlights of the villagers getting more distant.

Binod sat back down and gnawed on a piece of gristle. 'It's gone.'

As we slipped into our tents that night listening to the rustling of the cattle in their pen, I wondered if the tiger would return.

It didn't and I awoke alive and well. As I brushed my teeth with rainwater from a bucket it occurred to me just how many risks I'd already taken on this expedition, or at least what most people back home would consider risks. Of course the truth is, the locals had to deal with these dangers every day, whether it was tigers, landslides, earthquakes or just crappy brakes. I was glad to be going home, yet at the same time I felt sad to be almost at the end of my journey. I'd shared so much with Binod and felt I'd secured an affinity with these mountains, even though they'd almost killed me.

I could see why the people from Afghanistan all the way through Pakistan, India and Nepal held such stoic views. It was their lot to live here, so they might as well accept it with dignity and appreciation. It wasn't all bad. They had plenty of water, food, shelter and grazing, and when it comes down to it, what more do you need?

'It's not like the desert,' said Binod. 'We have everything we need.'

Binod had worked as a virtual slave in Saudi Arabia for thirty-one months ten years ago, to earn money to feed his family. So he knew what a desert was, and he felt lucky that he wasn't still in one. For me, despite the dangers, I felt like the sacrifices and the dangers were all worth it. I'd seen the top of the world and survived to tell the tale.

We left the mountains behind for a while as we emerged back onto the Terai at Belsot, just west of Lahan. Here we were stopped by the police and warned that the Madhesi people were still causing trouble. They told us that the borders were still closed and the Maoists had taken over some towns to the east. So we plodded on as fast as we could through the steamy flat lands, racing to the border with India.

Despite its trials and tribulations I was sad to say goodbye to the country to which I owed so much. Binod was sad to leave Nepal too.

'I'll miss Diwali with my family,' he said, visibly upset. He'd spent his evenings on the phone to Chandra and the kids and always passed on their humbling remarks. 'They say hello uncle.' It reminded me that while I was at liberty to spend my days wandering with little responsibility, Binod was a father and husband, and I needed to make sure he was safe. 'Family always comes first.' He'd tell me on an almost daily basis. He was right, of course, and if I'd gained any wisdom on this trip it was know-ing that you can never take anything, or anyone, for granted, because you don't know when it all might come crashing down.

India unfurled for the second time on my expedition in the form of West Bengal. The road we took passed through endless floodplains, shimmering rice fields and undulating tea planta-tions – scores of Bengali girls giggled under heavy baskets full of freshly picked leaves – the legacy of an empire almost forgotten by Indians today. Their thoughts of England were merely ideal- istic, rather than nostalgic, yet the signs were still there. Rusting agricultural machinery with stamps of King George; the 'coro- nation bridge'; British army camouflage on the uniforms of soldiers – some even wore, perhaps unwittingly, the Union Jack on their shoulders.

The highway jerked east, its course dissected by the vast expanses of the numerous tributaries that flowed south into the Brahmaputra. Alongside the road was a railway and as we walked, the scream of a train horn sounded every few minutes as cargoes of tea rumbled west and south, taking their precious loads to the cups of London, just as they had done a hundred years ago. To the north lay Darjeeling and the misty ranges surrounding Kangchenjunga, but where we were going was a wholly differ- ent Himalaya, untouched by colonialism, isolated from its neigh- bours and, if its own image was to be believed, a place of serene happiness and contentment. I could think of no better place to finish my journey than Bhutan.

17

The Dragon Kingdom

I thought I'd seen some stark transformations on this trip. Any journey will throw up variety, and travelling on foot through the Himalayas had already surprised me in just how different one day could be from the next. Within a matter of hours, I'd moved from lush tropical rainforest to barren empty plateaus. Crossing from Afghanistan into Pakistan, I'd changed from a landscape of windswept valleys populated by nomads who lived in yurts, to a settled, peaceful and warm paradise within the space of just a few miles. The borders had often astounded me with their power of separation; not just the landscapes, but also the diversity of people and culture. But none of this could have prepared me for the difference I encountered walking into Bhutan.

The Indian town of Jaigaon which sits on the Torsha river is representative of the other municipalities in West Bengal whose names I forget. It was crowded, filthy and noisy. Lepers sat in doorways missing fingers and noses; conmen and mystics plagued the streets and cows vied for supremacy of the roads with battered rickshaws, overladen lorries and minibuses packed with so many people it always surprised me that they could move. Nobody bothered to clean the streets because the monkeys and the cows would do it for them, and pigs waded around in the open sewers, delighted at the general lack of hygiene. Everyone, it seemed, thought it perfectly acceptable to spit vile globules of phlegm onto the pavement, or on someone else's feet, or to piss in the gutters in broad daylight. The whole town stank of shit.

'I've always wanted to go to Bhutan,' Binod said excitedly, as we walked through a small gateway manned by a smiling immigration official who didn't even ask to see our passports. Near by, cars and lorries were directed to pass through a large archway that was coloured with pictures of dragons and tigers, ornately illuminated with fairy lights. It was like entering a theme park.

On the far side we emerged into Phuentsholing and it was another world. There were no beggars or lepers. No car horns – everything was eerily quiet. Signs everywhere indicated that smoking cigarettes was illegal. So was 'spitting on the walls' – clearly a polite nod to the Indian truck drivers. Almost all the men and women sported the traditional national dress and all the buildings looked identical – large fortress-like houses with painted beams and decorative wooden frontages.

'It's so clean,' said Binod, looking around in awe at the perfectly manicured hedgerows that surrounded little parks and temples. Women wandered about in long silk dresses and there were fancy restaurants and coffee shops and not a shanty in sight. All the cars were new too; it seemed we'd left the subcontinent behind.

But there was no time to linger. According to the strict schedule we'd been given by the Bhutanese government, we had less than a month to get to Gangkhar Puensum – our final objective on the Tibetan border – the highest mountain in Bhutan, and arguably the eastern anchor of the Himalayas.

We left the town behind and climbed up into the hot, steamy forest that had, until recently, been an impenetrable barrier to invasion from the south. In fact, the first road hadn't been built until 1964, leaving Bhutan in perfect isolation from the rest of the world. Progress had been slow – the first Western tourists didn't come until 1974 – and even then there had been just twenty of them at the personal invitation of the King. Since the opening up, the monarchy had tried to keep Bhutan's traditional culture alive. Measures included the regulation on buildings, which had to be constructed in a traditional style, limitations on tourists to only let rich visitors into the country, and a restriction on TV and internet that was only lifted in the new millennium.

'You mean to say they didn't have any TV until 2003?' said Binod, bewildered.

'That's right,' said Jamyang, who had appeared in the entrance-way to the hotel.

'He looks like a government agent,' Binod murmured, nudging me at the sight of the man.

An enormous, hulking figure, Jamyang Darji was to be our Bhutanese guide and fixer while we were here. He looked perpetually angry and had the face of someone generally displeased with life. I'd been warned that we wouldn't have freedom of movement in our last country; part of the deal on being allowed to walk through Bhutan was that we'd have a minder who would look after our itinerary.

Jamyang was in his late thirties, of large muscular stature and wearing a black and red *gho* – traditional robes hitched up by a hidden belt. His legs were bare except for long socks and faintly ridiculous black, pointy shoes. He looked like a cross-dressing gangster.

'Does he know we are on a walking expedition?' whispered Binod in my ear, clearly upset at having his role as guide usurped by the stranger.

'I hope so,' I replied, genuinely concerned that this man was out to hinder our journey. But I also knew we didn't have a choice in the matter.

'Look, you're still my guide but we have to have this guy by law. Plus he can translate,' I said to Binod as Jamyang ushered us away.

Jamyang drove as we climbed the hundred miles to Thimpu, which took about four days. It was a relentless and beastly walk. I was glad to leave the jungle behind, although I have to say it was impressive. Endless muggy undulations of green with no break in the canopy. Unlike in India, I didn't see a single monkey. That was a good sign – there was no need for symbiosis here – they lived undisturbed in the jungle, along with tigers, leopards and probably a whole host of unknown species. The human population of Bhutan was altogether less than 800,000 people, meaning that for the most part, the country, though small, was largely unexplored wilderness and man's impact seemed restrained.

The road wound up in a countless number of uphill switch-backs that doubled, trebled and quadrupled the distance we thought it would be. Only occasionally we'd wander past tiny villages where families happily picnicked in the gardens amid a sea of prayer flags that fluttered in the wind. Like the people in their *ghos*, the houses were uniform in their identity and archi-tecture. I was amazed by the solid, impregnable-looking struc-tures that looked like modern survivors from the Middle Ages. They were beautiful in their own way and yet at the same time their uniformity felt oppressive, almost communist.

'It's the law,' reminded Jamyang when he stopped and waited. 'Nobody can build in any other style in Bhutan. In the villages, three storeys maximum, in Thimpu, six. We don't have skyscrap-ers, huts or flats. Even the factories must look like this. Everybody lives in these houses, and we like it.'

With no emotion he got back in the car. 'I'll see you in Thimpu.' With that he drove off ahead.

Binod shook his head. 'I thought the Bhutanese were happy people? He doesn't seem too happy.'

As we climbed above two thousand metres, the landscape started to change. The trees morphed from a blanket jungle of tropical green to a more subdued stumpy covering of pines and reddening shrubs that gave the scene a more highland, autumnal feel. There were scraggy cliffs and brown patchwork meadows. As we trailed alongside the roaring Wang Chu river, I was struggling to put my finger on what the transformed scenery reminded me of.

'It looks like pictures I've seen of Scotland,' said Binod.

He was right, although more accurately it was as if the Scottish Highlands had been projected onto the features of the Grand Canyon, perhaps with a Mediterranean sky thrown in for good measure. It was majestic, tough and terrifying all at once. The gorges and gullies were some of the most magnificent I'd ever seen and the pine forests seemed to cling on against the laws of gravity to mile-high cliffs. The amorphous panorama looked anything but Asian. Until of course we'd stumble across a clutter of multicoloured prayer flags strung between the deodars and firs, and then the sight of a Buddhist *stupa*, glistening gold in the bright Himalayan air would bring us crashing back to reality.

I walked ahead in peaceful solitude, enjoying the calm, relaxed feel of such an unknown, mysterious country. I imagined I was one of the first explorers to come this way, even though I wasn't. It was easy to imagine in a landscape like this. Binod, however, seemed to trail further and further behind. Every few miles I'd have to stop and wait for him.

'Are you okay?'

'I'm fine,' he said, 'just my feet are painful.'

But the way he'd crick his neck I knew it was more than that. I thought perhaps he was still suffering with his back after the crash. Either way he was getting slower by the day and I knew we had to get to the end soon, otherwise I didn't think he'd be able to finish or, more serious, he'd make his injuries worse. I tried to walk slowly from then on in but I was ever conscious of our deadline. There was no choice – we simply had to get to the northern border within the timeframe.

It was with relief that we reached Thimpu. It was a place I'd imagined and dreamed of since starting this journey, and it signified the last real stop before our final push. Thimpu is a bizarre town. Despite being a capital city, it's barely worthy of the title of city; with a population of fewer than 80,000, you can fit more people in Wembley football stadium. It must be one of the smallest cities in the world and it doesn't have a single traffic light. There's only one road in and out, and I counted the number of cars that drove past on one hand. It was peculiarly quiet, except for the howling of a few street dogs. It felt sterile – almost like a sanitised version of a Swiss Alpine resort. People moved about shiftily, looking around as if they knew that their happiness lay elsewhere – in the mountains and villages, and that life in the miniature metropolis was an unnatural sin.

I'd only planned on having one day of rest in the town but it turned out that our visit came at an opportune time.

'It's the King's birthday tomorrow,' Jamyang announced, smiling for the first time since we'd met. I had noticed the image of the revered monarch everywhere we'd been in Bhutan. Literally every single house and shop in the town had a Bhutanese flag draped from the wooden frontage, and the majority had a photograph of the King or his father adorning a balcony.

'Which is the King?' asked Binod.

'They're both the King,' Jamyang replied, shrugging away the seeming ridiculousness of the question.

'You can't have two kings,' I said.

'This is Bhutan, we do things differently here.'

Jamyang tried to explain.

'That's K5.' He pointed to the image of a younger man with long sideburns and a film star's good looks. He too was wearing a *gho*, but a yellow one, reserved for a king. 'He's the current King, the fifth in the Royal Line. And that – ' he pointed to the older man, 'that is K4, the father of the King. Who is also the King.'

'This is complicated,' said Binod.

'He retired in 2006. He got to the age of fifty-one and decided that he'd had enough so he gave the Kingship to his son.'

Jamyang was warming to his theme.

'Now we have a constitutional monarchy, like yours,' he said, nodding at me. 'The King, K5, is a progressive man and believes in development. That's why we have TV and internet now, and roads too. He thinks it will make us more in line with the rest of the world. It will add to our Gross National Happiness.'

'Your what?' asked Binod, even more perplexed.

Jamyang smiled sympathetically.

'Gross National Happiness. We have a ministry of Happiness here in Bhutan. We measure happiness as more important than Gross National Product and wealth. What's the point in money or development if it makes people miserable?'

Jamyang was beginning to grow on me. Despite his constant state of apparent misery he was actually a thoughtful, amusing and, he assured me, happy man. And it transpired he was neither a gangster nor a government agent, just a guide eager to get into the mountains and away from the town.

'Most tourists who come to Bhutan are French and sixty. They're the only ones who can afford it, and they just want to go and take photographs of the *dzongs* and monasteries. Not that many foreigners come here to go trekking, and almost none to where you want to go.'

I found out that in fact high-altitude mountaineering was illegal in Bhutan.

'It's because we don't have any rescue infrastructure here.' explained Jamyang. 'We only have one helicopter, and nobody has any experience digging white folks out of snow. It would be embarrassing to have a foreigner die in our mountains, so we ban it.

'But it's easier to blame the gods,' he continued. 'We tell every-one that it's bad luck and against Buddhist religion to scale peaks, and that shuts people up. Look what's happened in poor Binod's country.' He patted Binod gently on the shoulder.

'All those foreigners dying all the time on Everest, and the poor Sherpas dying with them. It's enough to make everyone sick, but the foreigners keep coming. You Westerners, we have no idea why you want to climb mountains. It's just stupid, don't you think? You just want to conquer things, plant flags and all that. We don't have that tradition. Except prayer flags, we stick those everywhere.' He grimaced.

'Well, we don't want to climb any mountains,' I said. 'We just want to walk to the bottom of Gangkhar Puensum.' I'd chosen the barely known peak as the end of my journey because it seemed an appropriate finish.

'We consider it the holiest mountain in Bhutan,' Jamyang said. 'It's the highest unclimbed peak in the world, and the highest in the Eastern Himalayas. Beyond it the mountains diminish into the Tibetan plateau. It's all downhill from there. In any case winter will be coming soon and you can't go any further.'

Binod smiled at this. I knew he'd be glad to finish. He'd missed Diwali with his family and I could tell he was ready for home.

He wasn't the only one. The chill and frosty mornings reminded me that it was almost December. I'd been on this journey since June – that was almost six months, and to make matters worse I'd just received a message from Ash inviting me to a Christmas party in London.

But first there were celebrations afoot in Thimpu to attend to.

'Well, since we are here, let's go and see the King's birthday.' If I was expecting a regal palace event I was sorely mistaken. Jamyang led the way through the deserted streets to the National Stadium where a crowd of *gho*-wearing locals jostled to try and get in through the doors. Jamyang pushed us to the front and presented our passes to a security guard who let us in.

We entered the stadium and it seemed the entire population of the city had beaten us to it. It was packed full of people, all in national dress, all smiling, all happy, all watching as traditional dancers lolloped around the field for the entertainment of the Royal Family. The royals were mingling with the people, wandering between the rows upon rows of orange-robed monks and bowing servants. It was like being at a medieval joust, except rather less fun.

'Do you think they're really all that happy?' asked Binod. 'It's quite, well, you know, boring, isn't it.' He said it quietly so that Jamyang didn't hear.

'I suppose that they are happy,' I said. 'I mean, it's all they know.'

I'd been thinking a lot about why this place laid claim to being home to the happiest people in the world. Bhutan had been virtually isolated from the outside world for so long that the people's happiness seemed to lie in their isolation and cultural identity. My own theory on the happiness of the Bhutanese was to do with building regulations. As odd as it sounds, I reckon that is what keeps Bhutan the way it is, and therefore unique.

263

Since the government legislates that all buildings must conform to traditional style and structure there simply are no shanties – and therefore no way for people to leave home to live somewhere cheaper. They are forced by necessity to stay at home (unless they can afford to build a new traditional style home themselves, in which case they are probably married and wealthy). It's this forced community spirit that ensures social cohesion and guarantees nobody really deviates from the norm. That – I think, as controlling and limiting as it sounds – is what makes the Bhutanese happy. Like the Dalai Lama said, it's having too many choices that makes you unhappy.

'The first tenet of happiness,' pronounced Jamyang, with total conviction, 'is good governance.' People want to be told what to do, he said. 'Nobody in Bhutan is interested in democracy. We love our King – we want him to be in control. Why do you in the West assume that people want choice? Why do you place such high value in freedom, when more often than not, it results in unhappiness?'

I looked at Binod, thinking that he'd disagree, given that he was so against the caste system in Nepal that had subjugated him so much and left him and his family in eternal poverty. It was only through change, and freedom of thought, that he'd been able to better himself and earn a decent crust. But he nodded his head in agreement.

'So is everyone in Bhutan happy?' I asked. It seemed an absurd proposition.

'No of course not, but we are happier in general. I think it's a combination of our cultural identity, family ties and Buddhist traditions of letting go. We have no hatred or jealousy here.'

I'd heard that in Bhutan women often had more than one husband. In fact sometimes a woman would marry two brothers to increase her family's productivity.

'It's true, but men aren't jealous. It's that simple. What's the point? Life is too short. Take the King – I mean K5. He is married to a beautiful woman.'

'Yes I've seen her photo everywhere – she's stunning,' I agreed.

'Not as stunning as his ex-girlfriend,' Jamyang sighed. 'He wanted to marry his wife's friend. She was even more beautiful.'

'What happened? Why didn't he marry her then?'

'Their star signs didn't match.'

'Are you serious?'

'Yes. We take astrology very seriously in Bhutan. He went to see a Lama and the Lama said no, you can't marry this one, it won't work, find another. So the King found another. Luckily she was hot as well.'

'And is he happy?'

'Yes, of course he's happy. He told the girlfriend to marry his brother so that he could see her, and now everybody is happy. It's all about living in the moment and accepting what you have. Dealing with it and not stressing too much. No point in worrying about the past or future. The past is gone and can't be changed. The future isn't here yet and will only change as a result of the present, so we must live in the present.' Suddenly the cross-dressing gangster had become a wise old preacher.

We left Thimpu and walked east over the black mountains towards Trongsa. Jamyang's words were ringing in my ears. Despite my thoughts of home I was determined to enjoy the last moments of my journey. Yet it was hard going as the weather closed in and my body ached with fatigue. It's always the same at the end of a long walk – your subconscious mind knows the end is near and lets your body start to fall apart. Like when an athlete 'hits the wall'; you just have to keep on going.

Binod was still struggling too; he'd lag half a mile behind and much of the time we'd walk in silence. I just tried to take in the beauty of the place. At Trongsa we passed an enormous *dzong* or fortress, which reminded me of a massive German castle, yet inside it was full of dancing monks dressed in orange robes. Outside, men in *ghos* played archery – firing arrows a hundred and twenty metres from a fancy compound bow, while their comrades cheered and jeered and danced and sang all day long. Giant weeping willows filled the valley; the wooden houses were all covered in festive lights and in the surrounding hills an explosion of red and yellow leaves made the scene almost perfect.

But not quite.

I felt that everything was not as it seemed. There was an underlying oddness, an unfamiliarity and strangeness all around. At Chimmi Langkar, On the corners of most of the houses, enormous penises were painted on the walls, many with wings, others with dreadful fangs. Some even had wild, evil-looking eyes, staring out from the head.

'What is this place?' asked Binod who was supressing a nervous laugh.

'We worship dicks,' answered Jamyang with a straight face. 'All these phalluses keep away evil spirits.'

He continued, quite seriously.

'There was an old saint who came and preached in Bhutan in the fifteenth century. He was a real womaniser who drank, smoked and "subdued" a lot of demonesses with his magical thunderbolt.' He winked. 'They called him the divine madman.'

I smiled at Binod.

'*Now* I know why the Bhutanese are so happy,' said Binod.

Behind the façade of modernity and development and cleanliness there seemed to be a mystical, almost Shamanist undercurrent to life in Bhutan. In spite of the image of a happy, pure nation there were hints at a darker, more superstitious existence.

'Myth and history are one here,' said Jamyang. 'At the Tiger's Nest monastery you should never question the fact that Guru Rinpoche arrived on a flying tiger, or that dragons exist.'

We reached Bumthang district on Friday the thirteenth of November. It was an ominous sign.

'Let's ask these boys for directions,' suggested Binod as we wandered through a small village called Hurjeh. Some school children were sitting in a bus shelter at the side of the road, all of them smiling and wearing miniature *ghos*.

'Hello, sir!' they said together in perfect English. 'Where are you going?'

'We are going to Chamkar,' said Binod.

The children were very polite. 'It's late, you should hurry, sir.'

They were right, it would be dark soon and we still had a few miles left to go, and when the sun went down it would become unbearably cold and the dogs would be on the prowl. We'd seen plenty of big black mastiffs. In the daytime they were chained up and even though they snarled and barked when you walked past, if you kept a good distance they were harmless enough. But at night they were sometimes let loose so that they could patrol the lanes and guard the village cattle from the wolves that inhabited the forests.

'There's bears as well,' warned the eldest boy, a smiling kid of thirteen.

'And Mirgula,' put in another, by the looks of it his brother or cousin. 'Tell him about the Mirgula.'

'What's a Mirgula?' I asked.

Binod laughed.

'What?'

'It's their name for the Mogoi.'

'What's a Mogoi?'

'A yeti!'

'Surely they don't believe in that?' I asked him.

'Yeti!' they screamed in chorus, all nodding enthusiastically.

'They live in the bamboo forest. My grandfather saw one once.'

One of the boys jumped up and put his hands above his head. 'They're this big. Like a man but with more hair.'

The oldest boy pushed his brother. 'No, they're like a gorilla, but white.' He flashed his teeth.

The smallest boy also jumped up and began to walk with his feet outturned.

'They walk like this; their feet point backwards.'

The middle boy mooed like a cow. 'This is their language.'

They were all deadly serious.

'But it's okay, you're big.' The eldest pointed at me. 'They don't eat people, they just kidnap boys and make them slaves. They make them cook and clean their holes in the jungle. But it's okay,' he repeated, 'they're very slow. They can't run, so if you see one, run very fast and you will be okay.'

The middle boy shook his head. 'Do you have a weapon?'

'No,' I replied.

'Not even a gun?'

'No,' I assured him.

'Take a stick just in case. They're very dangerous.'

'We shouldn't kill them,' said the eldest slapping the younger one with a disapproving whack. 'They're endangered.'

I thanked the boys for their sage advice and promised them I wouldn't kill the yeti if I saw him, and that I'd run very fast to which they all nodded their approval. We made quickly for Chamkar, the last town on the journey.

Jamyang was waiting for us at the Tamshing monastery, a small but ancient temple where shaven-headed monks sat under the shade of withered beams chanting the Buddhist mantras.

'Before we leave for the mountain there is something we must do,' announced our imposing guide.

He paused.

'Well you have met his Holiness the Dalai Lama, right?'

'Yes.'

'Did he give you any blessing?'

'Not really, just some travel advice,' I said.

'Then we must consult with the Lama here. Tshetrin Tharchen is a very wise man. He will tell your fortune and give his advice for the end of your journey.'

We entered the temple and walked upstairs along the creaky wooden floors. The doors were low and we had to bend down to pass through the threshold into a dark little room where an old man in an orange robe waddled around. He wore glasses and had bare arms and looked not unlike the Dalai Lama himself.

'Sit, sit,' he said hurriedly.

I looked around. On the walls were terrifying war masks with grotesque faces. Spears, ancient rifles and battle shields dangled from leather thongs. Old books and manuscripts gathered dust in a cabinet and the smoke from an incense stick hung like mist in the stolid shadows of the chamber. It reminded me of a wizard's den.

Jamyang sat down next to Tshetrin, the old monk, on a cushion, and Binod and I took our places by the window on his left hand. Outside the dirty glass pane was a cat meowing loudly, wanting to be let in. I watched a fat raven, as black as the night, hop among the rafters near by. Someone, somewhere blew on a horn, which rumbled deeply, echoing through the mountains.

'We are here to receive your blessing,' said Jamyang with his head bowed. The monk shuffled in his robes.

'We are on a journey. This man has been walking along the Himalayas and is almost at the end of his walk. We have just a short distance left to go – to the base camp of Gangkhar Puensum and we would like to know how we will fare.'

The monk began to chant and rock his head. His eyes were closed and he repeated the mantra 'OM MANI PADME HUM, OM MANI PADME HUM' over and over. In one hand he twirled a prayer wheel and in the other he rang a bell rhythmically, beautifully. It went on for fifteen minutes and I felt myself drifting into a meditative trance, almost against my will. I could suddenly see the appeal of being a monk, sitting, chanting and listening to the repetitive music of the bell.

The cat meowed again and the spell was disturbed. The monk opened his eyes but ignored the cat, as one of his servants placed a small box in his hands. It contained a set of dice. The monk held them to his forehead, whispering or praying something to himself, before throwing them back into the box. He stared intently at the results. Shaking his head, he withdrew the dice, put them to his forehead, prayed and rolled again. This time he frowned, as did Jamyang. Neither of them looked up. The process was repeated twice more, and two more times the monk shook his head.

The silence was broken by the monk. He muttered a few words to Jamyang.

'Well?' I said. 'What does he predict?' I remembered visiting the Aghori baba in Haridwar. Not again, I thought.

'That's all we get. Four rolls,' said Jamyang shaking his head.

'Each time the dice were rolled they came up with the same bad news. 'He says don't go up the mountain otherwise something bad will happen to one of you.'

'Who?' I said. 'What will happen?'

'I don't know,' said Jamyang. 'He just says one of us. He's done all he can to ward off misfortune, but still the prediction is the same. It we go up then one of us will face misfortune and not all of us will get to the end.'

18

Place of the Gods

Naptse was the end of the road. Nothing more than a few houses where semi-feral dogs lay napping in the yards, signified the beginning of the final push. Here we acquired twelve horses and four local men to lead them. We stocked up on provisions, hauled our tents, gas and food into the saddle packs of the beasts and swapped our comfortable trekking shoes for serious mountain-eering boots. We were already at an altitude of two and a half thousand metres but where we were going, we'd reach well over five thousand and it was likely to be cold. Very cold. The first biting winds of winter had already arrived, and despite the clear blue skies, I knew we'd be in for a rough ride. I tried in vain to put the monk's prophecy to the back of my mind.

Jamyang led the way. Gone was his *gho*, and now the brutish man looked far more at home. He donned his thermals and down jacket and hauled the latest rucksack onto his back, every inch the outdoorsman. I imagined he'd be very handy with an axe at felling trees.

The trail petered out from an easy stone-surfaced path to a twisting muddy track as we pushed north. We walked against the flow of a river which emerged some thirty miles ahead from the glacier of Gangkhar Puensum itself.

I thought that up here away from the roads and in the cool, clear air of the mountains where Binod would feel more at home, my Nepali friend would come into his own, but he was still complaining about his feet and lagged behind more than ever. I was worried for him. Up here there would be no rescue except a long ride out on the back of a horse. We pushed on. Despite his complaints he was as determined as me to finish this journey and set eyes on the magical mountain. It would take four days of hard walking, following the narrow path through an enchanted forest filled with thick bamboo where red pandas hid and wispy Spanish mosses dangled from the gnarled branches like the flowing beards of a yeti. We were walking into a fairy tale; a land of mystery and dreams.

It would be a suitable finale. Somewhere above the treeline and the weather-worn crags and heathland, we would get to the head of a nameless valley where our journey would end.

We walked into the chill winter winds. It grew colder as we ascended and the first fleeting glimpses of snow could be seen on the tops of the mountains that flanked the valley. The only sign of human intervention was the occasional string of prayer flags, hanging like ghosts from the skeletons of trees, almost transparent after years of neglect and frost. Sometimes we'd encounter shaggy yaks and their thin watchers, young men and women on the return journey after six months living in a stone *kraal* or a cave high up in the pastures.

'It's getting cold up there,' they'd say. 'You're going the wrong way.' They laughed, but it was an empty laugh. They were just relieved their shift was done and they could finally go home to their villages and families for the winter. I briefly envied them but reminded myself that my own six-month journey would also be over soon.

We'd walk for six or seven hours a day. It was too cold to set off before the sun had fully risen above the mountaintops and every day we'd try and stop walking before four p.m., leaving an hour of light in which to pitch our tents and boil some water. After that everything would be covered in a thin sheen of ice and our skin became numb to touch. The cold penetrated everything and made our bones feel old and useless. Even during the daytime, if the sun went behind a cloud there would be sudden shivers and an icy wind causing everyone to have to stop and put their warmest jacket on. The cold winter air seemed to be at odds with the cloudless sky. There still was no snow underfoot at the lower altitudes, but with each day we'd climb another thousand metres, and with it the thermometer dropped like a lump of horrid ice.

'We're lucky,' said Jamyang on the third day, just as we'd breached the treeline. 'Normally by now everything would be white with snow and you wouldn't even be able to see the mountains for the blizzards and the cold mist.'

I looked back down the valley into the endless forest. At a distance waterfalls dropped from nowhere, into nowhere, like bleeding wounds in the flesh of green. Nobody in the history of mankind had even seen them up close and the forest all around grew wild and untamed. Maybe there's a yeti in there somewhere? Or perhaps it was up ahead, in the open heath or in the crags of the snowy peaks.

Jamyang laughed at me. 'You won't find any yetis up there.'

'Why ever not?' I asked, putting on my best quizzical face at the onset of some banter.

'Ask Tenzing,' he replied, nodding in the direction of the old man leading the horses.

Tenzing was the old horseman who'd come with us from Naptse and owned the twelve creatures that now stalked us daily, stoically carrying our supplies. He was seventy-eight years old and very wrinkled. He had ten grandchildren. In the folds of his *gho* he carried a rusty sword and underneath his skirts a pair of knobbly knees marked a lifetime of walking. Jamyang translated.

'Yetis don't live in the snow. Everybody knows that. They live in the forests down there.' He was deadly serious, like the boys we'd met in the village. He believed.

'There's been no sightings in this valley recently, but maybe that way.' He pointed to the east, the wild east, where the mountains rolled off into oblivion. 'Or maybe Tibet.' He motioned wistfully to the homeland of his forefathers, the birthplace of the Dalai Lama, a place beyond my reach – beyond the great white wall of ice that was the impenetrable Himalaya.

I left it at that, not wanting to seem ignorant or sceptical. Who was I to argue with an old man of the mountains?

So we plodded on, leaving the mirgula behind, deeper up the valley towards the unseen glacier. Every step Binod took now seemed to be laboured.

'Is he going to make this?' Jamyang asked me as we walked along. He raised a questioning eyebrow, clearly wondering what I was doing bringing along a foreign guide who couldn't keep up. 'Maybe the Monk was talking about him?'

'No, Binod will make it,' I said. 'He won't give up.'

'What's his problem? He seems weak. I think he has no stamina.'

'It's not that,' I said. 'He's still not fully recovered from the accident, and he's not used to his new boots.' I was determined to defend Binod. As much as I liked Jamyang he wasn't the one who'd been with me all the way from India. He wasn't the one who'd been with me in that car, and he wasn't the one who'd saved me from an insurrection when I was nineteen.

Binod had to finish the journey, even if I had to carry him myself.

I looked back to where he was limping, a quarter of a mile away. The terrain was punishing. After the forest the valley widened to a potted moraine field full of enormous boulders, deep gulleys and water-filled channels. It reminded me of the Wakhan Corridor, with its steep-sided walls of rocks and sweeping plains. In the middle was the gushing river, icy cold and white. After we passed the three-and-a-half-thousand metre point, there were no trees and the only sign of life was the occasional yak. It seemed as though I'd come full circle. My guide trailed cautiously, stepping among the rocks so as not to risk slipping on their treacherous surface. I waited for him to catch up. Jamyang carried on ahead with the horses to set up camp with Tenzing and the other horse-men. It was one luxury we had. Many pairs of hands meant that even though Binod was slowing us down, the Bhutanese would race on and get everything ready for our arrival.

'What is it?' I asked him.

'It's the tendons, I think. I don't have any blisters.'

'Take your shoes off and let me have a look,' I said.

He did and as he slowly peeled off his socks I saw that his ankles had swollen up.

They were red and bruised. There was little I could do.

'Dip them in the stream. Maybe the cold water will reduce the swelling,' I suggested, and gave him some anti-inflammatories for good measure. 'Another ten miles and we'll almost be there.'

'I'm not sure I can do it,' he said looking down at his feet, avoiding my gaze.

'Come on, Sir,' I said, remembering how much it would spur him on.

He looked up and smiled. 'I feel like an old man.'

'Well then, get up, old man.' I pulled him to his feet and he hobbled on.

I'd tried to forget my own pain. The colder it got the more my arm hurt. In the tent at night I'd roll and turn over a hundred times in a bid to get comfortable. The biting chill would send shivers down my metal plates and a shooting pain that would wake me every thirty minutes from the little slumber I got. I was tired, exhausted and weak. My shoulder, still out of joint from the crash, was in no mood to forgive me for being strapped under the weight of a rucksack and it ached all day long.

But I was determined to carry on. I wanted to reach the base camp of Gangkhar Puensum, and from there, scale an unclimbed peak or ridge.

'Take your pick,' Jamyang had said to me the night before around the campfire.

'All the mountains are unclimbed here. Just don't go above six thousand metres,' he reminded me.

I looked at the map and saw a ridgeline, pointing like a gnarled finger into our valley, just a stone's throw from the foot of Gangkhar Puensum. It looked like the perfect finish. From the top we'd get views of the unattainable mountain and perhaps beyond, the Tibetan plateau. After six months of journeying I felt compelled to choose a significant end point – a goal to strive for, a mountain to climb – somewhere, anywhere to call the end. It was nonsense of course, but the idea of having an objective to reach spurred me on, however arbitrary.

Now I'd found it, and it was a day's walk away. We were almost there and as we rounded the final bend in the valley, I saw the mountain itself.

As I petitioned to Binod's pride and we stumbled on in the wake of the horses, she stood there up ahead. Beyond the wind-swept plain that was flanked by the grey-and-brown mountains, all nameless, all unexplored, was Gangkhar Puensum, rising abruptly from the terminal moraine like a sheer wall of glisten-ing crystal. It had the form of a giant white bat, its enormous wings held outstretched in perfect symmetry. The sky was perfectly clear and the highest peak shone like a glorious crown. I was speechless at its magnificence and stark beauty. Even Binod, who'd lived in these mountains his whole life, was almost moved to tears. Although I have to say that may just have been the pain in his ankles, of course.

Either way we were almost there. At the foot of the mountain I could make out the tiny shapes of Jamyang, Tenzing and the others scuttling about at the side of the river, preparing the set-up of base camp. They looked like miniature toy figurines against the vastness of the panorama. The horses rolled around in the dust, thankful to have shed their loads.

'I wonder what the monk's prediction meant?' Binod asked. 'He said there'd be obstacles and danger and that one of us wouldn't make it.'

He echoed my own thoughts. Even though I didn't believe in superstition, after so long spent walking through this part of the world I knew never to underestimate the power of spirituality and people's beliefs. There seemed to be some things we couldn't just explain away. Call it God, fate, karma or magic, I didn't want to bring any bad luck on the final part of the journey, so I hadn't mentioned it before. Jamyang had suspected we'd have heavy snow, but we'd been relatively lucky with the weather. Yes, it was cold at night, but it could have been a lot worse, and here we were, on the penultimate day before the end of the expedition, staring up at the clear heavens.

'To be honest, I think he must have been predicting you with your feet.'

It hadn't occurred to Binod that he was in fact the unlucky one and that the rest of us would escape intact.

He looked thoughtful for a while and then spoke. 'You're right. I mean, he was right. I think this is the end of the road for me. I don't want to put anyone at risk and my feet aren't up to it. I'll camp at the base and you go on up the ridge with Jamyang. Forgive me, brother.'

'See how you're feeling tomorrow, maybe you'll be okay.' I wanted to be hopeful. I wanted him to be there with me to the end, but deep down I knew that after the monk's words Binod had lost his appetite for any more risks.

He just smiled knowingly. 'Maybe.'

That night I slept fitfully. It was colder than any night before. Minus fifteen or twenty Celsius. The wind howled outside and I felt sorry for the horses that shivered uncomplaining as a layer of frost settled on their coats. The blackness of the night and the remoteness of the valley seemed only to add to the feeling I had of impermanence, of isolation from reality. The looming dark peak to the north appeared in my imagination as an impregnable fortress. I slipped and slid on my air mattress trying in vain to get some sleep. My feet were numb with the cold and every breath I took froze instantly on the waxy down sleeping bag. Crystals of ice appeared like twinkling stars on the inside of my tent and it all felt surreal. In the gloom I thought of Newby and Carless up in the Hindu Kush sixty years before, and their chance meeting with Thesiger. *Get a grip*, I thought to myself, *they didn't have it any better*. I dreamt of Thesiger tutting and calling me a pansy.

As I tossed and turned I thought back over the previous few months. Of the joys and hardships and friendships forged from five very different countries, where all the while, the omnipresent mountains had remained. Sometimes they were close, other times far. But they were always there – looming like giants in the background. Keeping some safe, and doing harm to others. They were capricious titans who did only what suited and when it suited. The mountains, I'd come to understand, were the masters.

Dawn broke slowly and I wriggled from my sleeping bag reluctantly, keeping my fleece hat firmly on my head and wrapping myself in my down feather jacket to keep away the morning chill. Binod was already awake and strolling around the camp. I was going to ask whether or not he was coming up the mountain, but I already knew the answer.

'Stay safe, brother,' he said looking up at the grey divider of rock. With that he handed me a Nepali flag. It was tattered and full of holes.

'Take it up there with you and bring it back to me please. I'm going back down the valley today with the horses so I'll see you at night.'

Jamyang walked over from his tent. As usual there was no smile on his face but he looked ready to go. He wore his gloves and gaiters and a death-metal bandana with a skull and cross-bones on his head. What a bizarre man, I thought.

'Are you ready, Wood?' he said. 'Let's get this done. It's my last one.'

'Last what?' I asked.

'Last expedition. I retire tomorrow.'

'Are you serious?' I asked, surprised.

'Yes, I'm tired of guiding. This is my last walk. After that I'm going to go into the printing business.' I struggled to imagine the lumbering hulk that stood before me looking like a mafia hatchet man, sitting at a computer making T-shirts with portraits of the King and Queen on them.

'Then it's a special day for both of you,' Binod said. I could tell he was sad not to be coming, but it was for the best. His feet were still swollen and as I looked up at the giant pile of boulders, I respected his honesty.

Jamyang and I set off in silence. At the edge of the valley we began the climb immediately. It started with a steep, grassy slope and we zig-zagged up slowly. Five metres left then five metres right. It was slow and hard going. Our legs were still stiff from the cold and as we gained altitude there was less and less oxygen to take in. The grass gave way to a fine layer of shale and loose stones that crumbled away underfoot. Above us the boulders gradually got closer until we were in among them. They were vast slabs of granite piled up on top of each other – the spilling remains of a million-year-old up-thrust. It looked like the earth has spewed up its guts and now we were scrambling among the offal. Some of the boulders were massive, bigger than cars, balancing precariously on top of smaller ones, and in between were dark crevices and deep holes that seemed to disappear into the very soul of the world. We struggled on cautiously, but with every step we became more and more out of breath. Jamyang looked more miserable than ever. I used the very last of my reserves to pull myself up, one boulder at a time, carefully placing my feet on the ledges and hauling myself up with my good arm. I was acutely aware of the weakness of my right limb and knew that there was no way I could rely on it if I needed to. I suddenly felt very vulnerable knowing that I couldn't trust my own body. This was madness – what was I doing?

It took almost five hours of terrifying scrambling to get to a little ledge just below the top of the ridge. As I looked around and up at the snow-capped mountains that towered above I was almost tempted to carry on climbing. The peaks looked so close and inviting with their glistening summits and virgin slopes. But they were all deadly and I didn't want to risk the wrath of the gods any more.

'I'm not going any further,' said Jamyang suddenly, sitting down on a rock as he wiped the sweat from his brow. 'This is where I finish. I suggest you do the same. Remember what the monk said?'

He was right. There was nowhere left to go. Up above, another fifty metres or so was a vast slab of rock that jutted skyward. It was the top of the ridge.

'I'm going up there,' I told him.

He shook his head and sighed. He threw me a ball of brightly coloured cloth, which I caught.

'What's this?'

I unfurled the bundle and found it to be an old string of prayer flags.

'Stick it up there, will you.'

So, armed with Jamyang's prayer flags and my own additions – a Union, Bhutanese and Binod's Nepali flag – I hauled myself up to the top using the very last of my breath and energy, alone.

It was worth it. The cliff dropped off to a sheer thousand-metre wall below and unfolding before my eyes was the valley from which we'd climbed. It was one of the most beautiful valleys I'd ever seen. I squinted to see the tiny dots of the horses disappearing off to the south, presumably with Binod limping along behind them. The valley ended abruptly to the north as Gangkhar Puensum soared into the sky, rising above us all; earth piercing heaven. Tibet rolled off on the far side amid a sea of white summits. There was nothing but perfect silence. I'd made it.

I wanted to shout something or whoop with joy but it seemed a shame to ruin the peace and quiet. I had done what I came to do, I'd reached the goal, but deep down I wished Binod could have made it with me.

I realised something when I was up there. This mountain didn't really mean anything. It wasn't the goal I should have been celebrating. This was just the end – it was the journey that mattered, not the destination. It was what I'd seen and done along the way. It was about all the people I'd shared tea with and who'd looked after me when I needed it the most.

I climbed back down to where Jamyang was sitting.

'What do you want to call it?' he said.

'I don't know, it feels a bit weird naming a mountain in this day and age.'

'Well you may as well, there's plenty of them to go round.'

I racked my brain as we descended the boulder field, slowly picking our way through the rocks as the sun directed its warming rays above.

'What's that?'

I suddenly noticed something at the opening to a small cave underneath a large boulder. I walked over to find a patch of sand that led into the hole. I picked up a small black object from the dirt.

'Is this what I think it is?' I said in astonishment.

The thing was a piece of excrement, hard like wood and yet twisted into the shape of a tadpole. It was full of digested hair.

'Yep,' he said. 'Snow leopard shit.'

I looked down at the sand again and noticed the unmistakable paw prints of the most elusive cat in the world. This must be his lair.

'Let's move on, just in case he's about. They can take down a yak,' said Jamyang.

I pocketed the scat and we went down the mountain.

'I think I'll call it Snow Leopard mountain,' I said.

Jamyang nodded in solemn agreement.

One of the horsemen was waiting at the foot of the ridge with a beautiful white stallion. It was the strongest and fastest of all the horses we had and took our bags with ease. We walked back down the valley to where the rest of the team would be waiting, ten miles away, near to the treeline where it was warmer and a campfire awaited.

I noticed that Jamyang was smirking.

'What's wrong with you?' I asked.

He looked at me and raised an eyebrow. 'I'm done. In a few days we'll all be home and I can retire.'

With the mountain to our backs we set off at a stroll.

'Do you really mean that?' You'll never go into the mountains again?' I asked.

He smiled properly now. 'Do you really mean it every time you say you'll never do another walk? I bet you said that last time.'

He had me there.

'I absolutely mean it, right now in this moment,' he said after a while. 'But to be honest I'll probably still be trekking when I'm seventy, just like you.'

We knew the route so we went at our own pace. The horse trailed alone, trotting along instinctively. Jamyang fell to the rear and I led alone. I picked a course through the gulleys and over the heathland, jumping from rock to rock and hopping over the little streams.

My thoughts returned to home, back to my family and to my life in London. I thought of what was to come. Of the endless rounds of parties and drinks and good food and cheese boards in Gordon's with Ash. I thought about my car and whether or not the tax was due soon. I remembered my little collection of treasures stuck in a storage box in Fulham. They would soon get to see the light of day again and take their place on a shelf in my new house just in time for Christmas. The lights would be up in Oxford Street now and mulled wine would be back on the menu. Maybe I would actually get a dog this time round.

I snapped myself out of the absurdity. 'Live in the moment,' the Dalai Lama had said. 'Stop concerning yourself with the future.'

And so I did. I suddenly felt very happy. I wondered if it was a sense of achievement. No it wasn't that. Relief that I was going home? Maybe, a little. But above all else I think it was the fact I no longer had a goal. I wasn't rushing to get somewhere. I was walking slowly and just enjoying it. The flowers seemed more beautiful and the skies more perfect that way. All the colours came alive and I noticed little things that I hadn't noticed on the way up. A blue magpie with an extraordinarily long tail scampered about the pine trees in search of a bite; a little vole poked up his head from the stream and somersaulted into the water. It occurred to me that what I'd been looking for all along wasn't to be found at the top of any mountain, it was always there, everywhere. When you can find the time just to be grateful for the air you breathe, then you'll be happy. Take away expectations and everything will come as a nice surprise. It had been my choice to climb that mountain and take this route or that, but I didn't have a choice any more. I was walking back down the way I had come; there was no other route. I didn't have to worry about getting anywhere on time now.

We reached the enchanted forest just as the sun fell below the pines and our breath turned to a cold mist. By the side of the river I could see the tents were already up and the horses were rolling around in the sand, rejoicing at being on their way home. They knew.

Binod was standing there waiting. I handed him the Nepali flag and we sat down on the banks of the river. We watched as the country fell into darkness except for the flickering glow of the campfire that was burning like the stars above the mountains.

Acknowledgements

Great things are done when men and mountains meet;
This is not done by jostling in the street.

I think I have to beg to differ with the great poet William Blake, whose words spurred me on along the way. No expedition is a one-man band, and success is necessarily the result of many months of graft and a hell of a lot of 'jostling in the street' beforehand. There are a lot of people I must thank for their own hard work, behind the scenes, at home and along the way.

I would have been completely lost without the encyclopedic knowledge and determination of my mountain guides: Malang Darya, Mehraj Mir, Jamyang Dorji and of course Binod Pariyar – I thank them for their great sense of humour and unfailing loyalty.

A big thank you goes to Jamie Berry for his creative genius and determination as a filmmaker throughout and to Alex Stockley for his contributions in Afghanistan and India.

The expedition could not have functioned without the expertise of Secret Compass, especially Tom Bodkin, Clare Howes, and of course Tom McShane who navigated the bureaucratic and logistical minefield with aplomb, as well as photographing it along the way too. Jamie, Alex and Tom spent a great deal of time with me and I regret not having the space to recount all of our wonderful adventures along the way.

A big thank you to everyone at October Films for all their hard work, particularly to Adam Bullmore, Jos Cushing, Martin Long, Uli Pflanz and Becky Rendall. I must also thank Group M for their financial assistance and John Hay at Channel 4 for his continued support, without which this expedition would have been completely impossible.

I owe the book to Rupert Lancaster, Maddy Price and all the team at Hodder & Stoughton for their guidance, patience and input; to Charlotte Tottenham whose editorial assistance was invaluable and of course my agent Jo Cantello who has been a pillar of support for the past three years.

I wish to also thank those incredible companies who have sponsored and assisted me with financial and material support over the past year: Craghoppers, IWC watches, Belstaff , Burberry, Leica cameras, Alt-berg boots, Flight Centre UK, Gurkha Leatherware, Osprey rucksacks, Sub-4 Orthotics.

And in no particular order, I am grateful to all of the following for either their words of wisdom, floor space, companionship on the trail, logistical assistance or cups of tea – sometimes all at once: His Holiness 14th Dalai Lama, General Sir Sam Cowan, David Forbes, Peter Wood, Ash Bhardwaj, Will Charlton, Sophie Bolsover, Shwetank Verma, Dr Simon Lambert, Balance Performance Physiotherapy, the villagers and clinical staff of Rukum and Musikot, Pooja Krishnamoorthy, Umanga Khadka, Professor Sher Ali, Mohamed Bashir, Raja Divraj Singh Jubbal,

Tania Shoal, Rehan Khodaijai, Amerjeet Thakur, Ramesh Kumar, Sophy Roberts, Christopher Giercke, The staff at the Windmill Hotel in Clapham, Emma Squire, Shernaz Italia, Siobhan Sinnerton, Dominic Harrison, Melanie Darlaston, Chris Sutherland, Huw Longmore, Michael Charlton, the late Hugh Carless, Martin Bell, Uma Paro, Jason Beverley, 77th Brigade, the Mera Peak 2009 Airborne Forces team, The Brigade of Gurkhas, Chandra, Bishal, Binita and Bishwas and of course my long-suffering parents.

Finally, my gratitude to the people of Afghanistan, Pakistan, India, Nepal and Bhutan for their generosity and unfailing kindness of spirit, especially all the villagers, sherpas and porters who kept me fed and watered in the furthest reaches of the Himalayas.

Picture Acknowledgements